CITIZENSHIP AND THE LAW
SERIES

General Editor
ROBERT BLACKBURN
Professor of Constitutional Law
King's College, University of London

TOWARDS A JUST SOCIETY

Law, Labour and Legal Aid

ALASTAIR HUDSON

PINTER

London and New York

First published 1999 by
Pinter, A Cassell imprint
Wellington House, 125 Strand, London WC2R 0BB, England
370 Lexington Avenue, New York, NY 10017–6550, USA

British Library Cataloguing in Publication Data
A catalogue record for this book is available from the British Library

ISBN 1–85567–546–3 (hb)
ISBN 1–85567–547–1 (pb)

Library of Congress Cataloging-in-Publication Data
Hudson, Alastair,
    Towards a just society: law, labour, and legal aid/Alastair Hudson.
        p.   cm.–(Citizenship and the law series)
    Includes bibliographical references and index.
    ISBN 1–85567–546–3 (hardback). – ISBN 1–85567–547–1 (pbk.)
    1. Legal assistance to the poor – Great Britain. 2. Public interest law – Great
Britain. 3. Law reform – Great Britain.
    I. Title.   II. Series.
    KD512.H83   1999
    344.41'03258–dc21   98–52855
                                                                             CIP

Typeset by York House Typographic Ltd
Printed and bound in Great Britain by Biddles Ltd, Guildford & King's Lynn

Contents

Preface

A wise old Labour politician once told me, rather confidentially, in the back of a London taxi pelting down Euston Road, that constitutional affairs and the reform of the legal system 'will never become major political issues in this country'. I thought then, as I think now, that he was wrong. Writing a year and a half after Labour's landslide victory in the 1997 General Election, Labour has begun to keep its promise to put reform of the constitution at the heart of its programme in the creation of the 'New Britain'. The state of the legal system, and in particular the reform of legal aid, has become a staple in even the tabloid newspapers. The performance of the Lord Chancellor and New Labour king-maker, Derry Irvine, both in terms of his proposals for the reform of publicly funded legal services and his taste in pineapple-studded, neo-Pugin wallpaper, has elicited the most pronounced satirical and analytical abuse directed at any Labour Cabinet minister. Both factors have ensured that the politics of the legal system are at the forefront of British politics, alongside reform of the constitution.

The subtitle of this book, *Law, Labour and Legal Aid*, indicates a central aim to place the issues of law reform and justice provision in the context of the broader discussion of regenerating the constitution and building the much-heralded 'New Britain'. In particular it considers the history of Labour's attitude to legal services policy. One issue that is explored in detail is the rejection of policies developed under the leadership of John Smith which pointed towards the need for an integrated set of policies which looked at the justice system in the round. In my time advising the Labour Party on its justice affairs policy, there have been important fluctuations in the party's ideological stance on a number of issues affecting the rights of citizens. Of particular interest at the time of writing is the development of ideas surrounding the Blairite 'third way' and, in particular for present purposes, the need for a public service ethos to emerge in the legal system.

The most difficult aspect of writing this book has been the composition of its title. In a few words, my aim was to summarize a disparate field of issues, both practical and theoretical, that would be raised in the text. The most common title for reports and policy documents in this area is 'Access to Justice'. Bodies as disparate as the Labour Party, the Bar Council, Lord Woolf, and the Consumers' Association have produced material bearing that legend. It is the common link between the many sound-bites coughed up in this area. In announcing his proposals for the introduction of conditional fees, Derry Irvine chanted the term 'access to justice' a dozen times per interview in a manner reminiscent of someone composing an advertising jingle.

Despite its loss of currency through over-repetition, it is an important starting point. The first problem with the vast panoply of dispute resolution systems that are available in the UK, is that access to them is denied to many citizens. Denial of access is rarely a result of express, substantive denial of access to a remedy. Rather, it is a practical problem of cost, of politics and of allocation of public resources. The result is the prevention of many individuals and groups from being able to pursue their claims and receive the remedies to which they consider themselves entitled. The key to the protection of most forms of rights in the UK is the legal system. For the most part, the issue is then the acquisition of legal representation. Many social welfare rights are not activated through the courts *per se*, but rather through the ever-growing labyrinth of tribunals, appeals procedures and alternative modes of dispute resolution that are available today. The most simple point is therefore that most people cannot afford lawyers and thus are denied access, in real terms, to the system.

The issue of politics is, then, what resources ought to be made available to ensure access to dispute resolution? In a perfect world, those who wish to bring claims would have access to the system by means of suitably trained professionals able to guide them through substantive and procedural rules. This will only work if those professionals are inexpensive or, more realistically, if the state pays for the advice and expertise of those professionals. The problem of public resources is also one of cost – legal aid is far too expensive, as is the maintenance of the legal system, to be sustained in its current form.

The question of access also operates at a number of levels. While financial barriers are the first hurdle, there are further questions to do with the content of the law itself. This book is not designed to deal with all of the substantive legal issues which might arise, instead it attempts to focus primarily on rights to the home and the treatment of the family in its concluding sections. The entry point to this argument is again political. The content of statutory legislation is a question of politics and of constitutionality. Whether there should be a Bill of Rights and the contents of that bill, are all important political questions. The further question is, what goes into the common law? The development of common law and equitable rights is a matter for the courts, and returns the vexed question of what is to be done with the judiciary? The focus here is on 'law' as a system. 'Access to Law' could have been a title for this book – as an easy bookshelf categorization as well as a description of its content. However, this would have meant ignoring a range of dispute resolution systems which are strictly outside law, although they may involve lawyers or may have legal results and ramifications. 'Access to Dispute Resolution' then presents itself as a clumsy and obscure title – if moving further towards the heart of the matter.

However, the range of political questions requires some definition of the subject matter of the book beyond the systems. While 'Access to Systems of Dispute Resolution' pulls the subject matter further and further into the centre of the issue, it sounds more like a title for a doctoral thesis than for a book. More significantly, we have yet to mention the 'citizen' as the subject seeking to defend rights and enforce obligations in the legal and quasi-legal systems of dispute resolution. This book will at least shake hands with the categorization controversy which surrounds the term 'citizen'. The constitutional lawyer will tend to talk of the rights of citizens but still nod back to the Royal prerogatives and acknowledge that the citizen is really a 'subject' of the Crown in legal terms. While this talk of 'subjects' may appear unenlightened, it does contain the seeds of constitutional truth. The legal root of power obtains from mechanisms and ceremonies which still see us as 'subjects', although the British Nationality Act identifies us as 'citizens'. I am also conscious that this book forms part of the Cassell 'Citizenship and Law' series. Therefore, it could carry the title: 'Citizens' Access to Justice' or 'Citizens' Access to the Systems of Dispute Resolution'.

The most important element that then remains outstanding is some purposive notion of the reason for this system – that is, a thesis. To reflect the forward momentum of the text in its title, there would need to be some contextualisation of the term 'justice'. While 'justice' is a laudable term, a book of this sort must necessarily occupy itself with some notion of what justice is. Once justice is discussed, it automatically starts to acquire inverted commas. Unfortunately, the title 'Access to "Justice"' (complete with inverted commas) simply seems too arched. Therefore, some qualification or exposition of the term 'justice' is needed. Justice can be defined in two directions at once. Either it can follow a primarily philosophical path, whose enduring complexity will generally fail to come down to cases, or, it can come down to cases right away and then struggle to reach any philosophical height greater than altruistic sentimentality.

The thesis behind this book is that it is more specifically 'social justice', in the centre-left conception that will be developed below, that should be read into the general term 'justice'. So then, the title becomes 'Access to Social Justice'. A book which really intended to cover this topic would need to look far further than law and its dispute resolving hinterland. It would need to consider social security benefits, housing, health, employment, education, the family and so forth. These concerns are within the remit of this book but not capable of full treatment by it.

By now we have reached the following: 'Social Justice Through Access to Systems of Dispute Resolution'. Another approach would be to turn the title around and talk instead of 'Social Justice Through Access to Dispute Resolution'. The temptation is now to call the book 'Susan' and leave it at that. But the quest for the right title introduces some of the main concerns of this text.

The core of the dilemma for the democratic left has been the strife between notions of the individual and the social. With the growth of discourse centred on human rights and the need for the creation of constitutional settlements, the left has found itself caught between a suspicion of centralised power and a desire for communal action. Indeed the greatest export from the liberal Western states has been the democratic and constitutional ideal. The leftist compromise has therefore been the need to sacrifice some of the rights of the individual for the success of the social.

The definition of 'the social' has moved towards a synonym with the term 'the economy'. As Thatcher pronounced that there was no such thing as society, the right began to define the sphere of action beyond the individual as being exclusively about economic activity. Consequently, unemployment became an acceptable casualty of the achievement of communal, economic goals. The left in Europe has been beguiled into accepting the elusive goal of the 'social market': meaning the achievement of monetarist economic goals but within a framework of generating social justice. The issue for this text is to unpick these attitudes to 'the social' in the context of the achievement of social justice.

The title for the book in this rightist context would then have to be 'Law, Liberty and the Individual', reflecting the civil libertarian bent that is often given to the role of law as a protector from oppression rather than a tool of social cohesion. However, there is a need to consider the means of the enhancement of those rights and the means of the realization of those individuals' goals. The creation of a political programme for government to achieve these goals requires an understanding of the social context in which individuals will seek to activate their rights.

The underlying conviction of this book is that the role of legal and justice systems is to act as a servant to all in society to converse about and to formulate their mutual rights and obligations. The concern of the justice system must be to enable the potential of the people to be unlocked. Therefore, the title of the book could become 'People's Access to Justice', in the vogueish spirit of the Blairite government, to act in the name of all the people. However, given that the justice system is then a place to converse about rights and to formulate their practical application to specific circumstances and to specific conflicts, it is political in the broadest sense of that term. It is a conversation about power. Legitimacy is lent to action by means of its sanction from the law or the justice system. Therefore, the title becomes something to do with 'people, power and social justice'. For the civil libertarian, in the guise adopted by the Blair administration, this is action in the name of the protection of the people by means of empowering them as individuals.

However, if it becomes responsive to a political project perhaps it is concerned with the delivery of social justice by means of appropriate constitutional and legislative change which is required to be enforced by courts and tribunals such that the title becomes 'Social Justice Now'. Perhaps that is a little too situationist, too much of a slogan. Its underlying purpose is to be found in another possible title: 'Achieving Social Justice'. The notion of a viable project is captured by this title. It is important to understand that any social change that is attempted by means of the reform of the legal system must be intended as an achievable result rather than a vague aim for some time in the future. However, that title is too portentous and too optimistic for the reform of the legal system alone. The legal system, and the justice system more generally, are merely tools for litigants to establish their rights rather than the sole resolution of the discourse about the content of those rights. What is central to the discussion is the importance law has as the language in which liberal democracies talk about the nature of rights and the mechanisms for their enforcement. Linked back to the earlier consideration of the need for access, a composite title looks as follows: 'Achieving Our Potential – Access to Rights for the Citizen'.

The synthesis of the foregoing must be to see the justice system as a tool within which both government and citizens are able to generate and produce resolutions to conflicts and re-definitions of rights and obligations as part of the broader context of regenerating the British polity. There is therefore a sense of a *processus*, an ongoing movement towards a goal of social justice. In a modernist conception it could be said that a just society is something which could be measured and achieved by diligent application of policy. This book is somewhat more pessimistic about the chances of success. Rather, social justice is a goal to be reached for, although possibly never attained. An ideology requiring development and improvement, without many concrete expectations that it is a standard which can be met such that sociologists and lawyers can close up their offices and walk out into the sunlight of a society beyond conflict.

Hence the eventual title of this book: *Towards a Just Society – Law, Labour and Legal Aid*. In the specific context of the new Labour, or *New* Labour, government, there is a need to set out the necessary course for the progress towards this goal of a just society in the context of access to law and the provision of publicly funded legal services. This book seeks to map some of the ways in which ordinary citizens, individually or collectively, can move towards a just society.

I am grateful to a number of people in the gestation and the writing of this book. Most of the ideas were formulated while working for the Labour Party as speech-writer and, apparently, 'wonk'. Paul Boateng was a friend and exemplar throughout that time. Important in the formulation of the ideas explored in this book were Nigel Warner and Liza Vizard without whose comradeship and affection little would have happened. Conor Gearty was a source of energy, advice and comradeship, and has been rightly described as 'writing like a prince'. I am hugely grateful to Rob Blackburn for giving me the support and the opportunity to explore more of these ideas. Latterly my colleagues at Queen Mary and Westfield College have made me welcome and energetic. In general I would like to thank my family for their support in developing my political self. Similarly, the members of Beaconsfield CLP who helped me to put this to work. This book is written by a Labour Party member, socialist, loyalist and activist in an attempt to contribute to the debate about delivering justice in Britain. Where it contradicts it is concerned to highlight our core values, where it argues it seeks to warn, and where it recommends it seeks to move us towards our shared conviction in the regeneration of a just society.

Alastair Hudson
Queen Mary and Westfield College
Mile End
April Fool's Day 1999

Introduction

It is social justice which requires that there must be access to the law
for all.   *Tony Blair, speech given to Sedgefield constituency,*
28 January 1995

The central assertion of this book is that reform of one part of the
'justice system' cannot achieve its goals in a vacuum from consideration of all other aspects of that system. As Tony Blair has said, and as
John Smith said before him, the purpose behind reform of the justice
system is the pursuit of greater social justice. The aim of any
programme of reform must be to work towards a 'just society'.[1] That
involves an increase in access to the system. It also involves a
programme of public education and a simplification of substantive
legal rules. The procedures of court-based litigation must be stream-
lined – however, that will not provide a solution in itself. The British
people must be brought closer to the means of dispute resolution as
a way of enhancing their own liberties and of unlocking their own
potential.

The defects in the current legal aid system

It seems to me that you cannot begin to talk about the English legal
system without making some reference to Charles Dickens's *Bleak
House*. The opening to that novel works every bit as well as an
opening to this analysis of the shortcomings in the English justice
system today.

> London. Michaelmas term lately over, and the Lord
> Chancellor sitting in Lincoln's Inn Hall. Implacable
> November weather ... Fog everywhere. Fog up the river,
> where it flows among green aits and meadows; fog down the
> river, where it rolls defiled among the tiers of shipping, and
> the waterside pollutions of a great (and dirty) city ...

1

And hard by ... in Lincoln's Inn Hall, at the very heart of
the fog, sits the Lord Chancellor in his High Court of
Chancery.

Never can there come a fog too thick, never can there come
mud and mire too deep, to assort with the groping and
floundering condition in which this High Court of Chancery,
most pestilent of hoary sinners, holds, this day, in the sight
of heaven and earth.

Jarndyce -v- Jarndyce drones on. This scarecrow of a suit has,
in course of time, become so complicated that no man alive
knows what it means. The parties to it understand it least;
but it has been observed that no two Chancery lawyers can
talk about it for five minutes without coming to total
disagreement as to all the premises.

The metaphor of fog is a particularly apposite one for the English
legal system at the time of writing. The modes of dress and address
have not changed since Dickens wrote of the Courts of Chancery (set
in a time before even the Victorian era in which he lived). Moreover,
the confusion caused to ordinary people, let alone lawyers, by the
complexity of law and legal procedure continues today. The groping
and floundering condition in which the British citizen finds herself
when confronted by legal matters flies in the face of any assertion that
we live in a democracy where all are equally subject to law and
protected by it. It would be better put to describe all as being *subjects*
of the law. In our democracy, law created both by Parliament and by
judges has replaced the monarchy as the locus of political power. A
citizenry which is not able to know the laws that affect it, nor of the
procedures of that legal system, are as oppressed as subjects of a
monarch dispensing arbitrary justice.

Logically, the only institution which can stand in the way of this
oppression is the legal profession, able to advise citizens how to
respond to law and (in the case of judges) to interpret and apply law
in a way that is fair. The fundamental issue is that the costs of
bringing a dispute to law are so prohibitive that most citizens are
unable to do so. Alternatively, if some money can be found to meet
the fee, lawyers are able to drag out proceedings and increase cost and
complexity such that many are forced into settlement against their
real interests. In this way law is capable of being oppressive. The
business of this book is to examine this democratic shortcoming and
to explore some of the means of reforming the system to alleviate
some of the problems that result. At a fundamental level, this is a
book about social justice. A concept difficult to define in the abstract
but dealt with for the purposes of this book as a result of ensuring

equality of access to law and an equally accessible means for all citizens to activate and protect their civil rights.

The introduction to Labour's policy document *Access to Justice* states that,

> the principle of equality before the law ... is now under
> threat because, in practice, it is meaningless and worthless to
> the millions of people who can no longer get proper access to
> legal advice, assistance and representation.[2]

Both the legal system, and the legal aid scheme that funds it to the tune of £1.7 billion annually, are overly reliant on lawyers and expensive court-based litigation. The heart of the political problem is that there is no new money to spend on publicly funded legal services and the maintenance of the court system. To manage the increase in demand and spiralling cost, there is therefore a need for a more fundamental refocusing of the structure of publicly funded legal services.

The grail for this discussion is a means of enabling all citizens to access legal and quasi-legal structures. Political priorities urge the system to find a way of achieving that without cost to central taxation. The current legal aid system, whether seen as a US-style judi-care safety net or as part of the welfare state, has become very unfashionable. In its place are urged a number of initiatives to place the onus on lawyer and client to find alternative means of paying a lawyer's fee – whether based on insurance or a parcelling out of the winner's award of damages. However, it appears that there is no single replacement for a legal aid system funded directly out of taxation, by contributions from clients and through costs awards, which will meet this book's call for greater social justice. There is no single, comprehensive system of justice provision in this jurisdiction or in any other which could replace legal aid in its entirety. The question is, then: 'How can legal aid be provided differently in particular types of case so that the citizen receives an equivalent or improved form of representation and justice, in line with the pursuit of social justice?' And, furthermore, what fundamental alterations can be made to the courts and tribunal systems to improve their responsiveness to the needs of ordinary citizens?

As considered in the remainder of this book, it is possible that the development of franchising of legal aid services can contribute to the control of cost and the monitoring of quality of legal advice and representation, despite having been formulated originally as a cost-cutting measure. The cost of legal aid can be monitored because the fees of these firms can be controlled by a dialogue between them and the Legal Aid Board as to the line between cost-effectiveness for the firm and for the Board. The result would be that by maintaining the level of the legal aid budget at present levels, more representation could be provided for more people than at present. Rather than rely upon central legal aid funds, there *may* be circumstances in which it would be reasonable for some parties to take out insurance against successful litigation. While some suggest movement towards a system similar to the Japanese system of compulsory insurance for health (payment through taxation to purchase insurance for legal costs), this movement away from the welfare state motivation of the 1949 Legal Aid Act is resisted in this book on grounds that it transforms all citizens, weak as well as strong, into independent economic actors to be dealt with merely as consumers rather than afforded viable democratic rights as fully-fledged citizens.

In continuation of this political theme, it can be argued that where public resources are being used, there ought to be some public recognition that some types of case are of greater utility than others. The argument runs: why should a centre-left administration allow millions of pounds to be used by the apparently wealthy (as in the Maxwell litigation), when other taxpaying individuals are not able to bring actions against their employers using legal aid? The extreme cultural shift that the Blair administration's proposals for a Community Legal Service proposal represent, is personified most clearly in the movement towards a system of *vertical* eligibility for legal aid, rather than simple *horizontal* eligibility on the basis of income. These issues are developed in Part III, *Publicly Funded Legal Services*.

The essential element to be borne in mind about publicly funded litigation is that legal aid is a payment of money from central taxation directly into lawyers' pockets. The question whether or not the legal aid bill is too high, is really a question about whether or not too much money is being paid to lawyers. The important measurement to be taken is the number of citizens who are enabled to enter into the justice system and participate in the discourse about the nature and content of their rights and responsibilities, rather than whether or not lawyers ought to be entitled to receive higher fees from the public purse. Restrictive practices in the legal system which parcel out work between QCs, junior barristers and solicitors – nothing less than an informal cartel formed by professional expectations – maintains standard fees at a high rate which has led to the current high level of the total legal aid bill. It is important to consider the extent to which voluntary agencies and advice agencies should be enabled to provide these services and make claims on the legal aid fund where they can demonstrate the necessary competence. It will be argued that the deconstruction of these restrictive practices are necessary to improve the democratic rights of ordinary people.

The acid test must be the quality of the justice that is made available to every citizen and not the commercial viability of the legal industry.

The reform of civil litigation procedures

The thrust of the reforms and alterations proffered by the lawyers themselves is for a tinkering with the detailed rules of their procedures. The irony of technocratic restructuring as a sop to the political need for fundamental change, is that the lawyers will insist on retaining their Regency codes of dress and Edwardian modes of address so that the practice of law remains as rarefied as ever it was. Subtle changes to the Rules of the Supreme Court will only have an impact at the margins for some of those who are currently able to litigate in any event. It will do little to increase access or secure broader social justice.

The example considered in some detail in Part IV, *Components of Delivery*, is the report prepared by Lord Woolf into civil litigation procedures. The easy criticism of the Woolf Report into the reform of civil litigation is that his strictly procedural reforms alone are unlikely to make any more litigants come to law. The problem for litigants is often not the concern about the delay involved in litigation, but rather the cost of paying for the first consultation with a lawyer. One particularly regrettable feature of the Woolf Report, however, is that the importance of a case is not necessarily to be measured by reference to its significance to the parties but rather by reference to its cash value. The very fact that a litigant will be required to rebut a presumption of lack of importance merely underlines the fact that those of restricted means are being relegated in the juridical scheme of things, at the expense of high-cost cash worth commercial litigation in Lord Woolf's recommendations. The instinct for the lawyer in coming to the reform of the law is to measure the profit involved in different types of case and to work backwards from there, not to consider the citizen's democratic rights.

Lord Woolf's fundamental aim was 'to improve access to justice by reducing inequalities, cost, delay, and complexity of civil litigation and to introduce greater certainty as to timescales and costs'.[3] There are also a tranche of specific objectives within that broader remit. Lord Woolf has expressed the opinion that the system of civil justice ought to be, 'accessible, efficient and just'.[4] He described the current system as being 'expensive, slow, uncertain and unequal'.[5] The last identified problem is interesting. It has hints of the statement of aims of the Legal Action Group which called for 'equal access to justice for all'. In Lord Woolf's opinion, people are not afforded an equal opportunity of justice if the system operates to deter them from seeking or obtaining access to justice.

One central issue explored in Part IV is between judicial control and party control of litigation. Is it an interference by the judges to set down timetables for the conduct of litigation? The answer to this question might depend on a more fundamental view of the role of the civil legal system in this regard. There are two competing views. Woolf considers that involving judges at an earlier stage will increase the likelihood of the issues being defined sooner and the parties reaching settlement. Zander's view is that involving judges at an earlier stage will increase the cost of litigation by requiring parties and lawyers to attend court sooner in cases which would probably settle in any event. He argues that at present more than 50 per cent of cases settle without court order.[6] Therefore, the introduction of judges into the decision of these cases is more likely to impede settlement than to hasten it. The social role of law is the key question here. While there is no denying the extent of the crisis of feasibility facing the English legal process at present, there is a great danger of ignoring the purpose of that same system.

Civil law is generally treated as being a homogeneous entity. The Woolf Report treats it in this way for the most part. For a lawyer, it is easier to think of one case as being the same as any other. It has the happy side-effect, at least superficially, of removing any hint of bias. Unfortunately, as set out earlier, the current organization of the legal system means that there is a power imbalance in the system at the moment. What is necessary is the disaggregation of types of case. Rather than seeing all litigation as being the same, it is only possible to remove imbalance by recognizing the differences between cases.

One good example is the need to treat personal injury cases differently from other types of litigation. The problem with personal injury litigation is that most cases will settle. By requiring parties to go before a judge at an early stage in the proceedings will lead to a front-loading of costs and prevent early settlement in many cases. The way in which this form of litigation is necessarily conducted (relying on the production of expert evidence which frequently removes the need to go to court) marks personal injury cases out as needing separate treatment. This is another example of the need to look at cases vertically rather than horizontally.

Alternative dispute resolution

The over-concentration in legal affairs policy on court-based reme-dies, which are overly expensive and inaccessible for most citizens,

6

has created the need to introduce alternative methods of more *appropriate* dispute resolution. Where law prevents access to viable solutions and remedies, it denies the litigants access not only to their rights but also access to their own potential. The argument that is classically put is that alternative dispute resolution (ADR) offers some capacity to think more constructively about the resolution of disputes.

Two main concerns arise. First, some institutions and groups of economic actors use alternative means of dispute resolution to keep their disputes apart from the courts and thus privatize their own fields of endeavour. One prolific example of this is a large amount of work done by arbitrators and disciplinary panels in financial markets in disciplining traders who have transgressed exchange rule-books. The danger is that the law's control is abrogated if disputes are not taken to law but rather to some insider who interprets the market's own rules as the market sees fit. The second concern is that some tribunals are created to deal typically with disputes concerning the poor or disadvantaged, such as social security tribunals, where lawyers are discouraged from appearing. In these contexts, the dispute resolution procedures appear to be de-skilled and the concerns of the poor to be subjected to a 'second class' form of justice. Alternative dispute resolution therefore raises concerns at both ends of the spectrum as well as offering a much-vaunted means of enabling citizens to access justice inexpensively and rapidly.

As considered below, there are a number of senses in which the reorganization of advice agencies and the broader use of computer-based technology also offer a means of opening up access to justice to citizens in alternative ways. The introduction of groundbreaking, new technology will undoubtedly revolutionize the conduct of litigation and facilitate a reduction in the pressure on central taxation. The reorganization of law centres, Citizens' Advice Bureaux and the other private charitable organizations which offer similar services, is necessary to co-ordinate the scarce resources which exist in terms of equipment, reference materials and human expertise. The use of this technology will enable the advice agencies to offer a unique new service that will be in great demand from ordinary people.

A Ministry of Justice

Amid this maelstrom of calls for change, and potential avenues for change, there is a need to co-ordinate justice policy more efficiently and accountably. The democratic problem surrounds the role of the Lord Chancellor as Speaker of the House of Lords, senior judge,

Cabinet minister and political apparatchik, rolled into one body. There is therefore a fusion of constitutional roles in one place. Developments under Lord Irvine in relation to the powers of the Lord Chancellor personally to approve rights of audience in court indicate an ever more disturbing accumulation of power in one place.

For a socialist, the creation of a central Ministry of Justice offers a suitably state-ist response to the problem. Matters of justice should be the responsibility of an elected, Cabinet minister who is accountable directly in the House of Commons. The creation of a central ministry would also recover the scraps of the justice system which are administered in other departments. The new Ministry of Justice proposed in Part V, *Models for Reform*, would organize the sharing of premises to reduce cost, and the extension of the support functions to ensure efficiencies that are translated to the citizen in a palpable improvement in the quality of justice received.

Policy concerning all the Industrial, Social Security and other tribunals must be centred in one place so that efficient working practices, costs savings and better administration can be concentrated together. Much of the savings in costs will come from 'hidden' reforms to the legal system. A Law Foundation would be created to examine the legal system, modelled on a similar body to that found in New South Wales, Australia. Its role would be to examine methods of improving access to justice and the reform of technical procedures which hamper access to justice or increase cost unnecessarily. Similarly, a National Advisory Service is necessary to bring together the diverse functions carried out by local government, the Citizens' Advice Bureau network, and law centres. In tandem with a form of National Legal Service, the ability of the citizen to receive advice and support can be greatly increased without great cost.

The political problem: Rhetoric and resources

Before considering the detail of proposals to reform the legal system, it is worth considering the exigencies of day-to-day politics and the need to manage a public sector budget. The problem of control of the costs of the legal system (let alone the need for radical alteration of that system) had been an intractable one for the Major administration and promises to be equally challenging for the New Labour administration. The issue of budgets and system management are the bane of modern government. A statement made by Labour MP Paul Boateng, when shadow spokesperson for legal affairs, is illuminating:

The Labour Party's central aims and values focus on the need
for strong communities which are able to sustain themselves
as part of a successful society.[7]

This attitude underlines the way in which politicians still want to
speak about the aspects of government which they seek to *manage*:
that is, they wish to conceptualize the problems rhetorically.[8] The
political problem is one of balancing ideological will with available
resources. As will be considered later, the solution to balancing that
equation may be to pursue bloody-mindedly the logic of that
political rhetoric.

The focus of the New Labour government's proposals[9] is on '*the
consumer of legal services*'.[10] This highlights another potential problem
with the future of the legal system in political terms. As the problem
is seen as one of consumption of legal services, the civil liberties aspect
of access to the most mundane forms of legal advice and assistance is
constantly downplayed. The legal system remains a system isolated
within its own terms of reference — fenced off from the broader
discussion of constitutional, political and national renewal.

The Labour Party's chief proposal to achieve this refocusing of
resources is to create a Community Legal Service[11] incorporating a
radically reformed legal aid scheme and far greater provision for
alternative dispute resolution. Coupled with this will be the reform
of the franchising scheme, extended to control the cost of access to
justice and to set high standards for the quality of services provided
by franchise-holders. The renewed focus on the *consumer* of legal
services must mean changes for the legal profession.[12] What it fails to
hit upon is the need to focus on the end-goal of a just society and not
on the trendy rhetoric of consumerism.

The heart of the political problem is that there is no new money to
spend on publicly funded legal services and the maintenance of the
court system. To manage the increase in demand and spiralling cost,
there is, therefore, a need for a more fundamental refocusing of the
structure of publicly funded legal services. Labour Party policy in
this context has undergone great change since 1992. It can be
segregated into three distinct phases. The first phase is policy under
John Smith, the second under the leadership of Tony Blair in
Opposition, and the third manifestation is policy under Lord Irvine
as Lord Chancellor in the New Labour administration. It would be
easy to overemphasize the differences in these drifts in policy. There
are some differences in detail. At the time of writing, Sir Peter
Middleton has completed a review of civil justice and legal aid policy
at the behest of the Lord Chancellor, Lord Irvine which has informed
much of the Access to Justice Bill 1999.[13]

New directions under Labour

There has been some rapid development of policy under Lord Irvine. The first notable factor is the determination of the new Lord Chancellor not to be bound by official party policy. The Labour Party election manifesto was, necessarily, less detailed than their subsequent policy document *Access to Justice*, but in an interview with the *Observer* newspaper soon after the election,[14] Lord Irvine set out some policy stances which appeared to be in conflict with published Labour Party policy. Foremost among them was the abolition of plans to reform judicial appointments. Proposals to introduce a lay voice into appointments to the bench and to the creation of new Queen's Counsel, providing accountability in the selection process, were thus laid aside in a few comments to journalists.

In Part II, *Theories of Social Change*, we shall examine some of the main underpinnings of the 'third way' suggested for Anglo-American politics by politicians like Tony Blair and non-politicians like Giddens. Giddens's principal intervention in this debate[15] has reclaimed a number of important themes of the left, such as equality, which had previously been thought lost in the sea of change. In examining the development of Labour government policy in this area, it will be important to ask why there is so little ideological linkage between the reform of law and of the constitution, with the progressive rhetoric of Blair and thinkers like Giddens, when there is so much obvious overlap in the subjects which they are discussing. In part this resolves itself in a lack of imagination among lawyers and policy-makers when considering the ways in which constitutional change will be *put into action* through law and quasi-legal structures. Indeed the position of the Lord Chancellor has become an interesting one since May 1997. His most famous public words, rather than being an express commentary on constitutional or legal reforms, has been his announcement that he considers himself to be in similar mould to Wolsey – the Chancellor at the time of Henry VIII who ran the Kafkaesque Star Chamber and was ultimately beheaded.[16]

It would be of some great concern if the reluctance to embrace progressive policy-making in the area of legal affairs were the result of an all-powerful Lord Chancellor blindly staking out a programme of politically convenient cost-cutting, rather than surveying the orchard root and branch prior to cutting out dead wood and planting anew. The irony may prove to be, as developed below, that only radical and citizen-friendly policies of the left are capable of delivering greater access at proportionately lower cost. The Access to Justice Bill (still awaiting Royal Assent at the time of writing) is considered in detail below.

NOTES AND REFERENCES

1 The expression 'a just society' is that used in the new Clause 4 of the Labour Party Constitution.
2 Labour Party, *Access to Justice* (London, Labour Party, 1995); see Appendix.
3 *Ibid.*
4 Speaking at the London School of Economics, 30 January 1997.
5 *Ibid.*
6 *Judicial Statistics*, 1994, p. 30, Table 3.4. See, for example, the *Report of the Personal Injuries Litigation Procedure Working Party*, (the 'Cantley Committee'), 1979, Cmnd. 7476, para. 9.
7 Sometime Labour Party spokesperson on legal affairs, speech to the Labour Party Conference, Brighton, October 1995.
8 As the Foreign Secretary Robin Cook has said, 'In Opposition you wake up in the morning thinking about what you are going to say today; in government you wake in the morning thinking about what you are going to do'.
9 As expressed while in Opposition, it should be noted.
10 As set out in numerous places in Labour Party, *Access to Justice* (London, Labour Party, 1995); see Appendix.
11 On the Community Legal Service, see Part V, *Models for Reform*.
12 See generally, Labour Party *Access to Justice, op. cit.*
13 A report published by completion as, *Review of Civil Justice and Legal Aid. Report to the Lord Chancellor by Sir Peter Middleton* (Lord Chancellor's Department, September 1997).
14 The *Observer*, 27 July 1997.
15 A. Giddens, *The Third Way: The Renewal of Social Democracy* (Cambridge, Polity Press, 1998).
16 Lord Irvine's most infamous public spending decision is his spending of £59,211 on wallpaper for his official apartments; see *inter alia* the *Guardian*, 2 December 1997.

Part I

Rethinking Justice Provision

1

Conservative Approaches

It's the characteristic of our Western societies that the language of power is law, not magic, religion, or anything else.   *Michel Foucault*[1]

INTRODUCTION

Before coming to examine the detail of the new political thinking that is growing up around the Blair government, it is important to conceive of the link between political policy and justice policy. The politics of the legal system and of related justice systems have tended to stand outside the mainstream of British politics. The core of debates about the economy and the welfare state have not impinged too closely on the development of ideas concerning the reform of the legal system. This chapter aims to consider a number of separately identifiable political attitudes and to link them specifically to legal affairs policy. Some of the components of that political thinking are examined in greater detail in Part II, *Theories of Social Change*, together with their practical impact on the discussion of well-understood debates relating to the trade-off between equality and liberty, and the possibility of creating a notion of achievable social justice. This Part, *Rethinking Justice Provision*, aims to put that debate into the context of the reform of the legal system.

The movement of the underlying political debate, fashionably enough, at the end of one millennium and the start of another, is for a third way between the old dogmas of left and right – and even away from the static positions of the reactive centre. The Blair administration has sought to encourage the development of a 'third way' as a political model,[2] aping Clinton's triangulation policy by moving forward between extremes of policy and pursuing Giddens's strategy from *Beyond Left and Right*.[3] While British politics has undergone seismic change with the end of consensus politics in the Thatcher era and its re-creation with the advent of New Labour, the legal system

15

has remained caught within its own autopoietic world, talking in its own language and conceiving of reform in connection with its own norms rather than in the context of the broader political debate.[4] The Thatcher governments failed to implement profound change in the face of opposition from vested interests within the judiciary and the legal professions.[5] The possibility for change has come with the election of a Labour government which is prepared to discuss fundamental constitutional reform and thus open up the way for a discussion of the way in which justice is delivered.

Political treatment of the legal system has tended to be discussed in a jargon and in relation to issues disseminated by the legal profession and the legal system. The staples of political discourse are not put to work in the context of the reform of law or access to justice. In recent years, the growing family of reports, policy documents and proposals invoking the now tired and under-analysed expression 'access to justice' have begun to emphasize the need to consider this area in the language of political reform more generally. While the Blair administration has begun to develop an identifiable set of principles to underpin its policies, its programme for the reform of the legal system, once in office, has lost touch with its core political convictions.

As explored in *Modelling New Labour's legal affairs policy*, consultation papers, speeches and other policy ephemera issued by the Lord Chancellor's Department has shown a tendency to confuse a number of different political creeds without attempting an explanation, for example, of how the language of human rights and the language of free markets can be effectively brought together in one political programme. The result, it is suggested later in this book, is that the policies which are being developed fail to match the political requirements of the Blair administration.[6] This section will first examine the various possible political approaches to the reform of the legal system before analysing both what is meant by the New Labour project in intellectual terms and how the pronouncements of Lord Chancellor Irvine fall to be analysed.

The Labour Lord Chancellor's Department does not appear to have its intellectual hand on the tiller of reform. While the statements of the problems to be faced are, for the most part, uncontentious, the proposed solutions lack a framework of principle which can inform a programme of coherent reform. That is not to say that legal affairs policy is symptomatic of a government without principled direction. That is not this writer's view. New Labour does have a set of ideological underpinnings: even though at times they appear contradictory and at times they do not deal expressly with many of the concerns of critics and loyalists alike. The aim here is to map out

16

those varied contexts. Significantly, this book seeks to apply those principles to the legal affairs context explicitly – to explain a means of shoring up the gaps in the programme of the current Lord Chancellor.

In terms of justice provision (that is the delivery of access to justice through courts and other structures and tribunals) future reform must move in line with the development of general political thinking rather than be relegated to a closed systemic discussion among lawyers of practices, policies and principles which only they are trained and competent to understand. Lawyers seek to exercise power in this context by claiming the sole right to discuss the detail of the reform of the legal system. Law has acquired its own power base primarily because liberal democracies are structured around a parliamentary politics which exists to debate and to create law. Delivery of those laws is then treated as a secondary factor to be monitored and controlled by technocrats, rather than being considered as an issue of politics in the same way as healthcare and education. The following discussion aims to tease apart not only the different strands of general political thinking but also the manner in which those different approaches inform policy on justice provision.

The political discourse of law

As Foucault maintains in the extract quoted at the beginning of this chapter, the language of law is at the centre of the discourse of power in Western society. For the individual, it is in the arena of law that questions of rights and power are decided. Where there is no access to law, there is no power. Without power there are no effective rights and no real obligations. The issue of access is dominated by the lawyers themselves and by political decisions as to the availability of public resources. While the political debate is effectively restricted to those legal actors, the only two groups of people who are able to access our justice system are the very wealthy or those who live on income support levels of income. The majority of British citizens, typically those who are in work or who have only modest savings, are unable to gain access to legal advice because they cannot afford it.

What is implicit in the regular trumpeting of the phrase 'access to justice' is an understanding that law occupies an important symbolic and practical place in the Western, democratic model. It is not true to say that most citizens have regular contact with the legal system – appearance in court for the non-lawyer is a rare occurrence. Many citizens will live long and fruitful lives without ever having to enter a court building. However, citizens will come into daily contact with the effects of government-through-law. The logic of democracy is that governments are empowered by democratic mandate to rule within the confines of existing law by creating new laws. Law is the exercise of power in that political sense. Therefore, it is essential to the logic of liberal democracies, built around the notion of the rule of law and the function of politics being to create law and thereby govern, that the law is capable of access by all citizens in equal part. Legitimacy for governmental action is achieved by law-making through constitutional means, as well as day-to-day electoral legitimacy through the lens of the media's treatment of politics. As Foucault said, 'it is as if even the word of the law could no longer be authorised, in our society, except by a discourse of truth'.[7] Law acquires the mantle of truth and probity precisely because it is law, made through the appropriate democratic mechanisms.

Without wishing to short circuit the voluminous jurisprudential treatment of the role and nature of law, at this stage it is important to accept that law does occupy a pivotal role in the logic of the way in which government in the UK is conducted. The creation and implementation of law is the whole point of government. That creation and implementation of legal right and responsibility is the manifestation of governmental power. Therefore, access to law is a vital part of making democratic politics work for citizens in such a society. Consequently, it must be right to begin any discussion of the reform of the legal system with a reference to law's role in relation to rights and responsibilities. However, that is not enough to explain the intellectual context of the discussion of law. Consideration of 'access to justice' prevents an understanding of the legal system as a political arena in itself and treats it merely as a conduit. The truth is that access to legal advice and representation is itself a feature of the presence or absence of political power. Therefore, the following discussion will take it as read that law occupies a central place in the logic of democratic politics and turns to consider the manner in which well-understood political positions fit into the rhetoric of law reform.

The development of policies to deal with the reform or restructuring of the legal profession have suffered from under-theorization. The legal system is only addressed as a political question when it has become too expensive and it therefore needs to be controlled in the same way as any other increase in public spending. The Lord Chancellor's Department budget is considerably smaller than the giants of public spending like Social Security and Defence. However, its relative anonymity in terms of size is not a reason for its marginalization from mainstream political debate.[8] What is lacking in current debate about legal affairs policy is a way of looking at the legal system in a political context that links it to other problems of public policy. To increase access to law it is necessary to think differently about the larger system that gives us law, solves disputes and gives advice to citizens more generally.

Identifying the key political issues

There are three predominant issues in the legal affairs debate: legal aid, access to democratically conferred rights, and the receipt of advice from publicly funded legal services. At the core of the debate is legal aid.

Since 1993, legal aid has become a political issue in its own despite years of comparative obscurity since the late 1940s. 1993 is the most convenient date to establish the coming-of-age of legal aid because that was the year in which two things happened. First, on 1 April 1993, John Taylor, the then Parliamentary Under-Secretary to the Lord Chancellor's Department announced an alteration to legal aid eligibility levels in respect of civil cases. The result was that approximately 14 million people were removed from eligibility for civil legal aid. While the Conservative government protested that only a few thousand people who had actually claimed legal aid in previous years would now be removed from entitlement, the political motivation behind the change was to remove the right to have lawyers' fees defrayed out of public funds from a large section of society (about one-fifth of the total population).

Second, the probity of legal aid provision to apparently wealthy individuals defending white-collar fraud charges began to receive coverage in the tabloid press. The connection was made between one of the demons of the tabloid press, 'fat cat fraudsters', and the exploitation of public money to fund their expensive legal defences. Once this idea had lodged itself into the collective mind of the tabloid and quality press, legal aid became a feature of the coverage of Maxwell, Levitt and other headline fraud trials. This increased attention culminated in the green paper 'Legal Aid for the Apparently Wealthy' which sought to develop policies to meet growing public concern about the abuse of public funds.

What was never discussed in this analysis of the role of legal aid was that dimension which connected with the ability of citizens to enforce their own rights. In the public discussion of the 90s buzz-word 'community', little was done to connect legal aid to the growing enthusiasm for self-help initiatives in local communities, and action taken by groups in protecting their own interests. Clearly litigation to establish the balance of rights and responsibilities between groups and local authorities or other groups of citizens is one important means of generating and protecting self-interest.

Legal aid is generally considered to be an economic question of the amount of money that is available, in some way, 'to pay for justice', as though expenditure on legal aid necessarily correlated with the acquisition of a given amount of justice. This is the result of an avoidable confusion which inhabits all discussion of legal aid. Legal aid does not buy justice – rather legal aid defrays lawyers' fees. There must be a gulf between the achievement of social justice in political terms and the payment of lawyers' fees. Much of that legal aid money goes to acquire advice and representation for citizens.

However, there is no central control of the manner in which that translates automatically into the provision of justice. Aside from the issue as to whether or not a legal outcome is just or not in all cases, there is a necessary reluctance for the political to intrude into the sphere in which lawyers and judges seek to reach solutions away from political concerns. Politics is seen as being a partisan activity which should not sully the purity of legal endeavour. That is to ignore the political motivations of some litigation and to hide from the necessarily political results which law imposes. For example, in a dispute over ownership of a property: someone gets the house and someone has to find somewhere else to live. At a very mundane level, that is political, reflecting a decision as to the comparative rights of people to occupy property. If a trade union brings an action against central government that is political in a sense which would be understood by any newspaper. All that legal aid is doing in that context is fanning the flames by making more litigation possible.

So a new understanding of legal aid's role is important. Legal aid acquires access to both a system and a reservoir of knowledge to which the ordinary citizen would not otherwise have access. The legal system is the arena in which the discourse about the nature and contents of rights and responsibilities in their application to practical cases, takes place. As considered in Part II, *Theories of Social Change*, the law takes from society a number of areas of debate and moulds them into a stylized form of proceeding. It is at this level that the citizen requires access to a reservoir of specialist knowledge: knowledge both of the substantive rules by which that system operates and knowledge of the ceremonies (pleadings, preliminary hearings, trial, modes of address, and modes of dress) which the legal system employs. Legal aid is therefore, in a real sense, about *access* to knowledge and to the possibility of participating in the ceremony of putting law into practice. At that level legal aid does two things. It makes the means by which the legal system decides disputes, a system which can be accessed equally by all who receive legal aid regardless of their means. It also bridges the world in which the disputes arise, and the world in which they are resolved.

That legal aid occupies an important place in accessing the system of justice is not a novel proposition. However, it is too common that legal aid as a means of accessing the system is conflated with the dispensation of justice itself. Legal aid facilitates; it does not guarantee results. Legal aid permits some form of access only to the advice of lawyers and to the courts system. Nothing has been said yet about the power of the Legal Aid Board to deny or restrict legal aid in given cases, that will be considered later. What is important to unpick at this stage is the fact that legal aid is available only for court-based solutions. It does not, at the time of writing, enable access to other forums such as employment tribunals or social security tribunals. Therefore, legal aid is about access to legal remedies rather than about access to the justice system more broadly. One of the strengths of the Access to Justice Bill is the possibility of applying this funding to non-court-based disputes.

While legal aid is at the heart of legal affairs policy discussions it is a symptom of the way in which the system was organized as part of the welfare state settlement. This introduces the second theme: access to democratically conferred rights. The purpose behind the creation of legal aid was to provide access to few lawyers practising in the UK after the Second World War. As explored below, it is not necessarily the case that legal aid was introduced solely as a means of supplying a further welfare benefit. If it had been meant to be a welfare benefit, it could be expected that it would have been linked more closely to the structures applicable to the provision of other welfare state benefits. The legal aid structure has never operated on the welfare state model, having been administered by the Law Society rather than an organ of the state, and having been means-tested rather than available on the basis of universal entitlement.

What is more interesting about legal aid in the context of the creation of the welfare state is that it broke the preserve of the civil courts as being a place where only the wealthy could go. Significantly, in terms of criminal courts, the defendant was able to acquire legal representation at no cost to herself. Therefore the law became something which could be activated by any citizen who fell within the legal aid scheme's eligibility criteria. The strength of the legal aid scheme was that it permitted access to democratically conferred rights and, more importantly, to their enforcement by legal means rather than by extra-legal means such as force, revolt or industrial dispute. The court was no longer a place where the poor were oppressed by magistrates imposing the criminal law. Instead the courts became a place where it was possible for ordinary people to go, in the company of their lawyers, to bid for a new settlement in the content of the common law and in the framing of the rights-responsibilities equation.

In public law, before the introduction of a large amount of legislation in the twentieth century (to do with public order and latterly with human rights), the common law contained most of the detailed rules which went to make up the British constitution. The question begs itself as to whether a random accumulation of common law rules can really be described as a 'constitution' just because public lawyers feel that those rules deal with issues of constitutional significance. In the absence of greater public education about law and the contents of citizens' rights (considered in Part V, *Models for Reform*) the legal system is the only forum in which those rights are discussed.

Therefore, the ability to confront government, public bodies and other individuals in courts and other tribunals opens up the possibility of discussing those rights. Furthermore, it opens up the possibility of discussing those rights in a forum which has legitimacy enough to pronounce on the nature of those rights by virtue of being a legally-constituted tribunal. While these assertions are not jurisprudentially novel, they form another essential element in the political understanding of legal affairs policy.

Politics therefore needs to translate the legal context into strictly political contexts. Legal aid has a role in the administration of law but it also has an impact on public finances. The economic policy aspect of law has been considered in so far as it relates to legal aid. Given that legal aid is about advice as well as representation, the general availability of publicly funded advice forums is of importance. Social life involves a number of situations in which the individual and the collective (and/or the corporate) meet. It can be in the context of public, governmental bodies like schools, local authorities services or hospitals; or it might be in terms of private, corporate bodies such as retailers, insurance companies, and non-profit-making organizations. Typically, collective entities will have knowledge, or procedures, or social goods which the individual wants to access. The collective will frequently wish to provide means of advising the individual how to access those goods, or else it might be regulated in such a way that it is required to give advice, or it might wish to retain its exclusivity by making access difficult to the uninitiated.

In this way, retailers will seek to make it easy for potential customers to find the goods they require and will seek to provide payment mechanisms which are both easy to understand and attractive. They will employ assistants to advise on the best products and the most efficient payment mechanism. An informal advice system is thus generated. Statute requires local authority to provide certain benefits to specific people together with advice workers and internal means of appeal. Consequently, formal means of advice and representation are set in place. However, these mechanisms would not be described as being strictly a part of the legal system because they do not involve lawyers and judges, although they are prescribed by law and result in judicial review if they are not properly carried into effect.

Thus society can be seen as a web of these goods, whether they be retail goods and services, or social goods. The individual will desire access to all of these at some stage. To achieve that, the individual may require advice and possibly representation in dispute resolution. Talk of closed systems emerges from seeing society as a matrix of providers, desirers and deciders in this way.[9] Some of these functions we would describe as legal. Typically, as I have already done, this is done by restricting the term to those claims which come before a court or which involve advice given by lawyers as to the content of the parties' rights and obligations (be they civil or criminal). However, if we were to talk about 'justice' rather than simply about 'law', many more of the advisory and adjudicatory functions carried on in society more generally could be seen as falling within that system. In terms of a policy towards publicly funded advice services, it is important therefore to look beyond law into a number of other contexts, even though the core of the political debate remains transfixed by the legal system simpliciter. As made clear in the *Introduction* to this book, discussion will therefore be of the justice system in general rather than simply the legal system.

In considering the various approaches to policy it is important to recall the contexts in which justice affairs policy operates. In short they are threefold: the democratic, the economic and the autopoietic. The democratic context is that considered above: access to justice is about the possibility of there being a properly functioning constitution in relation to which citizens are able to define their rights and their identity. To rehearse the point, liberal democracy rests on the rule of law. Therefore, it is essential to that logic that the law is evenly applied and evenly accessible. To have inequalities in access, regardless of inequalities in the substantive legal rules, violates the core notion of the rule of law. The rule of law is not a pure construct. In practice it is not possible to deny complete equality of access beyond allowing all parties to appear before a judge. Some parties will have access to better lawyers. Chance will mean that some parties will be able to adduce more complete evidence than other parties. Prejudice or discrimination will result in some witnesses being considered to be more credible than others.

The economic problem is the relentless rise in the legal aid budget. Less frequently discussed is the cost of maintaining the judiciary and the cost of upkeep of the court system. In terms of economics the justice system is both a drain on public funds and a part of the economy which impinges on commercial activity and allows lawyers to make money. The public policy issue focuses on the control of the budget relating to legal aid expenditure above all else. As with all departmental budgets, there are a number of fixed costs built into the system. In the case of the legal system it is the cost of running the courts, maintaining buildings, meeting judicial and administrative salaries, and so forth. Therefore, the attention is centred on the variable portions of the budget relating to criminal and civil legal aid. This budget has attracted attention because of its size relative to other expenditure and because of its rapid growth in recent years.

The other aspects of change have revolved around the mooted need to reform the judiciary, to make it more socially representative, and the legal profession, both to make it more representative and also less given over to restrictive practices. This has collided with economic considerations as the lawyers (both barristers and solicitors) have sought to protect their businesses. The removal of the solicitors' monopoly on conveyancing has resulted in the Law Society advocating the erosion of the barristers' exclusive rights of audience in higher courts. In turn the Bar has sought to argue for an independent Bar in which the commercial status quo is maintained. The professions' arguments in relation to reform of the legal aid scheme revolve around commercial protectionism – typically a resistance to any proposal to introduce fixed fees and therefore cap the earnings potential from particular areas of work.

The autopoietic context is the nature of the legal aspects of the justice system as a closed system. This book's focus on 'the justice system' is prescriptive rather than necessarily descriptive. A descriptive analysis would be required to look at the legal system as something distinct from other social actors and systems. It has its own badges of legitimacy bestowed on those who are made judges and on those who are accepted into the legal profession. Those people are educated to speak a language and to perform in ceremonies which have been created by lawyers over centuries.[10] Allowing such an important part of the democratic framework to have become so occultist is not in the best interests of social justice. Defenders of the status quo would consider this description hysterical. However, it is an accident of history, as with the remainder of the British constitution, that lawyers are still required to wear antiquated Regency court dress when representing their clients in many courts. It was no accident historically that the law was something imposed on the masses and litigated by the well-to-do. In the time of the Blair government's focus on the 'people' as the social body in whose name they seek to act, remnants of a feudal past merely re-emphasize the fact that the legal system generated its modes of dress, thought and expression at a time when it was literally a closed system, in that access was expressly denied to many, and continues in practice to be closed in terms of autopoietic theory and political practice at the turn of the millennium.

With that thumbnail sketch of the context, it is important to turn to the political categories of thought which could be brought to bear on it.

Five categories

The discussion of the preceding key issues to the following five categories of approach to legal affairs policy is this author's own attempt to delineate the lines, but it does draw on archetypes of five separate, established points of view: (1) the new right, (2) bureaucratic cost management, as was practised by the Major administration, (3) the legal establishment, (4) the new, democratic-socialist left (dubbed 'radical centrism'[11]) and (5) the more traditional left associated with the protection of the welfare state. Each of these political agendas is also adaptable to the politics of the legal system, and this is the focus of this chapter. The remainder of the book will seek to apply each of these approaches to the various contexts of the reform of the legal system. In particular the thinking of the Labour Party under Blair is taken apart and reconstructed in Part II, *Theories of Social Change*.

THE FREE MARKET APPROACH

The free market approach is the Thatcherite ideology transposed to legal affairs policy – even though the Thatcher administrations did not translate their monetarist and libertarian politics explicitly to that area. Subsequently the Social Market Foundation and the Centre for Policy Studies have come to look at legal affairs policy in the light of free market reforms of the National Health Service:[12] in short, to encourage block contracting of legal aid so that monopolistic providers of services control provision in geographic regions, rather than to enable the citizen to select any lawyer and permit that lawyer to recover her fees from the Legal Aid Board. Therefore this section seeks to apply free market principles derived from Hayek[13] and Nozick[14] to the justice system.

There is a narrow distinction between the cost management

approach considered below and the free market approach considered here. The reason for creating this distinct category is to examine two particular issues: first, the assumption that there is such a thing as a market in legal services, and, second, the use of the language of consumerism. The free market approach proceeds on the basis that there are markets in legal services and that the best approach to the legal system is to treat it as one would treat any other market.

The basis for the free market approach is that the state should withdraw from inter-meddling with society except to the extent that it can be justified as being necessary. This will produce a concomitant reduction in public spending and allow the market to step in to perform those activities from which the state has withdrawn. The underlying aim is to engender greater liberty in the individual and to allow the pure heat of the market to fuel increased prosperity. The law occupies a role as a means of self-help for the individual or corporate body to activate their own rights in the absence of interventionist government.

Free markets, block contracts and the legal system

The issue is, then, how to bring market discipline to the operation of the legal system, such that there is a reduced need for public spending on it. The primary contention of this book is, apart from the genuine concerns as to whether or not the market is a suitable means of protecting access to essential rights, that there is no such thing as a properly functioning market in the legal system in any event. Therefore, market-based solutions would be inappropriate without fundamental reform to the system such that it could be said that a market had come into existence.

The discussion of free marketism in the context of legal services is, as indicated above, based on the treatment of legal aid rather than the democratic or advice service issues which are considered in Chapter 7 in the section *Public service ethos*. The starting premise is that the legal aid budget has reached a critical point and must be controlled. Given the model of Major's reforms to the NHS, the translation of those principles to the legal aid system is superficially attractive. The anterior question is whether or not the reforms of the NHS, with their dramatic increase in bureaucracy, lengthening waiting lists and service reduction, ought to be considered to be a useful model for the reform of any system in any event.

In terms of legal aid it would require the Legal Aid Board to be organized regionally with legal funds being allocated on a regional basis. Therefore, the extent of central control would be the allocation of funds to each region within the framework of agreed criteria by reference to which that money should be distributed. The regional offices would then set their own budgeted criteria for the way in which spending should be prioritized within that region. It would be open to solicitors who had been granted a block contract by the Legal Aid Board to claim legal aid to cover their fees from the regional fund. The solicitor would only be able to claim legal aid in respect of work which fell within the scope of their contract. Each contract would enable solicitors to carry out work in a particular field.

Therefore, solicitors' firm X would be contracted to provide housing law services in the region, whereas firm Y would be contracted to provide matrimonial law advice and representation in the same area. Neither X nor Y would be the only firm in their region entitled to provide that service. Rather, a number of firms would be contracted. Claims against the fund would have to be made in accordance with the local plan. In respect of each firm, there would be a maximum which they would be entitled to claim in a given region in a given financial year. Solicitors would be buying into the system in the same way that doctors buy health services under the reformed NHS.

The rigours of the market would ensure, it is said, that efficient firms would survive. Similarly, the work done by solicitors' firms would be forced to become cost effective because it would be required to fit within the constraints of the annual regional budget. The violence of the logic of the market is that it is public money and public allocation of contracts which is funding the firms and not the straightforward relationship of seller and customer. The fixing of the levels of the block contract do have the effect of allowing central control to manage the level of public spending on legal aid in a way that is impossible in a system which is purely demand led. Ironically then it is the reverse of the usual free market logic: rather than allowing demand to generate the market's activity, central government would be interceding to prevent it by controlling the supply.

Block contracts have a number of potential shortcomings which are examined elsewhere. Primarily, there is the risk that funds will run out before the end of the financial year and perhaps prevent a case which is in mid-stream from being worked on further until more money is available in the next financial year. The process of making decisions as to priorities on a regional level necessarily means that some cases will be prevented from coming to court because a political decision has been made to deny them access to public support. This is the antithesis of the free market's focus on liberty.

In enhancing freedoms the free market solution is to enable citizens to barter with lawyers in a way which makes litigation profitable to the lawyer even though the citizen is unable to pay and public funds are not available. It rests on the parties' freedom to contract. Under the system introduced in the Courts and Legal Services Act 1990, citizens are allowed to form conditional fee arrangements with their lawyers which are popularly known as 'no win – no fee' agreements. In short the lawyer is paid out of any damages that are won for the citizen, with the risk that no fee is therefore payable if the case is lost. These arrangements are considered in greater detail in *Contingency and conditional fees arrangements* (Chapter 8 below).

The Labour Party has accepted the logic of block contracting and of the use of contingency fees for the purposes of its Community Legal Service discussed below and in detail in Part V. This is perhaps surprising given the fact that the Labour Party is focused on the creation of a just society and yet these policy proposals are market-based and not in any way directed at socially just conclusions. Rather than being based on the New Labour priority of social justice, the policies are based instead on the other non-partisan priority of public spending control. This is explored in more detail in *Modelling New Labour's legal affairs policy* (Chapter 2).

However, before it is possible to take this free market approach any further, it is first necessary to consider whether or not there is such a thing as a market in legal services.

Is there a market in legal services?

The legal system has never worked on the free market model which the Lord Chancellor's Department under the 1979–1997 Conservative administration had long considered that it did, or ought to have done. There is no such thing as a 'free market in legal services'. At the high-water mark of free market-ism under the Thatcher administration, the then Lord Chancellor Lord Mackay sought to introduce reform of the legal professions. The Departmental budget began to grow rapidly out of control despite operating under a guiding ideology which was committed to the control of public spending. It is a disturbing irony that spending on legal aid grew by 600 per cent between 1979 and 1997.

The theory of the free market was that by liberating the economy from regulation and control ordinary citizens would share in an increased national prosperity. In the context of legal services the closed shops of rights of audience and the solicitors' conveyancing monopoly were defended vigorously against Mackay's reformist aspirations, albeit ultimately unsuccessfully given the passage of the Courts and Legal Services Act 1990. It was the end of the conveyancing monopoly as part of the liberation of the housing market which fuelled the calls for greater reforms of the professions to enable solicitors to perform more of the functions reserved historically for the Bar.

What the Conservative administration between 1979 and 1997 did not do was challenge the ponderous legal system or the restrictive nature of legal services provision in general. At no time were measures taken to create a viable market place for ordinary citizens to gain access to justice. Rather, the eligibility criteria for civil legal aid were tightened such that 14 million people in the UK fell outside its scope. Effectively access to the legal system was taken away from anyone in work who was not rich enough to pay privately for legal representation – ironically the same demographic cross-section which made up the electoral backbone of the Tories' success at four successive elections. It is this impossibility for the majority of the population to access the legal system which makes it impossible to talk of a free market in legal services. A free market requires a broad range of suppliers who are able to offer comparable goods and services at a broad range of prices. Typically that range of prices will include a range of qualities of service, of back-up support, added extras on expensive models and budget features on the inexpensive. In the case of access to the legal system there are private lawyers for the wealthy and legal aid lawyers only for those on social security benefit equivalent incomes.

To underline how far removed the legal services area is from ordinary markets, it is instructive to compare it with an established retail market place – such as the one for motor vehicles. This market ensures that there are not only a broad range of vehicles used for a number of purposes (family saloons, long-distance cars for sales-people, executive cars for status, large vans for deliveries, lorries for road haulage), but it also provides for a second-hand market so that most people are able to acquire some form of vehicle. A rich family is able to afford a brand new, large family saloon in the same way that it is able to afford legal advice from a private practitioner.

An individual in receipt of incapacity benefit might be able to buy a very cheap, old, second-hand car which has passed through the hands of a number of owners – albeit with the added costs of compulsory insurance and a road fund licence. She is able to do so because the market provides for less desirable goods than the new family saloon but goods which are potentially within her price bracket. The social security system may also provide for some other form of vehicle under a motability scheme. On the basis that her need is for a means of transportation, even if she cannot afford her own car, there is public transport (buses, trains and even taxis and ambulances) which will be able to meet her transportation needs. Therefore, a combination of a market in privately-owned vehicles and a mixture of the social security system and public transport will satisfy her needs. Legal aid will be available, generally, to someone in receipt of benefits in her situation and therefore she will be able to receive legal advice and assistance at no (or low) cost to herself.

The problem is demonstrated by the analogy in relation to those who are in work. A person in work will be able to enter the car market and buy a cheap car, or obtain a bank loan or hire purchase facilities for either a new car or a used car. The broad range of the market makes this possible. That person is not able to enter a market for legal services. The lawyers will charge their usual fee. The individual may choose to suffer the cost of that fee from her ordinary income, or incur debt to cover the fee, or simply be deterred from taking legal advice and allow her action to lapse. The point being that there is no alternative source of advice which can meet her requirement for assistance and representation in the same way as a lawyer at a lower cost; whereas the need for transportation can be met by entering the market for a cheaper car. Typically, advice agencies will not be able or willing to meet the full range of services offered by a lawyer to private or legally-aided clients. The unadvised individual is required to represent herself or simply submit to her inability to act in the legal system. She is totally disempowered. At least someone in need of transportation can always get the bus.

Similarly, the entrepreneur, hero of the free market ideal, is unable to acquire legal advice and assistance at any other price than that demanded by the private lawyer. Transportation can be acquired at market prices or hired, whereas legal services remain out of reach of most people. The introduction of contingency fees is heralded as the means by which this lacuna can be filled. However, as considered below in *Contingency and conditional fees* (Chapter 8), this assumes that the individual's claim will be sufficiently valuable for it to generate enough money to meet both the claimant's needs and the lawyers' fees. It is submitted that this will not be the outcome in the vast majority of cases.

In the legal system there is no such thing as a 'market'. There are publicly funded legal services for those who are either very poor (legal aid) or those rich enough to make themselves appear very poor (legal aid for the apparently wealthy).[15] There is then legal service for those individuals and corporate entities (large businesses, charities and so forth) wealthy enough to afford lawyers. For the rest of society there is no ability to access any other form of *legal* service.[16] There is no 'budget' form of legal advice. Some high street solicitors are prepared to cut costs to bring in business. Fees are always open to negotiation or are left on a contingency basis. However, those fees are never open to negotiation in the same way that even non-NHS dentists are prepared to charge only £10 for a consultation and check-up.

Having accepted that there is no such thing in the legal service deserving of the term 'market', it should also be accepted that there are a number of reasons *why* this is so. First, professional restrictive practices.[17] Second, over-complexity in the system's rules and practices.[18] Third, the legal system operating as a closed system whereby lawyers dictate the substance and form of discourse.[19] Fourth, a lack of alternative mechanisms of dispute resolution.[20] While these points are discussed in more detail in Part IV, *Components of Delivery*, it is perhaps enough to say at this stage that the composition and structure of the legal system enable lawyers to maintain artificially high prices because they are shielded from competition with other professions and service-providers.[21] There are therefore tangible and intangible barriers to entry.

Despite the impossibility of a market in legal services in the legal system as currently organized, public policy focuses too much on the business that lawyers do and on the citizen as a consumer. This language is inappropriate; the presentation of the citizen as primarily a consumer is particularly so.

The language of consumerism

One significant trend in policy-making in respect of legal services, continued in the discussion of the cost management approach below, is that of considering the citizen seeking to come to law as being a 'consumer' of legal services. As considered above, there is no free market in legal services and therefore there is an initial problem with this consumerist rhetoric. The consumerist language appears most clearly in the propagation of contingency fees as a replacement for legal aid. The contract between the lawyer and the litigant is presented as the consumerist relationship found between purchaser and retailer, requiring that the purchaser receive contractual rights against the seller.

The heart of the objection to the language of consumerism is that it obfuscates the real nature of the business of the justice system: the allocation and resolution of social rights and responsibilities. Social justice is something which is desirable in itself, however the components of the term are defined. It is not something that is necessarily comprised of goods which are to be bought and sold. Therefore, the conflation of 'consumer' with 'customer' starts us off on the wrong foot. It supposes a citizen is only worthy of consideration once she has made payment or given value. Whereas, rights and responsibilities ought to be concerned with the content of the rights and obligations of citizens as human beings rather than as economic actors. The right to access law and the justice system is something which must be available to all citizens and groups with *locus standi* on grounds of their existence rather than on their buying power.

The language of consumerism is not the best context in which to discuss access to justice in any event. The rights of the consumer are the rights of someone with access to services or goods to be treated appropriately. There is a more important anterior question in relation to law as to the ability of people to bring claims to law or other systems at all. It is this problem of access which encapsulates the constitutional and democratic deficit in relation to the justice system in the UK. Aside from the substantive questions of the content of rules once a question is brought before a court or a lawyer, is the simple question, 'How do I gain access to such advice and representation?'

Further, the language of consumerism encourages policy-makers to stray into a mindset whereby the economic questions are placed before the democratic issues of access. The attitude of the policy organs of the Lord Chancellor's Department demonstrate a reflex commitment to the reduction of the budget and the introduction of reforms which will restrict entitlement to claim legal aid to contracted lawyers. This bureaucratic insistence on consumerist models has led to a cross-party consensus on the introduction of block contracts for legal aid franchises and in particular their acceptance by the Labour government, even though in Opposition it was implacably opposed to such initiatives. The justifications for these policy foundation stones are the need to control public spending, to achieve efficiency in the courts system through the alteration of procedural rules, and the creation of an efficient market in legal services by allocating block contracts. Consequently, the policy initiatives focus on the detail of budgeting rather than on the broader picture of the need for systematic restructuring of the justice system. This thread is considered in relation to the cost management approach.

The problem with market-based approaches to justice

There is no market in social justice. Therefore it cannot be said that any economic market will prioritize issues to do with social justice. On the basis that the purpose of the legal system, and the other areas of concern in this book, is to resolve disputes concerning social and legal rights and responsibilities. It is suggested therefore that social justice is a question which cannot be left simply to market forces.

The suggestions with regard to block contracting reflect the inability of market thinking to prioritize the citizen before the control of spending or the management of economic indicators. Placing the citizen first would entail a system which looks at the range of possible means of justice provision beyond the straightforward use of lawyer and court-based solutions, it would also ensure that there is equality between citizens before all else. It is also difficult to see how a system which carries within it the likelihood of reduced access to dispute resolution chimes in with the free marketeers' agenda for greater freedom. Rather than being set free from oppression, most citizens are precluded from taking steps to protect their freedoms. They are equally free to fail to protect themselves. Ironically the alternatives would appear to involve greater choice than the policies which have been advanced by the free marketeers.

THE COST MANAGEMENT APPROACH

Conceiving of the justice system in terms of economics is the bridge between the free market approach and a second policy dubbed here 'the cost management approach'. The cost management approach prioritizes the need to cut the Lord Chancellor's Department budget over other policy concerns as to justice or economics. Therefore it follows the monetarist edict that public spending must be controlled or reduced. It is an economic system management approach, meaning precisely that; it assumes that the legal system is to be treated as a system which should be managed in the same way as any other system which makes demands on public funds. Its ideology is most clearly identified in the policies of the Major administration, as outlined in a Lord Chancellor's Department consultation paper:

> [To] introduce a system of block contracts covering the type,
> quality, volume and price of services to be provided . . .
> improve the targeting of funds towards areas of need,
> particularly where suppliers can provide high quality advice
> at less cost than the present court based approach.[22]

The language used here is that of markets and of consumers. It supposes that, rather than deploy centralized state provision of services, publicly funded legal services should be delivered by lawyers holding block contracts. The attraction of the block contract is that it contains contractual terms between central government and the service provider as to cost, efficiency and regulation. This contractual mechanism could be used to ensure quality in service; however, most Labour government policy proposals have focused on cost savings in the same way that their Tory predecessors did.

It is interesting that the language of contract used by this approach has not been wedded to the Blairite commitment to a social 'contract with the people', with a nod to freedom of choice and quality of service. This absence is particularly strange given that Lord Irvine has championed a form of the block contract. The traditional legal aid system has always operated on a bare contractual model in any event. Private sector lawyers invoice central government or one of its agencies, and are paid for providing a service to the population providing they have some certification from the Legal Aid Board.

The goal of this Cost Management Approach is to seek effective and economical solutions to problems in the interests of the litigant on a case-by-case basis and in the ongoing interests of the taxpayer. It requires centralized budgeting control to the extent necessary to create a discipline for setting priorities. Therefore, the thinking is that there should be regulation and controlled cost of legal aid to public funds made possible by a system of block contracts operating within an overall predetermined budget. In creating the much-vaunted but still ill-defined[23] Community Legal Service, the role of the proposed government agency would be that of an overseer concerned with targeting needs and priorities. The buzzwords of this cost management approach are 'effective', 'economical', 'discipline', 'block contract' and 'budgeting'. In line with the emphasis on the consumer is the need for these goals to be achieved for the benefit of the purchaser of the services. The emphasis is not primarily on civil liberties nor is it on a discourse of rights and obligations. Behind this economic system approach lies an idea of individual freedom based on the free market model: that is, individuals with money ought to be free to acquire services to meet their needs. That is fine so far as it goes, but it only includes those people with enough money in the first place.

The discussion of this model cannot be confined to the purely Thatcherite. The Community Legal Service proposal under New Labour, for all the protestations that it will seek to do something other than create compulsory competitive tendering,[24] sits very close to a supply-led attitude to public funding of legal services. Rather than provide a budget which meets demand for legal aid and the other services that come out of that one budget, the Community Legal Service would attempt to control the availability of funds, thus cutting supply and rationing the availability of service.[25] One of the great concerns about this means of providing the service is that it will develop monopoly providers in particular regions where some firms have block contracts and other firms do not. Large contract holders will tend to swallow the personnel, clients and business of smaller firms who do not hold contracts, and the availability of a market will shrink.[26]

As discussed above, the political problem necessitates this new approach. Funds are limited in the politics of the 1990s and therefore service is limited. However, at least half of the problem is the reluctance to look at entirely new ways of providing the service. A legal system which focuses on the old-fashioned demands of the legal profession will fail to operate within the new strictures. The cost management approach appears to be rather one dimensional in that it contains no rhetoric about the social place of law. Surprisingly it did constitute the thrust of Conservative policy under the stewardship of Lord Mackay with some prefatory mention of the importance of law and the use of the obligatory term 'access to justice'. For example, in the Tory Lord Chancellor's Green Paper *Legal Aid – Targeting Need* (1995), the core principle was stated to be:

> [To] introduce a system of block contracts covering the type, quality, volume and price of services to be provided . . .
> improve the targeting of funds towards areas of need,
> particularly where suppliers can provide high quality advice
> at less cost than the present court based approach.

Here we have a mixture of cost management rhetoric with that of establishing and meeting social need. The most clear example of this is the reference to 'high quality advice at less cost' which conflates the need to supply a service with the priority of cost control. It is important that advice must be of 'high quality'. Importantly, there is no talk of lawyer and citizen but rather 'suppliers'. We return to the rhetoric of consumerism in which the citizen is merely a consumer and the lawyer is a supplier of an economic service. Taking on the cost effectiveness priority, in line with Conservative NHS reforms, funds are to be targeted according to 'areas of need'. Such areas could either be categories of case or, in the case of the cost management approach, geographic areas which are required to budget for likely need and to apply available resources within the confines of that budget to the isolated priorities.

THE LEGALISTIC APPROACH

The legalistic approach is not necessarily meant to sound as pejorative as it may appear. Within the legal system the lawyers will, of course, insist on having their say. It may be supposed therefore that the legalistic approach will prioritize the role of lawyers and the nature of the legal system as a closed system, in which reform is effected by means of altering the rules of the system and not by addressing more general issues to do with the interaction of that system with other aspects of society. The debate as to the reform of rules of procedure, and amendments to substantive legal norms, are generated in the specific language of law and communicated among lawyers. The central statement of this attitude appears in the Woolf Report *Access to Justice*,[27] a study of procedural rules commissioned from Lord Woolf by Lord Mackay, the Conservative Lord Chancellor. Lord Woolf produced the following analysis of the relevant goals:

> A civil justice system should: be just; be fair; at reasonable cost; at reasonable speed; be understandable; be responsive; provide certainty; be effective.[28]

This introductory statement of principle mixes concerns about justice with a commentary on the need to control costs, while attending to the lawyers' greater concerns about delay in litigation. This catalogue of goals is vague enough to convey little political purpose but is broad enough to demonstrate a canny appreciation of the political context within which reform of the legal system is to be carried out.

The approach of the Woolf Report is termed the *legalistic* approach principally because it does not seek to address any political or sociological considerations beyond the courtroom, unlike the other approaches.[29] In defence of Lord Woolf it should be said that there is evidence of a preference to extend the scope of the Report beyond procedural rules and into the detail of legal aid policy and issues of social justice.[30] However, the remit given to Lord Woolf necessarily restricted the scope of his deliberations to legal matters. Lord Irvine has accepted the Woolf Report as half of the necessary process of reforming the legal system alongside reform of civil legal aid.

The focus on solely legal questions of procedure had the benefit of preventing Lord Woolf from making difficult suggestions as to an increase in public spending, while requiring a focus on cost cutting purely within the scope of reform of procedural rules. This process is systemically interesting. The political system focuses on the cost management approach and the need to control public spending. The legal system is allowed to recommend legislation relating solely to its field of competence. Lord Woolf could not resist transgressing that boundary in his summary comments to the Report:

> It is essential that the reforms of legal aid should take into account and support the recommendations I am making.[31]

This statement reveals the deliberately narrow ambit given to a judge who wanted to talk about 'equality' rather than simply procedural rules. In a set of proposals which would greatly increase the cost to the legal aid budget without alterations elsewhere, Lord Woolf suggested that legal aid be made available for alternative dispute resolution procedures. Some of the other suggestions are more tentative and obscure. For example it is suggested that legal aid be available for 'unbundled' legal services provided by barristers and solicitors: a commentary on the need to restructure the professions. Further, it is suggested that a new system of 'in-court advice centres' be created to help the litigant. This proposal would involve a politically sensitive restructuring of law centre and Citizen's Advice Bureaux provision. Interestingly, none of this section of the Report is taken up in any of the policy discussions raised by the political parties. These questions are addressed in Part V.

The legalistic approach as put to work in the Woolf Report focuses on the need to stream different forms of civil litigation. Cases which are worth £3,000 or less are restricted to the Small Claims Court where litigants are discouraged from having legal representation by withdrawal of legal aid; cases worth £10,000 or less are restricted to the fast-track procedure in which cases are disposed of under a fixed, statutory timetable with restrictions of the length of legal argument at trial; cases which are worth more than the fast-track limit are heard under a case management system which involves judges at an earlier stage in the litigation to prevent the usual drift of litigation towards increased delay and cost. This schemata is discussed in much greater detail below.[32]

Lord Woolf introduced a stylized language of equality into the Report. As it is put, 'parties of limited financial means will be able to conduct litigation on a more equal footing' under the legalistic approach.[33] Equality is not invoked as a means of redistribution or of more general equality of opportunity in this context. The parties are to be made equal by ensuring that both know the length of time a case will last and the probable cost of litigation. All that is achieved is equality of information. More critically it does nothing to make the parties equal either in a financial or a democratic sense. Lord Woolf therefore hopes that 'advice centres' will be developed to help disadvantaged litigants.

By ignoring the social context of the legal system, the legalistic approach seeks another means of evaluating claims. The most accessible means of measurement is the financial worth of the case to the parties. In Lord Woolf's grand design, 'procedural judges' would be required to take account of 'the parties' financial circumstances' in allocating cases between the streams. The upshot of this procedural device is that the poor, whose claims have little financial impact in absolute cash terms but possibly enormous impact in relative cash terms or in personal terms, will be restricted to the lesser forms of justice where lawyers are excluded or where litigation is necessarily curtailed. Given that the lawyer writing the report, Lord Woolf, is not empowered within his autopoietic structure to expand the availability of publicly funded legal services, and therefore the disadvantaged litigant is restricted to a cheaper kind of justice. The regrettable result of Lord Woolf's well-intentioned reforms would effectively constitute the reintroduction of the Victorian division between one set of courts for the rich and another set for the poor. The very establishment of 'worth' to the litigant as the lodestar by reference to which the allocation of the case will be treated, ensures that money becomes the measure of a citizen's access to civil justice.

Lord Woolf accepts that the straightforward financial division of cases between streams of court procedure is not suitable in all instances. Therefore, exceptions are made in two categories of case: housing and multi-party actions. Housing is the best example of litigation which may well revolve around rent arrears or disrepair damages which amount to less than the £3,000 limit. However, housing cases may involve hardship to the litigants which far outweigh the financial cost, such as eviction and homelessness. By admitting of such an exception, Lord Woolf accepts that his system is not susceptible of universal application. Having accepted a limitation on the universal applicability of his cash-driven logic himself, Lord Woolf does not go the extra step and accept that different legal cases may need to be treated differently under the new framework of procedural rules. He does not go on to consider whether other forms of case may similarly fall outwith the scope of his recommendations. It might be appropriate to measure commercial cases by reference to their cash worth, but cases to do with access to housing or welfare benefits are likely to involve their own complexities while concerning only small amounts of money. It is not possible to create absolute standards in this way. By centring on the legal system alone it is necessarily the case that other means of providing appropriate (from the standpoint of the litigant, not the system) resolutions to disputes are overlooked.[34]

The further example of personal injury litigation is instructive. The suggestions for the introduction of greater court involvement at an earlier stage of litigation proceed on the understanding that the parties can be encouraged to settle sooner than otherwise they would. However, in the case of personal injury litigation it is clear that the majority of cases settle once the parties have exchanged expert evidence without the need to proceed to full trial. The effect of requiring an early court hearing would be that the parties would incur the cost of a hearing which would ordinarily be avoided by settlement after the exchange of expert evidence. This must be true of all cases which turn on expert evidence as to the facts and future damage. However, it was only the motivated lobbying of the Association of Personal Injury Lawyers which prevented the same rule being applied across the board as to the desirability case management. Therefore, the desire for certainty and uniformity in rule-making, in contradistinction to what is perceived as being costly judicial anarchy, is likely to increase the cost of litigation in some cases: thus failing the sole political purpose behind the remit given to Lord Woolf.

Typically the legalistic approach will look to timetables for litigation and the business of procedural justice. In assessing the merit of different cases, regard is given to the financial weight of the case and the complexity of the legal arguments. At the level of procedural justice, the solution is sought in combined sets of court rules rather than in the restructuring of the profession or the opening up of alternative avenues of representation, advice and assistance. The salvation of the system is identified in the reform of court procedures in the same way that the problems are identified as being in those same procedures. The use of the Woolf Report to cut costs is, as considered in Part IV *Components of Delivery*, a potentially poisoned chalice. Woolf is unlikely to make the legal system cost less. The fear is that it will actually cost more. More to the point, Lord Woolf is unable to address head-on his own particular agenda of removing inequality. That is the business of a system which places movement towards social justice at its centre.

NOTES AND REFERENCES

1 M. Foucault, *Power/Knowledge: Selected Interviews and Other Writings 1972–1977*, ed. Colin Gordon, (Routledge, 1980) p. 201.
2 T. Blair, *The Third Way: New Politics for the New Century*, Fabian Pamphlet 588 (London, The Fabian Society, 1998). See also A. Giddens, *The Third Way: The Renewal of Social Democracy* (Cambridge, Polity Press, 1998).
3 A. Giddens, *Beyond Left and Right* (Cambridge, Polity Press, 1993).
4 See, for example, G. Teubner, *Law as an Autopoietic System* (Oxford, Oxford University Press, 1994); N. Luhmann, *The Differentiation of Society* (New York, Columbia University Press, 1982).
5 See, for example, the Law Society, Bar Council, and the policy behind the Courts and Legal Services Act 1990, considered in Part IV, *Components of Delivery*.

6 Part V, *Models for Reform*.
7 M. Foucault, *The Order of Discourse* [1971] in R. Young (ed.), *Untying the Text: A Post-Structuralist Reader* (London, Routledge, 1981), p. 55.
8 Although there are those who would argue that its relatively diminutive size is a reason for simply increasing spending on publicly funded legal services.
9 See Part II, *Theories of Social Change*.
10 It can be little wonder that so many lawyers become members of masonic lodges.
11 After Tony Blair's own talk of the 'radical centre' in British politics, see T. Blair, *The Third Way, op cit.*
12 Lord Mackay speaking to the Social Market Foundation in November 1996.
13 F. Hayek, *The Road to Serfdom* (Viking).
14 R. Nozick, *Anarchy, State and Utopia* (Oxford, Blackwell, 1974).
15 See, for example, Lord Chancellor's Department consultation paper, *Legal Aid for the Apparently Wealthy*.
16 Typically, advice agencies do not have rights of audience before most courts and some tribunals – nor are their workers necessarily qualified to give legal advice.
17 The nature of the professions is considered in more detail in Part IV, *Components of Delivery*.
18 See the discussion of Lord Woolf's report into reform of the civil justice system (pp. 164ff.).
19 See, for example, the discussion of A. Giddens, *The Third Way* (Cambridge, Polity Press, 1998) and G. Teubner, *Law as an Autopoietic System* (Oxford, OUP, 1994).
20 As set out below, there is a broad range of available dispute resolution, but the discourse of substantive law remains the locus of political power.
21 At a practical level this is visible in the lawyers' retention of rights of audience in court and the demand-led nature of claims on the legal aid fund, and also at a more abstract level in that lawyers ensure that it is only those trained in the legal arts who are able to conceive of legal claims, serve suitable proceedings, and perform an effective advocate role in court.
22 Lord Chancellor's Department consultation paper, *Legal Aid – Targeting Need* (HMSO 1995), Cmnd. 2854, p. 21.
23 At the time of writing.
24 See Lord Irvine's speech to the Bar Council Conference, October 1996.
25 The Community Legal Service is considered in Part V, *Models for Reform*, p. 199.
26 This approach grew out of the Conservative government's need to control spending on legal aid. The proposals made as to block contracting grew out of the reforms of the National Health Service and compulsory competitive tendering in local government.
27 Lord Woolf, *Access to Justice – Final Report* (HMSO, 1996).
28 Lord Woolf's Interim Report, *Access to Justice* (HMSO, 1995).
29 That is not to say that Lord Woolf was content to operate within the remit assigned to him. The discussion below as to the detail of Lord Woolf's Final Report indicates some of the desire to look beyond these legalistic confines.
30 Speaking at the London School of Economics, 30 January 1996.

31 Lord Woolf, *Access to Justice – Final Report* (HMSO, 1996), p. 9.
32 See Part IV, *Components of Delivery*, p. 123.
33 Lord Woolf, *Access to Justice – Final Report* (HMSO, 1996), p. 7.
34 Lord Woolf does call for greater use of alternative dispute resolution through-out the Report, while being unable to step outside his remit.

2

Left of Centre Approaches

Not even the apparently enlightened principle of 'the greatest good for greatest number' can excuse indifference to individual suffering ... The student of politics must therefore seek neither universality nor immortality for his ideas and for the institutions through which he hopes to express them.   *Aneurin Bevan,* In Place of Fear[1]

THE WELFARE STATE APPROACH

The welfare state approach harks back to a traditional socialism within the Labour Party, but also draws more closely on the policy approach of John Smith's leadership of the Labour Party. There is a tension in placing these two approaches under one banner. The former refers to the genesis of legal aid under the Attlee government's creation of the welfare state after the end of the Second World War. It would be a mistake to understand this as being socialism as understood by state socialists. Rather, it is, as Habermas has described it, the 'welfare state compromise'.[2] In short, capitalism is accepted as the core organization of the economy but the excesses of market-based economic freedom are to be mitigated by a welfare state which seeks to ensure the health, housing and minimum level of wealth of the population. There is a tension between the democratic collectivist vision of the welfare state and an emerging view, accepted by Smith and the Commission for Social Justice, that perhaps some level of inequality is acceptable in certain contexts, such that our attention should focus on relieving the poverty of the poorest rather than on redistributing the wealth of the richest.

The tension between John Smith's programme and the received absolutism of the traditional welfare state view is not located in an acceptance of some market-based economic structures in areas like employment policy. In truth, Labour had never really espoused anything other than an acceptance of capitalism by supporting protection for workers through trade unions against that system of capital. The dissonances between classical Labour traditions and the reforms introduced by Kinnock and Smith became most explicit in the work which the Commission for Social Justice undertook in the period before Smith's death. The Commission was moving towards dismissal of equality as a key goal of policy. Smith's vision, and the work carried on under his patronage, is strongly in line with the welfare state position because it focused on ensuring the prosperity of the totality of the population by preserving the institutions of the welfare state. As the Commission for Social Justice explained in *The Justice Gap*,[3] there are necessary inequalities in many contexts: the disabled will rightly receive an unequal amount of healthcare compared with the otherwise healthy able-bodied person, and the unemployed will receive more employment-related benefits than those in well-paying jobs. It is said that it is possible to justify some inequality therefore in the allocation of welfare state benefits. The objections to this stance raised by Cohen (1994) and others are considered in greater detail in Chapter 3, *Equality*.

If legal aid were to be understood as a universal welfare state benefit, it would require uniform access to legal advice and representation at no cost for all citizens. To achieve this end it would be necessary for the state either to pay lawyers in private practice to represent any citizen who can demonstrate entitlement. Entitlement in this sense could be restricted to legal advice in connection with other welfare state benefits, housing or specified categories of case. As such that would be an explanation for the way in which the legal system is currently organized. The more orthodox mechanism for legal aid as a universal welfare state benefit would be for the state to retain a large cadre of lawyers in a national legal service, mirroring the employment of doctors and nurses in the health service.

As a universal benefit, free at the point of use for anyone who requires it, the system would be unwieldy and very expensive. Unlike a health service, there is no obvious result or measurable point at which the system could tell when it had done enough to have discharged its obligations to the citizen. The conduct of litigation or the giving of advice is only comparable to health service professionals in that it would involve the employment of large numbers of professionals. Instead, it is likely that this structure would require the state's lawyers to be reserved for particular types of litigation. One regularly mooted suggestion is the creation of a national legal service to deal with criminal cases to mirror the prosecution function of the Crown Prosecution Service. The detail of these proposals is considered in Part V.

If legal aid is to continue to be means-tested, but also considered to be a welfare state benefit for the disadvantaged, its structure would be required to be somewhat different. At one level it would be no different from the current structure in that an eligibility limit would be set according to which a citizen would have to demonstrate a level

43

of income below that prescribed limit, but beyond which the citizen would be entitled to legal advice and representation in any category of case. Viewing legal aid as a welfare state benefit would require it to be different if it restricted the type of case which could be dealt with under the benefit scheme. The system would operate only for the benefit of the disadvantaged but be restricted only to particular areas of advice and representation such as social security, criminal defence or housing cases.

The difference from the current system is the focus not solely on levels of wealth but also on areas of social need. By specifying that only prescribed categories of case are available to be dealt with under the scheme for those who are disadvantaged, it is possible to direct public resources to those issues which are considered by political decision to be in particular need of public funding. The system comes closer to a supply-led welfare state benefit by selecting more precisely the contexts in which it will be available, rather than being demand-led by any citizen falling within the eligibility criteria to be used for any purpose desired by the claimant.

The shortcoming with this principle is that it does not move away from the provision of legal advice and assistance to a category of the underprivileged except by picking the types of case which can be heard by it. In practice this might mean adding hearings before industrial tribunals to the list of subjects which are covered by legal aid and the removal of (for example) commercial disputes to balance the legal aid budget. There remains the question of whether the service is then to be provided by lawyers in private practice or by means of a national legal service organized by the state. The cost and bureaucratic problems of transition between the current private lawyer, demand-led system to a system organized by the state is a disincentive to its introduction by any government.

The core issue which is still not addressed by the welfare state approach is that of the category of people who remain outside the system, in short anyone in work who is not prosperous will continue to be outside the system. This disempowered constituency is difficult to calculate with precision. It includes anyone who has an income in excess of income support but who is not able, or willing, to pay lawyers' fees which might range from £50 to £1,000 per hour depending on the type of case.

Reconsidering eligibility and class structure

A redrawing of the understanding of the class structure in the UK is necessary. Those who are reliant entirely on benefits which keep them below income support income levels might be dubbed the

LEFT OF CENTRE APPROACHES

'benefit-dependent class'. At current estimates one in every five households in the UK is entirely reliant on benefit – although a number of them will be on levels higher than income support. At the higher end of the wealth scale are those who are comfortable and feel no financial insecurities. Such people are able to afford private legal advice and therefore would probably make no claim on a national legal system in the same way that many of them would elect to buy into private healthcare plans – the 'secure class'.[4]

The remainder, a 'new middle class', are a section of society who are probably in work or in receipt of a level of income above income support, but who are not entirely financially secure. This, it is submitted, constitutes the majority of the British population. These people are unable to afford private legal representation for substantial legal issues beyond limited advisory work – such as house convey-ancing. This constituency, the new middle class, would probably fall outwith a means-tested legal aid scheme. If this constituency remains outside a reformed scheme, those people will not have been made able to access the justice system and the project can be described as having failed. This scheme is similar to Hutton's 40:30:30 society, considered in Part IV, *In Place of Injustice*.

The universal welfare state benefit approach meets the challenge of including the whole of the new middle class in the same way that they are included in entitlement to treatment from the National Health Service. The downside is the necessary cost of providing legal services on that scale by using lawyers in private practice. It is unlikely that legal aid rates, even if controlled under block contracts or franchising, would be able to pay for the foreseeable rise in demand caused by including the new middle class into eligibility. A national legal service could only achieve this increased service at similar cost to present levels if the salaries of its lawyers were kept down and a backlog of cases was allowed to mount up. As such the universal welfare state approach appears impracticable on this level.

The intractability of this problem is the same as the intractability of the control of legal aid under any of the credo considered hitherto. The solution lies in taking a more holistic view of the problem than is possible by focusing solely on legal aid as a means of widening access to the justice system. The dilemma from a democratic view-point is to increase access to the justice system generally. Therefore, it is important to provide access to appropriate means of dispute resolution at low or no cost to the citizen, depending on the dispute in issue. For example, in family law cases, the largest drain on the total legal aid budget of any legal category, increased use of media-tion and counselling for stages of the process of divorce where lawyers are not necessary would generate a great saving to the legal aid budget. The creation of a coherent structure of advice centres by merging law centres and Citizens' Advice Bureaux, currently organized separately and funded out of different governmental budgets, would create economies of scale and a greater number of access points for citizens. A number of such ideas are considered in Part V, crossing the rigid fence which currently divides discussion of the legal system from discussion of any other justice provider.

For the welfare state approach this ability to focus on the removal of social injustice by means of appropriate advice and representation services makes it possible to bring together a number of disparate organs of central and local government to provide better advice and information for the citizen. By locating it within the framework of the welfare state it is also possible to discuss political priorities in the justice provision aside from the block contracting logic of simply assigning money to fixed budgets. The third political issue in legal affairs policy, after legal aid and democratic rights, is the nature of publicly funded services. By subjecting the justice system to the same process as other welfare state benefits, it is possible to decide what types of activity are to be funded from the state purse and which activities are considered to be appropriate to be self-funding or organized in a different way. There is a requirement politically to create a ministry which is both accountable to the House of Commons and capable of looking across the full range of policy affecting justice policy and the means of delivering advice and representation to citizens.

Shortcomings in the welfare state approach

The radical centrist approach, considered below, is perhaps best identified in its reaction to the welfare state attitude. The shift from a society in which the welfare state structures of the 1948 NHS might have been easily transferred to the legal system, to a society in which the creation of such structures is considered impossible by the radical centrists, is grounded in the fact that expectations have changed. Citizens have developed in two ways since the heyday of the welfare state. First, the needs of citizens are no longer uniform. A comparative increase in prosperity has also brought with it a conviction among what was once the working class that they are entitled to aspire to different things. The process of lifestyle choice has generated a different social context. For the legal system this has meant that citizens come to it with a broader range of problems, seeking new forms of rights and responsibilities. Consequently, it is not possible to provide identical care or service to each person. The service provided by public services is required to be moulded to the demands of the user.

Second, citizens are used to responsive and professional services being provided to them by the private sector. Consequently, the public sector has been forced to introduce quality monitoring schemes, complaints procedures and more efficient information technology equipment to meet the demands made on them at a political and an individual level. It is this second feature of the development of citizens' expectations which has shown the legal system to be an anachronism. In no other sphere of life outside the court room would it be acceptable for professionals to charge so much for doing so little, for the service to be cancelled or delayed in the manner that court proceedings are frequently delayed, and for the system to be orientated to such an extent to suit the convenience of its actors (specifically, judges and counsel).

The state of the modern legal system as a service is best summed up by the dichotomy between two states of affairs. On the one hand the circuit judges' residences while on circuit, replete with butlers and major domos, alongside the Bar mess with its wood panelling and servants. On the other hand the ordinary litigant suffers the sterile sensibilities of the public canteens, reminiscent of an airport lounge, where prosecution witnesses are required to wait with the accused or the family and friends of their opponents, awaiting the judge's pleasure. In no other part of our public life would the swaggering arrogance of the legal system, with its outmoded dress codes, masonic customs and oppressive architecture, be suffered by the public. It is the public that the law ought to serve. Not the public who ought to be required to bow their heads at the legal altar. As considered below in relation to radical centrism, the new focus on performance in the management of the public sector marks a radical development in the democratic accountability of public services. Its introduction to the legal system and the justice system more broadly is an essential part of rejuvenating the quality of justice provision in the UK. This issue is taken up in the context of the growth of radical centrism below in Part V.

THE RADICAL CENTRIST APPROACH

This section considers the theoretical approach to reform of the legal system which might be taken by the Blair government. To speak in the conditional sense of 'might' may seem peculiar given the fact that there is an existing Blair government with a programme of law reform. However, that programme of legal affairs reform is not closely tied in to the politics of the 'radical centre' – one of the terms used by Blair to describe the new ground his administration is seeking to create in British politics. In Part II, *Theories of Social Change*, some of the driving features of this politics are considered in greater detail. First it is important to place the radical centre politics in the context of Labour policy of the past.

As mentioned previously, the Labour Party has never sought anything more radical than social democracy on a European model.[5] There is no political movement or party in the UK which approaches the question of law or, arguably, of civic rights, in a way which purports to do more than produce some greater social 'fairness'.[6] A truly Marxist organization would seek to ignore law on the basis that it would wither away after a proletarian revolution, or would at least be used as a part of the engine of revolutionary change in property relations. It is an unfortunate part of the internecine strife on the left in Britain that the term 'socialist' is frequently taken to be synonymous with 'Marxist', by both modernizers and traditionalists in the Labour Party. The term 'social democratic' is advanced as meaning an approach concerned with 'social justice' and 'realising the potential of ordinary people'[7] rather than relating specifically to the short-lived Social Democrat Party of the 1980s in the UK.

The second reason is that much of the discussion of human rights among lawyers does not seek to redress any of these imbalances. As Conor Gearty has explained:

> The [European Convention on Human Rights] contains no guarantee of equality. It accords the same 'human rights' to corporations as to the rest of us. It largely accepts and protects the pre-ordained allocation of property in society by presuming that '[e]very natural or legal person' should be 'entitled to the peaceful enjoyment of his [or her] legal possessions'.[8]

The concern of this social democratic model is to address the pre-Marxian socialist notions of social justice and equality of opportunity to achieve greater democratic empowerment. To that extent, the approach taken is a development of the 'social democratic approach'. However, its claim for socialism (properly so-called), is that a system of dispute resolution that removes power imbalances between litigants is, straightforwardly, an engine of equality. The law, and the systems that surround it, should seek *in their practice* to be transparent as between litigants. Once there are disaggregations of power between individuals at the level of *access* to justice, that is, in the context of procedural rules, the operation of substantive legal rules will necessarily be biased.

However, radical centrism loses its connections with either socialism or social democracy when it begins to move away from equality as a core goal. In its place a number of other ideas crowd into the foreground. A 'just society' is one of the core goals of the Blairite Clause 4 of the Labour Party constitution, together with 'liberty' and 'community'. As Blair puts it, his concern is with 'social-ism' rather than 'socialism' as properly understood. That is, a concern with community and the values which communities ought naturally to espouse within a framework of enlightened prosperity in a competitive market economy. This is a very different vision from the communal endeavour propounded by collectivist socialists and the trade union movements, such as Stanley and Beatrice Webb (authors of the original Clause 4 of the Labour Party constitution). The rigorous language of competition is the foundation of radical centrist prosperity rather than the security of a planned, supply-led economy. Community is expected to be self-generating to some extent through self-help groups and enlightened self-interest. Law should form a component of this self-definition by enabling citizens, either individually or in groups, to define one another's rights and responsibilities. Access to that law is therefore necessary to permit this growth and social regeneration. It is important to measure the detailed rhetoric of Blair's project, as set out below, against the rhetoric being used specifically in relation to legal affairs policy.

The radical centrist approach is personified by policies such as the creation of a Community Legal Service which employs vertical eligibility criteria for access to resources; expansion of alternative dispute resolution; use of the information superhighway for advice and education; and the reform of the legal profession and the judiciary. The strength of the social democratic approach in this context is its unspoken determination to weaken the stark dividing line between the legal system and other social systems.[9] The Labour government's proposals should not be represented solely as a social democratic approach, any more than Lord Mackay's proposals should be considered to be solely based on the economic management approach. Rather, each takes some of the other.[10]

Mapping the politics of the radical centre

At the time of writing, there is a flurry of terminology flying about the Internet and the plethora of study seminars in an attempt to define the new force which many believe is emerging in Europe and the US. It has been hailed by some as the 'third way' or the 'radical centre'. Its central conviction is that times have changed such that old ideologies are no longer useful in their entirety. Rather, the best of those ideologies is to be taken and wedded to a new settlement of the relationship between the individual and the state, between the private sphere and the public. In ideological terms, it accepts that times have moved beyond the convictions of left and right, requiring some new epithet to indicate that, rather than simply establishing a new point on the left/right spectrum, the new politics occupies an entirely different dimension.

This new politics has proved difficult to discuss and to conceive of, either because it requires an entirely new language to be discussed properly or because it is simply a vacuous exercise. Understood from the point of view of a Labour Party emerging from received notions of its socialism, however, it is rather easier to make concrete. The received notion is that the Labour Party has always been a socialist party. If by 'socialism' what is meant is Marxism, then that is simply mistaken. The Labour Party grew out of the trade union movement with a politics grounded in securing social justice for the working class at the beginning of the twentieth century. Its socialism is properly described as social democracy on the European model. There was never an attempt to replace capitalism as the primary means of organizing economic life. Its greatest hour was the creation of the welfare state in 1948. Itself a compromise between capitalism and state socialism, it provided universal benefits which were both available to all and free at point of use. The National Health Service was the jewel in the Labour Party's crown and has remained a monument for the Party's Bevanite tendency.

The New Labour project has grown out of a Party wedded to its welfare state institutions and its trade union heritage into successive attempts to embrace the electoral affections of the British people increasingly desirous of liberty and suspicious of inefficient state industries and institutions. The response has been to develop a language of interdependent rights and responsibilities in which the desires for a rhetoric of freedom can be tempered with a missionary understanding of social and communal obligation. This model of a radical centrism which talks of self-help for citizens matches very closely a vision of a justice system in which those same citizens are able to define the extent of their rights and the responsibilities of other actors in their community. This happy coincidence of rhetoric is a theme continued later.

It is important to understand the precise intellectual framework which marks out the Blair project from Gaitskell's attempts to reform the Party, Kinnock's policy review initiatives, and Smith's system of policy commissions. The reasons for change are justified by a series of significant social changes which require a different context for the debate about public services (aside from the economy in general, as well as constitutional reform). The coming together of the development of global economy outwith the control or sanction simply of the nation state, the growing use and opportunities offered by information technology, the end of pre-war social uniformity and a developing determination for higher standards through greater choice, has meant a changed ethos among Labour policy-makers.

Whereas the Labour Party had once argued for the protection of jobs in the public sector as a means for ensuring economic security for its historical constituency, the New Labour focus on the nature of the service provided to the user of that service then requires concentration on the democratic relationship between public bodies and citizens. Mixed in with much of this discussion in speeches and the media is the lazy language of consumerism. Lazy in that it suffers from all the faults associated with consumerism in the free market approach considered above, and in that it avoids a mature debate about the content of democratic rights between public bodies and individuals. The democratic context is also there: the core principles are identified as justice, liberty and progress all of which were famously wrapped up in Blair's vision of an 'age of achievement'.[11]

The core political objectives beyond those principles, in the context of the provision of public services, are social inclusion and autonomy. Social inclusion is at the heart of the welfare-to-work agenda, Gordon Brown's determined programme of putting a nation back to work, and the (at times long-stop) Social Exclusion Unit looking at initiatives to strengthen communities. Progress is at the heart of Blair's mission for his 'young country' both in terms of economic initiatives and symbolic gestures such as the Millennium Dome and the emphasis on 'cool Britannia'. Autonomy operates both by giving power to the individual and by giving responsibility to local authorities and community organizations rather than retaining that power at the centre. The legacy of increasing centralization of power under the Thatcher and Major administrations, together with its fragmentation through quasi-governmental bodies like the Next Step agencies, has been to change the Labour Party's view, in the majority, as to the desirability of holding power at the centre.

In contradistinction then to centralized power held at a distance from 'the people', the talk of the third way is for the individual to connect with the community. Interestingly government's role is seen to be setting standards and regulating overall performance against centrally set objectives. The context of 'community' is therefore more critical, something which is analysed more closely in Part II. It might involve greater self-help, greater power for local government, or new regional assemblies involved in setting local priorities. The leading ideal of the community agenda (as opposed to the communitarian agenda considered below) is for decisions which have a local impact to be decided locally, or at least as closely as possible to the place of impact.

By reducing the role of the state in the provision of public services, it is hoped that reinvigorated local communities will evolve to provide local solutions. In this way devolved budgets follow the granting of responsibility to those local communities. (It ought to be said that the term 'community' is itself up for grabs, as considered in Part II.) The role of public services is redefined by some commentators[12] to be to enhance the opportunities of individuals and communities rather than to respond specifically to alleviate need. Existing public services are seen as having been designed at a time when needs were more uniform and were made by a less demanding public. The NHS of *Carry On Doctor* is seen as an inefficient, anachronistic creature of its time. The command economy controlled from the centre is not considered to be sufficiently responsive to local needs to provide the particular form of service which specific communities or regions may require. Therefore, devolution of responsibility is preferred together with an increase in accountability for those local providers. Public service providers are consequently required to incorporate a new set of functions to enhance the efficiency and accountability of the services they offer: performance management, bench-marking, local scrutiny, incentives for good performers, and sanctions from the state in the case of under-performance. The redrawn public service structure aims to provide more than simply rights of access but also rights to information and rights to shape the services available.

From Old Labour to New Labour

Old Labour, as it has come to be known, is best identified with the 'democratic collectivism' of Sidney and Beatrice Webb, authors of the 'common ownership' version of Clause 4 of the Labour Party's constitution. The NHS was the most complete statement of that collectivist project, providing for universal benefits and services made available on the basis of total equality and common ownership. Provision of services was made entirely on the basis of need and without reference to any other criterion. In effect, public services were demand-led but the important demand element would be 'need' and not any other entitlement. The counterpoint to this is the civic activism propounded by Marquand who advocates devolved responsibility.[13] Access to social goods would be demand-led backed up by supply-side investment on the basis of Brown's well-known post-classical, neo-endogenous growth model in which the state invests in those projects which contribute to growth in the economy and society rather than simply pump-priming. The movement away from needs-based provision is matched by budgeted, planned provision of access to services. Rather than being orientated around the composition of the service-provider, the service-provider itself becomes performance orientated, giving rise to greater consumer power and moving away from an expectation of uniform provision.

A legal service

The concept of service is to all intents and purposes absent from the legal system. Goss has identified the three main goals for public services as being to invigorate democracy, to integrate better a fractured society and to develop the concept of social capital.[14] These principles for the reshaping of public service accord with the view of the legal system as a means of ensuring citizens have access to a means of protecting their rights. Yet they do not form a part of the way in which the courts, the judiciary or the legal profession operate – despite the creation of a Courts Services Agency. Compared to the local government ethos of the Citizens' Advice Bureau or the law centre, the system of courts and the judiciary are not responsive to social pressures in the same way that senior members of the NHS are required to be. NHS managers are required to meet performance targets and undertake monitoring. The thought of a judge being bound to put into practice a mission statement on a user-focused system of working seems an intriguing one – albeit a democratically exciting one.

There is a need for the legal system to move into performance management so that it is delivering a *service* to citizens. Currently, local authority services are required to live up to performance criteria whereas the legal system as currently organized does not.

Continuing importance of the welfare state model

The radical centrist view has rejected traditional welfare state thinking. The institutions of the welfare state as designed in 1948 are dismissed as being unresponsive and unsuitable for a society moving into the twenty-first century. As indicated above, some of this dismissal by the free market tendency is vogueish rather than fully worked through. However, it is a useful context in which to consider the reform of the legal system, being a part of society never subjected fully to the attentions of the architects of the welfare state. The new conception of the local authority as a provider of *services* to the public rather than being monolithic institutions from which that public ought to wait for beneficent gifts of assistance, is a useful starting point for any discussion of the legal system. As considered throughout the discussion of the radical centrist approach to legal affairs policy, the legal system does not match up to the responsive and community-sensitive structures which are demanded from other public service providers, although many other aspects of the justice system (more broadly defined) do necessarily because they fall under the control of local and central government. Two main issues arise. First, how can the legal system be made more responsive to its users? Second, how does the critical question in the welfare state as to whether services must continue to be free at the point of use, apply to legal aid and other publicly funded legal services?

The relationship of the legal system to its users forms much of the theme of the discussion in Part V. Together with the need to control the flow of money from public funds to lawyers, is the need to ensure that the public purse is acquiring a suitable level of advice and representation for its citizens. The legal service is not being provided by the state at present. However, much of the justice system is being provided by the state by means of mediators, counsellors, local authority employees in welfare, housing and other departments, and in centrally funded advice agencies. The dissonance in treatment between those various means of delivery has been considered above and the possibility of comparison with the NHS is explored below. To remove these differences, a more comprehensive public service ethos is necessary for the legal system to integrate itself into the working practices of the broader justice system and the rest of the public sector.

The second issue surrounds the fact that legal aid is currently demand-led: the solicitor or barrister makes a claim for a fee which is paid by the Legal Aid Fund, unless there is particular reason to consider it to have been excessive. Better that the state set out a tariff for the services which it buys from lawyers in private practice instead of settling their bills when levied as fixed fees. The question which arises from this is whether the litigant should be entitled to receive 100 per cent of the aid free. At present there is a system for contributions depending on the litigant's means. A different system would be to acquire fixed price advice or representation services from the lawyer, with the option for the litigant to pay for greater service than the state is prepared to provide by means of a top-up to the state funded tariff.

Comparing the National Health Service with the justice system

A further option for the alteration of the system would require the citizen to pay a flat fee before being entitled to receive the benefit.

This is already a mooted possibility for access to NHS healthcare. However, the difference would be that the healthcare flat fee would be paid to the NHS whereas the flat fee in the legal aid example would either have to be paid to the lawyer, which seems to be something lawyers would frequently have to waive to attract some clients, or be paid to the Legal Aid Board to be paid, in effect, back to the lawyer as part of the fee. It might lower the legal aid budget in part but its attractiveness otherwise is limited. This movement away from universal services free at point of use is an element of the contingency fee proposals advanced by Lord Irvine whereby the litigant is required to contribute the cost of an insurance premium to cover the lawyer's fees should the case be lost. The only mooted advantage of requiring the litigant to pay part of the legal aid cost is to give that person a stake in the litigation, thus discouraging fruitless suits. However, it seems more likely to discourage the genuine litigant who is reluctant or unable to afford the up-front fee.

In seeking to develop a new welfare state model which incorporates both the traditional and the modern in public service policy it is as well to compare the archetype of the democratic collectivist model, the NHS, with the justice system. Policy development in respect of the NHS has moved rapidly in recent years. In the face of enormous popular affection for the NHS, a number of quasi-privatization initiatives have been introduced. First, the introduction of NHS trusts has given local control over buying services to local hospital trusts. Similarly, general practitioners have become buyers of healthcare services from hospitals with budgets out of which they are required to meet the health needs of their patients. An interesting dichotomy has emerged between the GP's responsibility to the care of the patient and the responsibility for the use of public funds. The Private Finance Initiative, PFI, has begun a process of using private money to build or refurbish hospitals, then leasing them to the NHS. In all of this the NHS is being pulled between privatization through the use of private sector funds and greater local accountability hoping to make the service patient-led.

The NHS has received more political consideration and analysis than the legal system. Some of that analysis is applicable to the legal system subject to a few important failures in the comparison. The NHS is currently formulated on the basis of budgets whereas the legal aid system remains demand-led.

THE HISTORY OF LABOUR PARTY POLICY

The birth of the policy

There is a great difference between the policy of the Labour Party and the policy of the Labour government. The two need to be kept separately in mind. Aside from the development in thinking under different Labour Party leaders there is a clear division between the policy of the two organs. That this is possible is the result of the Labour Party forming its policy by means of vote and resolution of annual party conference. The policy of the Labour Party is contained in the 1995 document titled *Access to Justice*[15] (naturally) which was accepted by Labour Party conference in October 1995 in time to be included in the manifesto in a summary form before the 1997 General Election.

Between the Party's acceptance of the detailed contents of *Access to Justice* and the writing of the 1997 General Election manifesto, Lord Irvine made a speech to the Bar Council conference in October 1996 announcing that there would be a review of civil justice policy if a Labour government were elected in May 1997. Effectively, this speech overruled *Access to Justice* and constituted a declaration that a Labour government would not consider itself to be bound by the Party's policy. That much was nothing new: Labour leaders had regularly chosen to distance themselves from the radical edicts of Party conference once in governmental office. What was awkward about the announced review was that there was no detail at that stage as to who would conduct the review nor as to what its remit would be. In the event this became the Middleton Review, discussed below.[16] At the time, Labour's careful, informal and formal consultation processes, conducted by Paul Boateng MP, were destabilized by the announcement that the policy which had been carefully developed with the appropriate interest groups and explained to all other interest groups, would not necessarily be governmental policy after a General Election in any event.

Significantly, Lord Irvine had been a member of the policy working group which had put together the *Access to Justice* proposals adopted by Party conference in 1995, but which were rapidly shelved thereafter. Other members of that working group included Jack Straw and Paul Boateng. Similarly, Lord Irvine had been a member of the Democracy and Citizenship Commission set up within the Labour Party by the late John Smith MP to produce, *inter alia*, legal affairs and constitutional reform policy documents. A policy document entitled *Access to Justice* had been accepted by that Commission and the Joint Policy Committee before John Smith's death. The paper fell into the abyss of forgotten policy papers, along with the work of the Social Justice Commission at the start of the Blair leadership. Lord Irvine was a member of that policy commission also. Its chair was Tony Blair.

The following discussion will follow these policy papers in chronological order in an attempt to map the development of policy under the various organs of the Labour Party at different times. It will focus on the policy issued by Lord Irvine's department at the time of writing. But first it is important to introduce some of the discussion about the way in which the ideological roots of the Labour Party have changed from when Neil Kinnock was leader.

Components of 'Blairism'

The Labour Party's position on the detail of legal affairs policy has shifted since 1992. There has been some shift too in its intellectual underpinnings, in line with the transformation which Kinnock, then Smith, and then Blair have wrought on the Labour Party. Since the 1992 General Election the Party has moved from John Smith's humanist, ethical socialism to the Blairite approach, which will be explained in greater detail in this book as being a form of 'democratic socialism' based on neo-Gramscian ideas of a new nation and the generation of community. There has been a production of something new in the shift from old style Labourism, which was inclusive of all churches on the electable left from trade unionists, welfare state social democrats and centre-left modernizers, to an ethos derived from American, liberal ideals of a state which seeks to create a context in which individuals are given the freedom to make their own life choices within a broader community.

The major components of the Blair project and of the more general ideas organized around the radical centre are explored in Part II, *Theories of Social Change*.

Policy under John Smith

John Smith convened internal policy committees in five areas to redraw the Labour Party's programme in the wake of the 1992 General Election defeat. He replaced Neil Kinnock on a popular tide of support within the Party and the Labour movement. Smith managed to occupy an unlikely ground which reassured traditionalists that neither socialism itself nor the welfare state institutions of which the Party is so proud would be abandoned, while also reassuring modernizers that he would introduce sufficient change to secure victory at the next election. In truth, the campaign for the 1997 General Election started immediately after the 1992 election had finished, with the wide coverage of the Smith/Gould and Blair/ Prescott/Beckett leadership races. Labour benefited from the popular airing this gave to the discussion of its core values. The Democracy and Citizenship Commission was entrusted with, *inter alia*, responsibility for constitutional reform and legal affairs policy. Due to Smith's tragic death in 1994, the policy document had not completed all its ratification stages. However, as the most in-depth and far-reaching set of Labour Party policy proposals on the justice system to date, it merits some attention.

The paper was titled *Access to Social Justice through the Legal System* (*ASJ*). The title is an important change in itself. In line with the difficulties discussed in the Preface to this book in selecting a title which includes all the necessary standards, *ASJ* connected with Smith's own, principal concerns. While the Commission for Social Justice carried out its deliberations, the core concept of 'social justice' remained at the forefront. At a time of modernization of the Party and of its politics, the touchstone of social justice came to be the standard against which policy fell to be measured. It also constituted the talisman which would reassure all in the Labour movement that their one common aim, the removal of inexcusable unfairness, remained at the centre of its politics. *ASJ* therefore captured the spirit of this drive. The opening principles were:

1. To provide equal access to justice for all in society.
2. To improve the quality of the service currently provided by professionals in the justice system through investment in training and in people.
3. To reform the system of justice to make remedies more available, efficient and appropriate.

As a statement of central aims, these move no further than any other statement taken at face value. The use of the language of equality is, however, focused on a more traditional socialist message than the radical centrist position. The central social system is the 'justice system' rather than the legal system in particular. The opening words of the Report pursue this theme:

Labour's central requirement, on winning the next General Election, will be to instil in the British people a feeling of change and of improvement in the quality of their lives. By enabling them to provide for themselves, Labour will win the enduring trust of the people. To make these intentions concrete, the justice system must support them. However, looking at justice means looking further than simply at law. There is a need for justice at all levels of society; often in ways which are inappropriate for purely legal solutions.

As part of this attention to the broader context of justice, the central concern of equality was to be supported by means of a greater use of interactive technology which would bring the citizen closer to courtrooms and the system, and also bring advice workers closer to one another. As the Report continued:

> Therefore Labour will look to the new possibilities opened up by technology and alternative means of justice provision. The possibilities for justice reform are centred on new, developed systems of communicative technology and interactive data resources. Modern technology can enable citizens to educate themselves as to their rights with the assistance of the professionals that staff advisory agencies and legal aid practices.

Smith's modernizing influence is visible in the need he saw to renovate those social and constitutional systems which had lost the confidence of the British people by being both distant and out-dated:

> The justice system needs to be overhauled. It is outdated and has lost the confidence of a large part of the population. Labour will introduce methods of protecting rights that are easier to access and which offer more appropriate remedies than a system which is orientated solely around the courts.

Pivotal to the restructuring of the entire system would be a new political structure which would analyse the problems and pull the disparate areas of policy together. This structure would be a Ministry of Justice commanding a place in the Cabinet and effectively moving the justice portfolio from the House of Lords to the Commons. As explained in the following extract from the introduction to *ASJ*, the new Ministry would have occupied a pivotal place:

> The impetus for this change will come from the creation of a Ministry of Justice to which Labour is committed. The role of this new ministry is to centralise the courts system and the broad spectrum of tribunals and to improve their working practices to deliver better service to the citizen.

The possible composition and competence of a Ministry of Justice is considered in Part V, *Models for Reform*. Beyond these early statements of principle, however, were a number of detailed policy proposals aimed both at increasing equality of access to social justice and controlling the cost to the public exchequer, namely: activation of democratic rights, communication technology, alternative dispute resolution, a Law Foundation, restructured advice agencies, and enhanced support for the Law Commission.

The aim was an integrated approach to justice reform across the board. In terms of reform to legal aid it was expected that the new policy proposals would contribute both to the rationalization of the system and the reduction in its cost. Reduction in cost was expected to allow more citizens to be brought within the eligibility limits. It was accepted that there was 'no single replacement for a legal aid system funded directly out of taxation' – in contradistinction to the current enthusiasm for contingency fees as a partial solution to the problem. The use of franchising for legal aid providers was accepted as a means of ensuring the quality of advice being given to citizens by granting franchises only to those service providers who could demonstrate sufficient competence.

The judiciary was to be reformed by the creation of a Judicial Appointments Commission made up of lay and legal members which would advertise judicial vacancies, interview candidates and publish criteria for its decisions. Access to the magistracy would be extended by devolving power back to local magistrates' committees and introducing protection from discrimination at work for those who wished to serve as magistrates. The professions would be fused by means of being trained together. Furthermore, exclusive rights of audience would have been eroded in a fusion of the professions. This would have permitted solicitors and barristers to practice differently in client contact and advocacy but without the formal distinctions and restrictive practices associated with the two categories.

Within these specific policies was a further underlying theme to demystify the law so that ordinary citizens would find the system more approachable. This would have worked at a number of levels. First, court buildings would have housed more public services so that they were not reserved solely for lawyers and judges. Second, public education as to the law and the legal system would be increased and broadened in schools. Third, use of information technology would allow citizens to find out about their rights more easily. Fourth, substantive law would be recodified over time so that it would be more comprehensible to the layperson – perhaps by including a short summary statement of the effect of legislation at its beginning.

This policy document was altered under the Blair leadership.

The Access to Justice policy paper

The *Access to Justice* policy paper which was eventually published in July 1995, and ratified by Labour Party Conference in that year as Party policy, was a truncated version of the document produced for the Smith Democracy and Citizenship Commission, with some important omissions. The novel recommendations for a Law Foundation, for the innovative use of information technology, and for the creation of a Ministry of Justice were jettisoned. By far the most significant omission was the Ministry of Justice commitment. The press caught on to this deletion, in particular Duncan Campbell in the *Guardian* listed it among Labour's policy changes since Blair became leader. The more perceptive commentators would have understood that it reflected the different relationship between the leading candidate for the office of Lord Chancellor with the two leaders. Lord Irvine had studied law and been friendly with John Smith at Glasgow University: therefore, Smith would have been more likely to have been in a position to insist on the transfer of power from the House of Lords to the Commons. However, Lord Irvine was kingmaker in relation to Blair – having encouraged him to seek the safe seat of Sedgefield after choosing him for tenancy in his chambers. Blair would have found it awkward to displace the power base of his mentor. The issue was raised only once under the Blair leadership.

The Commission was reconvened under the chairmanship of Jack Straw to produce policy papers from scratch. Under the tight timetable for production and ratification of policy it was decided that the Smith document was too long and would have to shortened considerably. Furthermore, it was decided that no new bodies should be created because that would appear to be the establishment of new quangos, contrary to Party policy. In effect, *Access to Justice* shrunk both in length and in its reforming intent. One of the most significant issues became the extent to which the Home Office ought to acquire responsibility for some aspects of justice policy. It has been a feature of the Blair administration's approach to Home Affairs that responsibility for juvenile justice and the treatment of young offenders, one of the core manifesto pledges, has moved decisively to the Home Office.

The *Access to Justice* paper was the culmination of years of consultation with interested groups, as well as the professions. Despite its reduced scope it retained a zealous assault on the restrictive practices of the legal profession and the undemocratic impact of the selection and composition of the judiciary on the British constitution. The paper needs to be read in the context of a more general commitment to constitutional reform. The energy behind Paul Boateng's regular broadsides against the Bar and the solicitors mirrored the Party's determination to remove the voting privileges of hereditary peers. Also within it was an important theme: that justice provision was costing the taxpayer too much while delivering too little. The principle of legal aid as set out by the Attlee administration was preserved as the lodestar of reform while the lumbering inertia of the system itself was described as ripe for reform to continue to live up to post-war ideals.

Access to Justice is divided into five main sections: the community legal service, alternative dispute resolution, consumer rights, public education, and reform of the legal profession. The context of the Report is the removal of social injustice which was allowed to ferment under the Conservative administrations and the control of the spiralling legal aid budget. Much of the rhetoric in the document is concerned with the enlargement of 'consumer orientated reform'. This is an uncomfortable form of words, given New Labour's commitment to the advancement of human rights based on the civil entitlements of the individual. In line with the radical centrist approach to social reform, *Access to Justice* focused on rolling social change and the need for the justice system to empower citizens and facilitate their own self-help initiatives. In its Introduction, the paper provides:

> our justice system could and should be a vital public amenity
> for individuals and their families, empowering people to
> defend their interests, to assert their rights, to enforce the
> responsibilities of others to them and to challenge abuses of
> power and authority.

As part of this statement of principle in the new version, is an affirmation of the new Clause 4 of the Labour Party's constitution, which had constituted such a great victory for Blair in his project to change the nature of the Labour Party:

> As our new statement of aims and values makes clear, Labour
> is committed to working for a 'just society, which judges its
> strength by the condition of the weak as much as the strong,
> provides security against fear, and justice at work . . . and
> delivers people from the tyranny of poverty, prejudice and the
> abuse of power.'

The document's principal rhetorical flourishes were expounded by Boateng at the Labour Party Conference in October 1995 while speaking in support of the adoption of the policy. Somewhat to the surprise of some of the apparatchiks, the speech commanded a standing ovation from an audience of Party delegates which had never previously been brought to their feet by talk of the legal system before. When put in the context of broader social and political reform, the *Access to Justice* programme was capable of commanding much popular enthusiasm. Of course, the rhetorical buttons were easy to push. Criticisms of the legal profession are guaranteed to produce whoops of joys and judges are easily caricatured as aloof patrons of a Victorian, privileged class. Bonded to the rhetoric of 'rights for all', it could not have failed.

MODELLING NEW LABOUR'S LEGAL AFFAIRS POLICY

In the period since the May 1997 General Election, the policy of the Labour government towards the justice system has followed roughly the path which was set out by the Labour Party policies in Opposition – with one or two significant exceptions. It is important, therefore, to map out the development of Labour's policies before, in the remainder of this book, submitting them to analysis.

The Middleton Review

The all-encompassing review of policy promised by Lord Irvine in his speech to the Bar Council at the October 1996 Bar Annual Conference, culminated in a review conducted by Sir Peter Middleton, which reported to the Lord Chancellor in September 1997 ('the Middleton Review'). Sir Peter Middleton is a former Treasury official, it should therefore come as no surprise that the focus of the review was on cost management of the legal aid budget. The terms of reference of Sir Peter Middleton's review encouraged it to proceed down the road of cost management. The underlying political purpose was to make the Middleton Review dovetail with the Woolf Report into the reform of the procedural rules of civil litigation. The Middleton Review was the first policy-orientated act of the new Lord Chancellor in the field of legal affairs: it set out the ground for future policy development quite clearly. While dumping the Party's policy, attention was to be given to the budget's bottom line and the broader context of the legalistic approach to justice reform. Even though the Lord Chancellor was similarly in charge of constitutional reform, no part of the Middleton remit asked the Report to focus on the democratic dimension of legal affairs policy and the best trade-off between cost management and democratic socialism.

The terms of the remit given to the Middleton Review were as follows:

1. *To conduct a review of civil justice and legal aid to consider whether existing proposals for reform are the right way to deliver the following objectives:*
   (a) *to reduce the cost, delay and complexity of civil litigation; and*
   (b) *to gain better control of the cost of legal aid, better value for money for the resources available, and the ability to target those resources on the areas of greatest need.*

2. *To make recommendations on whether the current proposals are workable, whether they are likely to be cost-effective, what the priorities should be for their implementation (where appropriate), and whether there are alternative approaches that ought to be examined further.*

3. *In particular, the review is to consider:*

   (a) *whether the civil justice reforms can be implemented without imposing costs which outweigh savings both for potential litigants and the courts;*

   (b) *the means by which the cost of legal aid can be kept within limits which society can afford and is willing to pay in the context of the overall public expenditure ceilings to which the Government is committed, while giving the fullest possible weight to the important values of legal aid as a rights-based entitlement equally available throughout the country;*

   (c) *the interaction between the two reform programmes, including the costs/benefits of civil justice reforms to the legal aid fund, and the extent to which legal aid systems can reinforce the objectives of the civil justice reforms;*

   (d) *how far relevant aspects of the reforms (for example involving the not-for-profit sector, information services, use of ADR) might be developed to lay the foundations for a Community Legal Service.*

The Review constituted Lord Irvine's primary, personal policy initiative, liberating his department within the Blair administration from the commitments made in the Labour Party policy document *Access to Justice*. Taking each section of the remit in turn it is important to consider the priorities on which the review was to focus. The core question for the review was whether in focusing on the means of 'delivery of objectives', those were objectives concerning simply the control of public expenditure in respect of the legal aid budget, or whether there ought to have been a core objective concerned with the promotion of social justice. Is was not clear what precisely was meant to fall within the term 'civil justice'. As considered above, a number of issues might be said to fall within the political breadth of the term 'justice' in respect of civil law.

The objectives are then set out. First, 'to reduce the cost, delay and complexity of civil litigation'. At first blush, this appears to be a straightforward reference to the Report of the Woolf Commission into the reform of the civil justice system. Given the breadth of the problem and the context of the new constitutional settlement which the Blair administration was seeking to introduce, the question arises as to why these legalistic concerns are considered to be the more fundamental problems for the legal system than access to justice *simpliciter*.

Second, 'to gain better control of the cost of legal aid, better value for money for the resources available, and the ability to target those resources on the areas of greatest need'. The fundamental policy focus of the Lord Chancellor's Department appears to lie behind the expression 'better control of the cost' as part of the larger, New Labour commitment to 'keep within current spending limits', although as a matter of Lord Chancellor's Department internal policy it must be taken to mean 'slow the increase in cost'. More essentially, why is 'better value for money' selected as the criterion rather than 'better access to justice'? As mentioned above, the New Labour focus is clearly on the cost management approach. In that light, does the expression 'target' mean a need to adopt the Legal Aid Board's preferred model of vertical eligibility measurement for legal aid rather than horizontal financial eligibility,[17] or does it refer simply to the free market model of using block contracts to dispense legal aid? As a further anterior question, it is not clear within the cross-category development of Lord Chancellor Department policy how the 'greatest need' is to be measured. In theory it could be achieved in departmental cash terms or by reference to welfare state model of social need. In the context of a rolling cost management approach, it is not clear that social need will lead the constraints of cash limiting.

The second paragraph of the remit asked Middleton to consider 'current proposals' to decide whether or not they are workable. What is not clear is which proposals are included within that expression. A number of interest groups outside the Labour Party had produced proposals by this stage in time and therefore Middleton was being set loose on a number of proposals. The attempt was to leave the way clear for an affirmation that contingency fees, the Lord Chancellor's favoured approach as a 'quick fix' to legal aid funding, would be the most efficient reform proposal. The attraction of contingency fees to the political actor is that they would take a number of claimants out of the legal aid system immediately and thus cause a drop in the size of the legal aid budget. Furthermore the cryptic expression 'alternative approaches' does not make clear whether it is financial measurement exercises or different means of the delivery of advice and representation that are to be covered.

The primary focus for Middleton was then 'to consider: whether the civil justice reforms can be implemented without imposing costs which outweigh savings both for potential litigants and the courts'. The remit for the review sought change without increased cost. As set out above, it is not clear how this can be achieved without a more fundamental restructuring of the entire justice system. A number of broader issues such as the decoupling of matrimonial legal aid from the rest of the civil aid budget, and the democratic importance of access, would need to be considered. Although it is perhaps reasonable to ask a functionary to consider issues of cost and to reserve political questions for the politicians, it is not clear at what point in the review process Middleton's musings were to constitute part of the discussion about 'rights' in the UK.

The thrust of Lord Irvine's project is contained in the second theme which Middleton was required to bear in mind, namely: 'the means by which the cost of legal aid can be kept within limits which society can afford and is willing to pay in the context of the overall public expenditure ceilings to which the Government is committed, while giving the fullest possible weight to the important values of legal aid as a rights-based entitlement equally available throughout the country'. The phrase 'limits which society can afford', raises an older question as to the price that society ought to be prepared to pay to secure social justice. At the theoretical-political level, this question falls to be decided in a much broader debate about what constitutes 'justice'. To do otherwise would be to conflate legal aid with a total provision of justice once more. At a practical cost management level, change can be achieved within existing spending limits only if there is a radical overhaul of the means of providing access to justice. Simply concentrating on the figures for legal aid, in a vacuum from dealing with the greater question of restructuring the system for securing social justice, will result in a failure to cut costs and also fail to tackle the greater problems of breakdown in the social fabric and loss of communal identity.

The Woolf proposals for reform and the Middleton Review are seen as one complete project by Lord Irvine, prior to the introduction of the Community Legal Service. As such the remit refers to 'the interaction between the two reform programmes, including the costs/benefits of civil justice reforms to the legal aid fund, and the extent to which legal aid systems can reinforce the objectives of the civil justice reforms'. The question arises: 'How are the reforms to the civil justice system and to the legal aid fund to be seen as being linked?' There are links between Woolf's personal underlying programme to remove 'inequality'[18] and the notion of introducing 'civil justice'. What is surprising is the seeming dissonance between the 'objectives of the civil justice reforms' and legal aid in this sentence as though they were somehow separate. Given Woolf's own plea that legal aid reforms mirror his proposals, even though there are necessary tensions between those programmes at the theoretical and practical levels, it is a surprise that there has been little public examination of the distinction between those parallel projects (beyond the warm sweep of rhetoric).

Clearly, legal aid was created in the Legal Aid Act 1949 with a view:

> to make legal aid and advice more readily available for persons of small or moderate means, to enable the cost of legal aid or advice for such persons to be defrayed wholly or partly out of moneys provided by Parliament.

From its inception, in the early stages of the welfare state, legal aid was intended to contribute to an increase in social justice. The aim for the reform of both the civil justice system and the legal aid system must be social justice. Within the ambit of the new Clause 4 of the Labour Party constitution, this must require a system which works towards the creation of a 'just society'. A just society, in the context of legal remedies and systems of dispute resolution, must require equality of access to those systems. Hence the proliferation of reports and policy documents titled 'access to justice' and those which emphasize the importance of identifying 'need'.

There is an important gap between the civil justice reforms and the reform of the legal aid system. That gap is quite simply that neither review is addressing the central question: 'What is the best means of delivering access to justice?' The legal system has demonstrated itself to be exclusive and inaccessible, while the legal aid system has shown itself to be regressive and increasingly expensive. The better question might be: 'Are the priorities for legal provision correct?' When the budget is divided up in such a way that one third of its total is spent on private divorce proceedings, a considerable sum is not being directed at the relief of poverty.

The final part of the remit refers to the 'use of ADR' and the development of ideas 'to lay the foundations for a Community Legal Service'. The creation of a Community Legal Service is Lord Irvine's grand design. Beyond a catchy title for a system of block contracts, it is not clear precisely how it is expected to operate. At one level it operates as no more than a renamed version of Conservative proposals for block contracting and NHS-style trust reforms. Ideologically this may be problematical and may create political problems of presentation. For example, the current system gives preferential treatment to those with matrimonial disputes. Where a particular community takes money away from matrimonial disputes and puts it towards those bringing industrial disputes, there is no longer horizontal equality between citizens.

Civil justice reform

Lord Irvine's policy for the reform of civil justice falls into two halves: the replacement of much of legal aid with conditional fee arrangements and the implementation of Lord Woolf's proposals for the reform of civil procedure.[19] The approach is a fusion of the cost management approach (the reduction of legal aid spending) with the legalistic approach (the adoption of Lord Woolf's narrow reform package). It is anticipated that this intellectually timorous package will rejuvenate the legal system. In fact, the danger to the citizen posed by both of these reforms is enormous.

The worst-case scenario is that claims brought by ordinary citizens will be refused legal aid and will prove too small to convince a solicitor to enter into a 'no win, no fee' arrangement to represent them. The self-representing citizen will then be forced to submit her claim to a fast-track system of justice, again because it is not worth very much money. While it might constitute the difference between penury and comfort for the individual, the courts system will treat it as comparatively unimportant and accord it 'no frills justice'[20] to reach a resolution.

The Access to Justice Bill 1999 followed the 1998 White Paper in concretising Labour's legal affairs policy in legislation. The presentation of the Bill in its initial stages included a number of provisions which were subsequently dropped by the government during debate in the House of Lords in what appeared to be a negotiating tactic in allowing some provisions to fall by the wayside so that other contentious provisions could remain.

The kernel of the new legislation is the replacement of the classical legal aid architecture with a new body, the Legal Services Commission, with responsibility for public provision of legal advice and assistance in both civil and criminal contexts. The new Commission is charged with responsibility for administering the legal aid budget through the Community Legal Service ('CLS') for civil legal aid and through the Criminal Defence Service ('CDS') for criminal legal aid. The legal aid bureaucracy is therefore altered by the legislation but there is no alteration in the structure of legal aid, other than the development of contingency fees. Rather, such changes are left to the Commission (with the approval of the Lord Chancellor) to develop through regulation of the CLS and CDS.

The 1999 Bill sets out core objectives for the administration of legal justice:

> ... that persons have access to legal services and the
> machinery of justice which they would otherwise be unable to
> obtain on account of their means ...

From that objective it is difficult to isolate precisely what is meant by the 'machinery of justice'. At one level, this could refer to lifts in the court buildings or it might refer to access to any level of advice or assistance. However, the difficulty with the latter alternative is that the presence of Citizens' Advice Bureaux does mean that there is always *some* access to advice and assistance. Therefore, the provision ought to be taken to refer to access to court-based remedies or to remedies provided by alternative dispute resolution tribunals.

What is similarly unclear is the sense in which citizens are to be 'unable' to acquire access on account of their means. Without a welfare state form of eligibility limit, it is difficult to see whether a person who could afford access to legal services only by withholding the food from her children's mouths for a month would be 'unable' to obtain access to legal services. It is possible for her but practicably she is unable. With more complicated litigation, a citizen may be able to afford the preliminary advisory sessions and even to the initial trial but not to push the case to appeal. In such a situation, it would not be clear whether or not that person ought to be considered to be unable to access the legal system. To draw lines between cases requires a return to the system of eligibility limits, vertical eligibility differences between different types of case or a progression to an integrated welfare state system.

The role of the Lord Chancellor

One feature of the early days of the Blair administration was the level of attention that was lavished on the unelected kingmaker in the Cabinet, Derry Irvine. His beginnings demonstrated an accident-prone tendency in his own departmental press relations and in those of New Labour generally as talk of the cost of his wallpaper and bathroom fittings became a satirical staple on radio and television. At the same time as his disdain for high street DIY stores made the national press, the Lord Chancellor sought to introduce both the Human Rights Bill and the reform of legal aid to the public arena. The office of Lord Chancellor has received a fillip with the publication of the range of Cabinet committees chaired by the Lord Chancellor and his legendary proximity to the Prime Ministerial ear.

As will be considered below, the office of Lord Chancellor has been under attack for some time as an affront to the constitutional settlement in the UK, fusing executive, legislative and judicial functions in one office. The personal power of Lord Irvine is perhaps the most obvious example of fears as to ineffective checks and balances on the power of office-holders whose roles threaten the delicate equilibrium of the unwritten constitution.

The Lord Chancellor's personal voice is observable in LCD consultation papers in a way that it was not previously. Whereas in the past policy papers would usually be written in the third person, asserting facts and arguments, the new style appears to express the Lord Chancellor's own opinions and view of the facts directly in the text rather than adopting the more distant tone of the Conservative years. The result is a more obvious thumping of political tubs. Community-based policies are emphasized,[21] as are governmental objectives concerning fiscal control.[22] This tone is pursued by identifying issues which the Lord Chancellor personally wishes to see addressed.[23] A new style inhabits the LCD, even if the content of policy is moving in the same direction as under Conservative administrations.

Themes and (con)fusions

There are two fundamental defects in New Labour legal affairs policy: first, it fails to take an integrated approach to justice policy and, second, it fails to match a consistent ideology with targeted policy. The need for an integrated approach to reform is pursued for the remainder of this book. It is suggested, in short, that the only way in which it is possible for reform to be effective is if it examines the problems which citizens face as to dispute resolution and as to education about their legal rights. The present focus on cost-cutting ignores the democratic aspect to justice reform. More importantly, the failure to understand that there is a complex web of services and social need beyond the limited problem of the legal aid budget means it will be impossible, in fact, to cut budgets. Cost control and effective delivery of access to justice are only possible as a result of root and branch reform. Tinkering at the edges of legal aid eligibility will not deliver on the larger political project of the Blair administration.

The further confusion is the rhetoric of protection of human rights with the monetarist dogma of reducing public sector spending. The attention paid to the reduction of budgets as the pre-eminent priority of government has broad implications for the restriction of their role, mainly in terms of government becoming a manager of the taxpayers' communal bank account rather than being an engine for reform of social structures. The attention of the Lord Chancellor on cutting costs by using conditional fees, while failing to marry that to the other half of his brief to do with the entrenchment of civil liberties legislation. This new policy has been presented, together with unconvincing soundbites, in such a way as to imply an increase in access, whereas the truth is most litigants will now not receive legal aid and will not be able to reach a conditional fee arrangement with lawyers if the amount claimed is too low.

Justice affairs policy remains a backwater in the Blair project which has yet to be adapted to the reforming zeal that personifies much of the rest of the programme.

CONCLUSION: THE CONTEXT OF CONSTITUTIONAL REFORM

The reader will be able to isolate some themes running through this discussion. First, the area of reform of the legal system has been considered to be a problem of practice rather than theory for too long. Second, the principle of social justice is one which should lead this debate. Third, the solutions which may be required by the principle of social justice need not be jettisoned as part of a *realpolitik* assessment of available administrative resources. Fourth, the voguish and one-dimensional imperative of controlling of public expenditure (which has become an article of faith in the administrative organs of the legal system) has ignored, for ill, the social need for complete access to justice in a society in which social relations are transforming rapidly.

Another side to the New Labour policy is the abnegation of any element of welfare state-ism in the policy. In reasserting the necessity of increasing court fees, Lord Irvine has said: 'whilst I accept that citizens have what may be called a constitutional right to a court system, I do not accept that they have a right to a free court system'.[24] In short, there is no right to equal access to courts. For some people, high court fees will be a barrier to entry preventing them from bringing litigation in the first place. More fundamentally, it places another nail in the coffin of a justice system seen as an extension of the welfare state. The death of comprehensive civil legal aid was caused as much by this attitude to justice as by the rise in its cost.[25]

The core objective of a restructuring of this system must be that access to justice is made as broad as possible. To work towards this end, it is necessary to make decisions about the allocation of resources. The difficulty is that the legal system *in toto* is not capable of sustaining this core objective of wider access to justice in the way that it is currently organized. The solution therefore requires a programme of policies which address the systemic problem and do not simply chip away at parts of it. Unless you focus on the justice system as a means of generating a more just society, you will not get the priorities right. The call for reform is a call for justice; the call for access is a call for equality. To deny people the access to law is to deny them access to their rights. It is to deny them the access to the whole of their potential. In the words of the late John Smith, 'it is simply unacceptable to continue to waste our most precious resource – the extraordinary skills and talents of ordinary people'.[26]

NOTES AND REFERENCES

1 A. Bevan, *In Place of Fear* (first published 1952; Quartet Books, 1990).
2 J. Habermas, *The Philosophical Discourse of Modernity* (Cambridge, Polity Press, 1987).
3 Commission for Social Justice, *The Justice Gap* (London, IPPR, 1993).
4 See, for example, Hutton, *The State We're In* (London, Jonathan Cape, 1995).
5 See Elliott, *Labourism and the English Genius* (London, Verso, 1995).
6 See, for example, Gordon Brown's tract, 'Fair is Efficient – a Socialist Agenda for Fairness', which isolates 'fairness' as a suitable left-of-centre goal; Fabian Pamphlet 563 (London, Fabian Society, 1996).
7 John Smith, Preface to *Strategies for Renewal* (London, Vintage, 1994).
8 C. Gearty, 'The Cost of Human Rights: English Judges and the Northern Ireland Troubles', (1994) 47 Current Legal Problems 19, p. 21. Although provisions in the new Human Rights legislation in the UK include rights to accommodation if not a redrawing of property rights.
9 See the discussion of law as a closed social system, below.
10 The Labour Party's proposals contain intentions to develop franchising of contracts and of community-based legal aid provisions which some have difficulty in distinguishing from the Conservative Party proposals.
11 Speech to the Labour Party conference, October 1996.
12 See, Alan Milburn MP, *Mapping the Third Way*, Nexus conference, London 3 July 1998.
13 Marquand, *The New Reckoning* (Cambridge, Polity Press, 1997).
14 Goss, speaking at the Nexus conference, *Mapping the Third Way*, London, 3 July 1998.
15 Labour Party, *Access to Justice* (London, Labour Party, 1995); see Appendix.
16 See *The Middleton Review*, p. 63.
17 The distinction between vertical and horizontal eligibility is explored in *Publicly Funded Legal Services*, below.
18 As set out in Lord Woolf's address to the London School of Economics, 30 January 1997.
19 Lord Irvine, speech to the House of Lords, 9 December 1997; www.open.gov/lcd/speeches/1997/adjn-deb.htm.
20 To use Lord Woolf's favourite phrase.
21 As set out by Lord Irvine in a speech to the House of Lords, 9 December 1997; www.open.gov/lcd/speeches/1997/adjn-deb.htm.

22 Lord Chancellor's Department, *Access to Justice with Conditional Fees* (March 1998); www.open.gov.uk/lcd/consult/leg-aid/lacon.htm.
23 Lord Chancellor's Department, *Justice at the Right Price* (July 1998); www.open.gov.uk/lcd/concult/civ-just/fast.htm.
24 Lord Irvine, speech to the House of Lords, 9 December 1997; www.open.gov/lcd/speeches/1997/adjn-deb.htm.
25 The same point was made, more confusingly, in a speech to the Lord Mayor's dinner for Her Majesty's judges on 23 July 1997, where Lord Irvine said: 'I do not accept that there is a constitutional right of access to a free court system, anymore than I could accept that before the National Health Service was set up in 1948 ... a "constitutional" right to free medical services was being denied, although we all recognise that the health of the nation makes a high call on scarce public resources.'
26 J. Smith, Preface to *Strategies for Renewal* (London, Vintage 1994).

Part II

Theories of Social Change

3

Social Justice, Law and the Political Programme

INTRODUCTION

The following discussion is in truth a statement, a position. About how law is. Not about how law seems or how theories of law interact – but about how law is. And about how law ought to be.

Conceiving of the term 'law' is, of course, the central problem of jurisprudence. I am conscious that the following may well be a particularly unsatisfactory account for many legal theorists in that it seeks to be political and not logically impenetrable. 'Law' in this discussion refers to the institutions, cultures and systems which are discussed in Part V, *Models for Reform*. The ideas considered form a programme, or a position, growing out of the welfare state and radical centrist analyses as set out in the preceding chapters. The ideas explored below form a part of that programme.

Part II, *Theories of Social Change*, seeks to map the theoretical background to the reform of the legal system. The approach to reform of the legal system tends to revolve solely around empirical analysis carried out in patches and a compromise between the various vested interests of the legal system. The reforms which have been mooted by the Labour Party, and the reforms which were introduced or discussed by the Thatcher and Major administrations, have lacked any solid, intellectual understanding of the context in which change is sought, the outcome which is sought from change, and the political ideology which informs change.

In the reform of front-line political issues like education or the treatment of the economy, the intellectual, political and statistical backgrounds are well understood. Reform of the constitution, the content of systems of democracy and the reform of the legal system (together the 'justice system' in this discussion) have not been systematically connected to this mainstream discussion. In the twilight of the Major years there were attempts to mirror the introduction of block contracts in the NHS in the treatment of the legal aid system. The reason for this was a transplanting of a fashionable new right response rather than the result of focused analysis of the way in which the justice system operates.

The more general themes which inform the political debate and the generation of New Labour principles require some exploration in themselves and an application to the need for reform of the justice system.

The limits of jurisprudence

The detail of the discussion in this part is predicated on a simple premise: in the absence of sufficient access to justice it is not possible for jurisprudential theory to provide an adequate account of the nature and administration of law. The points made in the Introduction to this book about restricted access to justice and to legal services mean that law is something which is *done to* ordinary people and not something which is a tool,[1] or a contract,[2] or a system[3] which is in some sense owned by people. Rather, law is outwith their grasp: it is too expensive for them and too closed from them. Therefore, law cannot be a system which it is important to consider in jurisprudential terms before it has been considered in political terms.

Law is political in the sense that it involves the imposition of judgement on, and the exercise of power over, disenfranchised citizens. In that sense it is less important to consider the technical or philosophical nature of law than it is to account for it in political terms. In the following chapters I will attempt to set out a political theoretical account of law, rather than a jurisprudential one. It is possible to explain even a coercive legal system in which citizens are disenfranchised in jurisprudential terms. However, it is hardly useful if the result of that analysis is simply an acceptance that some citizens are disenfranchised. Law in the UK is primarily an issue of politics and power in a changing world.

To illustrate this point the analysis will consider a suitably dialectical account of the legal system in a social democratic context. MacCormick's essay, 'Legal Right and Social Democracy'[4] seeks to explain the history of the term 'social democracy' and its relationship to law by juxtaposing Hume's account of property rules on the one hand, taken together with libertarians like Hayek, Nozick and even Pushkanis, with the socialist account of law identified in Marx and in Rawlsian social contract theory.

MacCormick identifies the term 'social democracy' as one which has been used by Marxists but which was latterly appropriated by European welfare state socialists, and (he must acknowledge) that has more recently been claimed by the rejuvenated centre-left typified by the Blair administration. He identifies four principles standing at the heart of social democracy: that social justice cannot be realized through market institutions; that the state therefore has a role to play in economic life; that civil rights and liberties are nevertheless of great importance; and that the inclusion of property rights among those liberties negates the possibility of a collectivist reorganization of society. This conception of social democracy is advanced as the best one available, conforming to a respect for the rule of law and 'legal right'.

In MacCormick's account Hume 'treats of justice as the virtue we exhibit when we strictly respect other people's legal rights, especially their rights over property'.[5] Human beings are perceived to be primarily individualist but with a necessarily social element.[6] For Hume, property rules are required to be applied universally, regardless of any individually unjust result of such application. Further, the distribution of such rights have no basis in egalitarianism on the realpolitik grounds that such a policy would be impracticable, inefficient and pernicious. The benefit of this approach is that it is the rule of law which is the basis of government, rather than a discretionary and consequently dictatorial system. Hayek has made the link in this thinking with Kantian ethics – that is, that individuals ought to be free to act within the constraints of law.[7] The alternative would be a rigid government by reference to principles of *ad hoc* fairness which would make citizens subject to the discretion of the arbiters of fairness in that context.

The core of Hume's argument, as taken up by Hayek, is that individuals are free because they are equally constrained and unconstrained by law. At the heart of this position is the understanding that all individuals are equal before the law. In theory, that is indeed the case.[8] Law applies evenly in theory in that judges apply it without grace or favour. In practice, nothing is further from the truth. Citizens who are unable to afford a lawyer, or who are not sufficiently educated about the rights to which they are entitled, are less equal before the law than those citizens who can afford lawyers or who have access to the necessary knowledge.

The anti-thesis, which MacCormick identifies, is the Marxist thesis that equality before the universally-applied law is no guarantee of equal access to social goods. In its place is suggested a form of decisionmaking and justice allocation which is based on collectivist principles. Again, in the absence of the conditions upon which this thesis is predicated, it does little for the ordinary citizen. The Marxist position requires that there be a proletarian revolution which introduces the collectivist structures under which law would wither away. More generally, the form of social justice sought by this thesis (broadly an equality of outcome considered below) requires that no citizen is empowered differently from any other citizen. Under the legal system as currently composed, citizens are differently empowered because of their different access to the justice system.

Thus MacCormick's project is to correlate the 'Whig thesis' (based on liberty before the law) and the 'Marxist thesis' (based on a revolutionary, egalitarian distribution of power). MacCormick has a different sense in mind when he says, 'Justice is not teleological but purely and simply procedural'.[9] The more interesting sense for this discussion is that justice is to be isolated in its procedural aspect. This practical focus returns the analysis to the void which separates the citizen, and the disputes and problems of her lifeworld, from access to advice, knowledge and representation. In short which separates her from justice.

It is not proposed to pursue the detail of MacCormick's argument from there. Nor is it intended to pick out MacCormick from other jurisprudents for any reason other than that he develops a workable notion of social democracy – albeit, not one that is favoured in this text, as will emerge below. The core point is that jurisprudence is a logically posterior question to the issue of access to justice as considered in the following analysis of the political lodestars of a feasible strategy for generating greater access to justice.

Structuring the political project

As considered above, there is a need for the left to identify the nature of their project for the twenty-first century. The fall of the credibility of state socialism stemming from events in central and eastern Europe, and the rise of global capitalism, have encouraged the democratic left to seek a new language in the centre of politics. However, this new centrism, identified in the context of the legal system in *The Radical Centrist Approach* above, is not the ideologically moribund centre of the Cold War dialectic of left and right. Rather, it is an attempted synthesis of rightist and leftist concepts – welfare socialism with monetarist economic management, tough law and order policy with a concern for social cohesion, individual rights with communal responsibility. This Part aims to map some of the principal tenets of this 'third way', primarily by suggesting the most appropriate principles for such an emerging ideology in the context of justice policy.

There are a number of voguish concepts (globalization, reflexivity, connexity, communication and chaos) ranged alongside some staples of leftist thought (such as equality and hegemony). In the particular context of the justice system, as a *political project*, these concepts have a very specific correlation. The common thread is an observation of a changing world mixed with a desire to root out social injustice. First, it is important to consider the reason why a third way is being sought now, at the end of the 1990s.

Movements and change

The world has changed drastically, sometimes violently, in the past fifteen years. The globalization of economic power has reduced the ability of national governments to restructure internal economic relationships. There has been a revolution in information technology, with implications for education, leisure and the work place. At the same time society has become hyper-complex – as new power bases emerge, fragmenting traditional power structures. Employment relationships too have seen a shift away from traditional roles. Work and career patterns are no longer inter-generational and linear. Many of the staples of manufacturing industry and the coal industry have all but collapsed, and mass unemployment and non-unionized, part-time labour have become a central feature of the new economic landscape. The accepted social 'truths' of our society (of the family, of work for young people, of geographic communities) have been destabilized by the modernist, monetarist project. There is a disen-chantment among the 'jilted generation'[10] which now sees no place for itself in the social and political landscape of previous genera-tions.

The adopted challenge for the New Labour government has been to generate a new politics which captures the spirit of these funda-mental changes in society. Blair's insistence on the re-drafting of Clause 4 of the Labour Party's constitution was a necessary declara-tion of the ordinary values of the socialist project. Core socialist values of equality of opportunity, social justice and democratic empowerment are as vital now as ever they have been. They are the core around which the political philosophy of the new labourism is being constructed. These core values must be objectives as well as principles. The important task for the centre-left is to achieve greater social justice and not just espouse it, to realize equality of opportu-nity not just to preach it, to deliver democratic empowerment not just promise it. The new constitution must not just recognize these as principles but work towards them as goals.

The real danger facing the Labour government is its current lack of an identified political ideology. That said, the Labour Party does not need 'a big idea' to take them through to the next century. There are no apparent, big ideas left to be uncovered, other than to fuse old core beliefs with the new context. Rather, it needs to rediscover what it has in its fundamental concepts which people will understand to be true and with which they will identify. As Cohen has said,

> What the [New] Right did is no proof of what the Left should do. It is nevertheless extremely suggestive. It tells against looking for a 'big new idea'. That is anyway a futile endeavour, since you do not land a new idea as a result of angling for one, in the wide sea of intellectual possibility. New ideas standardly come from attempts to solve problems by which old ideas are stumped.[11]

There is a need for remoulding political theoretical ideas at the end of the 1990s because of the changes which have hit British society: economic globalization, the hyper-complexity of social institutions, the collapse of the manufacturing industry, the advent of mass unemployment as a long-term feature, the destabilization of social myths by the modernist project, the information technology revolution, the all-pervasive disenchantment of the jilted generation.

The importance of the project in political theoretical terms is that it will draw on both traditions to create a new, synthesized whole. The new thinking of New Labour is really a dialectics of the past. Rejecting the uselessness of both state socialism and market-based *laissez-faire* economics, this necessarily dialectical process must draw from what has not been discredited in both of these systems. In starting this new strain of thought, Labour has been forced into a position in which it has developed its headline ideas before an intelligent base has been able to grow to feed the specific policy and ideological processes that accompany a political party going through fundamental reform.

New Labourism, new values

To give birth to the New Labourism, the Labour Party must glean what it can from its socialist values and isolate those elements which can be translated to the new thinking.[12] What is clear, is that the Labour Party was never a socialist party on the fundamental Marxist–Leninist model.[13] It only ever advocated the reform of economic and social mores to improve the lot of the working class in a capitalist society. However, many of the fundamental values which informed the nascent Labour Party were of a Marxist or socialist kind. Notions of egalitarianism and emancipation from economic exploitation shared a common heritage with the Marxist project. As such, the social democratic aims of the Labour Party (never extending as far as the imposition of state socialism) grew out of a set of values relating to fairness which were comprehensible to the electorate.

However, in the socialist project there was a morality which sat outside the economic base of Marxism. To locate in the values of socialists only economic objectives is to miss socialism's emphasis on ideals to do with morality and social structures. Socialism has been engaged in a normative process which fleshed out values on to the bones of economic theory.[14] In short, there has been an implicit development of ethics while talking explicitly about economics. Post-Marxism, post-structuralism and critical theory have all been on their surface ontological programmes seeking to deconstruct the capitalist system and replace it with the leftist project. This has resulted in what has been described by Habermas as the 'welfare state compromise' of social democracy and Labourism. The issue here is whether the left should release its hold on an intention to govern or to exert economic power and concentrate instead on being a moral code which aims solely to work for the redistribution of social goods.

The end of old values

The old myths of our society have been destabilized by the modernist project. One of the most important examples of this destabilization process has been the dissolution of traditional 'communities' whereby individuals and families lived in close proximity to the work place, and shared communal facilities, values and aspirations. In seeking to erect a programme built on the concept of the community, the problem presents itself that such concepts no longer retain their traditional meaning nor does everyone understand them to mean the same thing.

This project still rumbles on. Habermas has taken the post-modernists to task for suggesting that the modernist project has been completed. It is more accurate to suggest that different aspects of the modernist project are in different stages of development and perhaps that the deconstruction school has arrived to pull down those ideas which are either redundant because they belong to another time or because they never had a valid claim to truth. In *The Philosophical Discourse of Modernity*,[15] Habermas begins with the claims of the French post-structuralists that they have moved beyond the philo-sophical subject and the concomitant need to return to reason understood as communicative action. This notion of the individual's role being replaced by communication bears a number of straightforward, definitional political complications when placed alongside an agenda which seeks to 'empower the citizen'.[16] However, the debate needs to be assimilated to the work of a modern party of the left attempting to reconstruct its intelligent base of ideas. The work of the modernizers, which continues outside the field of aesthetics in the forward march of technology and of the demands of the citizen.[17] The focus of this book is on achieving social justice through legal and related systems.

Mapping the change

The New Labourism is left in the position where it is attempting to draw from a heritage that has been irredeemably altered in many respects by market capitalism.[18] What the New Labourism requires is an avowedly intellectual exercise which will create a reservoir of principle from which the movement can draw as it goes forward. There is a sensible suspicion of new ideas for new ideas' sake. The revelation that the Labour Party does not need 'a big new idea' is the first reason for guarding against a junking of old ideas just because they are old ideas. However, politics has moved on, and New Labourism must seize the tide of this change to carry the Party forward.

Society has become hyper-complex.[19] The socialist and social democratic agendas are trapped in the mindset of a time when central government could control society and provide solutions on its own. Systems theory has led us to one, new understanding: that power relations have splintered. Foucault's analysis of the location of power[20] recognizes this splintering. He locates power in culture too, which is perhaps too diverse a target for government and therefore also too broad a target for a workable political theory. What is important is the location of, for example, much economic power in unregulated financial institutions.[21] Unless politics understands the power that rests in the hands of quangos and private sector organizations, it will be impossible to create an agenda which confers rights and assumes responsibilities. In the language of responsibility, it is necessary to locate the power and place obligations on the holders of powers rather than berating the disempowered citizen for a lack of moral exactitude. The role of law, as used by the citizen, will be to go where politics maybe cannot – to deal with the individual situation precisely.

There are two possibilities offered by the new technology. On the upside, public access to information will empower people and will allow them to shape their lives free of the strictures of public censorship and even of the demands of the work place (in the case of those able to work from home). Alternatively, technology will create a *Bladerunner* future in which people will be frightened to emerge from their homes, and will be fed pap through a million different cables, and in which vast electronics corporations will wield enormous power.[22]

The reality is that either scenario is possible. What is certainly true is that technology offers vast educational and vocational opportunities, and Labour must begin to rethink the way in which it views society and the structure of educational norms. The acceleration of communications and televisual technology has already had a profound effect. The Gulf War was fought and observed with the use of advanced technology. Instant communication tools like the photocopier and the fax helped to undermine communism in eastern Europe as the samizdat newspapers replaced the usual communication by word of mouth of the activities of other protesters.[23] The fax speeded up communications from weeks into seconds and created the momentum for the velvet revolutions. This rapid dissemination of information has had its effect on politics with the creation of 24-hour news coverage. The potential result is a world peopled by 'dromomaniacs' (people who are the tools of a technology that constantly overtakes them).[24] Alternatively, individuals can become self-serving agents using this technology to further themselves: harnessing speed to facilitate growth.[25] The effects of technology, on the meaning of individuality and the linguistics of communication, are altered by this radical termination of the power of speech and the pen.[26]

The relationships of international capital have moved the control of economic indicators, employment policy and so forth, beyond the scope of national government. We are in the third stage of international capital: we have progressed from the nineteenth-century model of the capitalist system, to the nation state, to the global market place where goods are produced and disseminated on a worldwide basis.[27] The globalization of power relations has made the development of international politics an essential aspect of the agenda of a political party that is organized round the nation state.

The 1990s has seen the rise of a new, indifferent youth culture. More than ever before there is broader access to narcotics of an ever greater strength, there is less prospect of finding work, and the breadth of coverage of populist anti-culture is more widespread. The advent of the 'rave culture' has created in many young people a feeling that tribal unity is only possible in the presence of narcotic intoxication and via particular forms of music. Rave music itself is directed exclusively at the anti-culture: it fuels its message with a technical sophistication that is designed to entrance the listener and manipulate thought patterns. Unless politicians centre on the fact that this generation does not consider itself to be rooted in any of the social structures that have come before, they will fail to develop a politics which can be communicated to this group. The politics of rave culture and the soma generation which is in danger of being produced, are real issues that political theory must address.

The role of a functioning, responsive legal system will be to shape the detail of the rights and obligations owed in this evolving society. To facilitate a discourse about the contents of the rights which exist and those which perhaps ought to exist.

EQUALITY

Equality is at the heart of most of this discussion. It will be argued below that equality is at the very centre of social justice on any model of the left, and in particular in the creation of a viable justice system. Although there are those who would analyse the operation of law predominantly in terms of freedom,[28] the logic of those liberty-orientated approaches is that there is no inequality inherent in the legal system. As considered in Part III, *Publicly Funded Legal Services*, I argue that there is exactly such an inequality in the legal system. For all to be free in a democratic society, all must be equal under the rule of law. The question is not really, 'Should we be equal?' but rather, 'In what ways should we be equal?' In the context of the rule of law, the logic of democracy requires that we be equal without compromise. The argument advanced in this book is that we should therefore be similarly equal without compromise in relation to access to law and legal remedies. The interaction between community and individual autonomy is considered below.

However, the notion of equality is a particularly problematic one. There are many different ways and times in which equality can be measured. The Blair administration is not focused on equality of outcome as one of its core aims, rather it is focused on the creation of a social market, a just society and on prosperity. Its social democracy is libertarian and aspirational, rather than egalitarian. For the first time the rhetoric of equality has been dropped by a Labour government in an attempt to distance itself from the slogans of redistribution and universal benefits, and move towards, what has been dubbed in this book, 'the radical centre'. In moving beyond the structures of left and right the main ideological casualty in discourse has been equality.

The content of the term 'equality' has become ever more difficult to pin down. Gordon Brown has spoken of 'equality of opportunity'[29] and even more generally, of 'fairness', as being among the key socialist goals. Echoing John Prescott's words, the New Labour project is applying 'traditional values in a modern setting' by leaving equality of outcome behind. To some that means effectively jettisoning those values and being 'value-less'. In fact, the Blair administration sees itself as working towards the development of different values – although it is still necessarily jettisoning some values as it goes. The primary casualty has been equality. The notion of equality has in Giddens' interpretation transformed into a concept of 'inclusion',[30] and to a notion of 'equal worth' in Blair's conception.[31] For Giddens, inclusion relates to an ability for all citizens to participate socially by virtue of a social investment state which will educate them so that they have opportunity, but which will also nurture them through the rest of their lives where that initial injection fails. Blair is concerned to provide opportunity and prosperity by ensuring policy which gives equal democratic worth to citizens. While both these conceptions have an impact on the economic context in which citizens live, it is apparent that equality is given a more spiritual (and thus a less economic) spin.

Ironically, it is in relation to access to justice that the notion of equality has the greatest claim to truth. The notion of the rule of law, underpinning the constitutional democracy revered by the Blair administration, is that there is equality before the law. To translate that aim into practice, it is essential that individuals have equal access to law and are equally subject to it. As considered in the *Introduction* to this book, the current structure of the legal system means this is not the case. What remains at issue is the type of equality that is meant and the manner in which it ought to be applied in policymaking in the context of the justice system.

It is in the sphere of legal affairs that equality is an easy concept to apply. It is an uncontentious statement in democratic societies that everyone should be equal before the law. It also follows that the standard of equality is something which can be different in different contexts. Rather than constituting resiling from principle, it is important to measure the appropriate social good and to conceive of the appropriate level of equality for the purpose. Thus in relation to welfare state benefits, employment-related benefits replace income in a way that makes the recipient unequal in terms of receipt of social goods but more equal in terms of income than unemployment would otherwise mean. However, access to the National Health Service is equal to all in that there are no eligibility criteria. Therefore, it is necessarily the case that there is no such thing as total equality in our society – it is not suggested that those in employment ought to be entitled to unemployment benefits as well as the unemployed. Therefore, in relation to access to justice it is important to understand the appropriate context of equality.

In opposition to the egalitarian socialist and social democratic viewpoint, is one based on the autonomy of the individual which emphasizes liberty rather than social structure. The libertarian position emerges from Nozick, who has referred to the autonomous subject as

> a being able to formulate long-term plans for its life, able to consider and decide on the basis of abstract principles or considerations it formulates to itself and hence not merely the plaything of immediate stimuli, a being that limits its own behaviour in accordance with some principles or picture it has of what an appropriate life is for itself and others.[32]

This individualist subject makes decisions and choices in a way that is unfettered. The measure of that freedom is therefore in its equal application. None should be more free than others to make these choices. The question arises then as to whether or not this is a useful way of considering equality. To be equally free to make mistakes or to succeed, necessarily means that equality is a transitory value which will apply to selected groups of people only for a short period of time until their life choices make them either unequal or simply different. The antithesis to Nozick's libertarian position is that of the social contract championed by Rawls. In *A Theory of Justice*, Rawls extends a conception of equality and social justice combined:

> Justice is the first virtue of social institutions ... in a just society the liberties of equal citizenship are taken as settled; the rights secured by justice are not subject to political bargaining or to the calculus of social interests.[33]

In the calculus of providing social justice through law, it is contended that only social institutions will create an environment in which individual citizens will be empowered to shape their own rights and responsibilities. As considered below, there is a trade-off between individual autonomy and the systemic pressures which come to play an important part in the discourse about rights in particular contexts. However, to ensure that individuals' liberties are protected, it is this writer's opinion that equality of power within the justice system is the fundamental criterion in the generation of social justice. To be free under the law must mean to be equally free to access that law. Beyond the question of access, which is the remit of this book, it is a question of politics as to the reform of common law if judges do not reflect social requirements in their judgements and as to the reform of statute through Parliament.

Equality of opportunity

Opportunity stems from the concept of personal autonomy. It is by giving power back to individuals that they are able to realize their opportunities. By investing in the citizen, the state enables the citizen. Central dictation of the pattern of an individual's life chances does give them the ability to meet their own needs or to realize their own potential. A similar approach is taken by Held in the context of his principle of individual autonomy, predicated on a notion of some pre-existing equality:

> persons should enjoy equal rights (and, accordingly, equal obligations) in the framework which generates and limits the opportunities available to them; that is, they should be free and equal in the determination of the conditions of their own lives, so long as they do not deploy this framework to negate the rights of others.[34]

This theory suggests that there are justifiable inequalities in our society. Rather than a reliance upon compulsory equality for all, there are circumstances in which an unequal distribution of social goods is permissible. An example of this might occur where an individual has a particular talent which is deemed to be of social benefit. An inequality of social goods to assist this individual to hone that talent would be a justifiable use of resources even where the individual is not *per se* in an economically unequal situation.

Opportunity, diversity ... and injustice?

There are shortcomings with this focus on opportunity, in that it permits of huge social injustice by encouraging unequal outcomes. Giddens has identified the shortcomings of equality of opportunity as the sole plank of egalitarian thought in the radical centrist position.[35] In his view, if the focus is simply on opportunity, without thought to a just level of equality of outcome, the desire of the radical centrist for social justice will not be satisfied.

The fundamental issue is then, to what extent are specific inequalities to be justified? And further, beyond choosing the grounds for inequality of treatment, opportunity to do what? These are normative claims which themselves need to be grounded in an intelligent base of concepts. There are inter-generational inequalities; these inequalities will emerge even on Rawls' 'year zero' approach to justice generation.[36] How do we manage the growth of the aged population and the need to alleviate the poverty of the elderly? Sen talks of a need to assess capability of individuals to act: a dynamic conception of equality of opportunity. James concentrates on the injection of equality of opportunity at infancy: providing universal nursery education, healthcare at birth and so forth, so that at least the start in life is equal. Opportunity, it is argued, will follow from this.

How does one conceive of inequality? What is the inequality displacement which we are trying to manage? Should a system of equality of opportunity favour diversity? The 'one-size-fits-all' approach to benefits does not take sufficient account of the needs of individuals. To work towards a socially-inclusive system of benefits provision, individuals must find that their needs are met by the system. The emphasis must instead be on the provision of services to individuals in communities. The development of a public service ethos which is committed to responding to individuals, rather than simply to carrying ideology into practice, is the necessary focus of all social services including the legal system.

The aim of equality of opportunity in today's context is better described as equality of access to life chances rather than a redistributive provision of an exact mean average of social goods. There are some individuals, communities or groups at whom benefits and social goods should be targeted, while retaining the emphasis on diversity.

How useful is equality of opportunity?

There are matters of degree in this view of equality of opportunity. While equality of opportunity is often considered to be a less radical idea than policy to ensure equality of outcome, the notion of making all citizens' opportunities equal is in fact a very radical idea when taken to its possible conclusions. It is in staking out the perimeters of this notion together with management of perception of ideas like stigmatized means testing that will determine the success or failure of the project.

This issue resolves itself in part into a discussion of what the state can enable people to do for themselves. In this radical centrist vision, the role of the state ought to be centred on isolating those who are not served by the system and therefore require assistance to ensure that their opportunities are equal to those of everyone else. To borrow the Labour jargon, to be 'tough on need, and tough on the causes of need'. This approach sits less controversially with a discussion of law, perhaps, than with a discussion of the economy. With reference to economic goals, the classical socialist position would argue for equality of outcome, such that there is no demonstrable inequality or economic injustice.

With reference to the justice system, a notion of law which is capable of being used by the citizen to defend rights and to advance aspirations, is a legal system based on some equality of opportunity. It is not an issue of outcome because the ultimate outcome is a question for the judiciary and the legal system. The only meaningful outcome is the ability to take an issue before a lawyer and before a court without the barrier of cost. But that is really a question of access, rather than a question of outcome. Whether access is the same as opportunity in this context is a narrower question.

Equality of access

The context of equality which is most apposite in a society where citizenship is predicated on a balance of rights and responsibilities conceived of and enforced by law, is equality of access. As Held imagines the operation of this principle:

> Democracy ... entails a commitment to a set of empowering rights and duties. To deny entitlement capacities in any significant domain of action is to deny human beings the ability to flourish as human beings and it is to deny the identity of the political system as a potentially democratic system. A democratic legal state, a state which entrenched and enforced democratic public law, would set down an axial principle of public policy – a principle which stipulated the basis of self-determination and equal justice for all and, accordingly, created a guiding framework to shape and delimit public policy.[37]

The pathway of the political debate about equality is well-trodden.[38] On the one hand, it is argued that it is the responsibility of government to ensure that there is equality of opportunity between citizens, as considered above. In the light of the change in work patterns which has seen the 'jobs for life' culture be replaced with mass unemployment, Labour has begun to argue for 'life-long learning' which would enable adults to retrain and thus be able to retain the opportunity to participate in the job market despite periods of unemployment or the obsolescence of their skills. The shortcoming with equality of opportunity is that it permits for inequality after the initial injection of equal preparation. In truth, its focus on the virtues of competition means that inequality is an economic necessity.[39]

The flipside to this initial equality is equality of outcome. This measures the traditional socialist concern that it is visible poverty and inequality which ought to be the object of political reform.

Therefore, policies such as the introduction of a minimum wage work towards the removal of inequalities, rather than the equality of opportunity approach which leaves citizens to their own devices once they have received the initial service. Brown's complaint is that equality of outcome has no sensitivity to effort or dessert, tending instead towards bureaucratic inertia by means of centralized regulation. Ensuring equality of outcome in legal terms creates difficulties. In terms of litigation it is impossible to ensure that the parties are equal in any meaningful sense without displacing the authority of the court to reach an unfettered decision.[40]

A third context of equality is equality of provision. This aspect focuses on the rights of citizens to receive public services. As an echo of the universality principle, it argues for all citizens to have equal rights to use public services as a result of their citizenship. The National Health Service is a good example. Regardless of income, a citizen is entitled to treatment regardless of the cost of that treatment. Where the principle has broken down in practice is by the introduction of prescription charges and the flat-rate charged by dentists.

The legal aid system, as explored below, is a very bad example of a social construct when measured against the principle of equality of provision. Public funds are only provided for citizens to pay the fees of their lawyers through legal aid if they are very poor. In effect, unless an applicant is on social security benefit, there is no legal aid available. There are millions of citizens who are unable to access legal services because of the prohibitive cost. However, their need is not sufficient to generate entitlement. There is no equality of provision.

Yet it is a type of equality which must be the fundamental principle in the provision of justice. Equality of access is central to a properly functioning legal system. Equality of outcome is not a useful concept in this context. The outcome of an application to court will be dependent on the merits of the case, the availability of credible witnesses, and the opinion of the judge on the proper interpretation of the law. The only meaningful outcome is in the context of a dispute being heard by a court, or otherwise processed by the justice system, in accordance with principles of fairness and procedural propriety.

Equality of access is closer to equality of opportunity. Each citizen is to be entitled to access legal services, regardless of wealth or other factors. The opportunity in this case is the access to advice and possibly representation in the resolution of a dispute or in the development of a legal right. In the context of law it is easier to achieve equal opportunity from the outset, and then leave it to the court to reach a decision on principles of fairness. The only weakness is in respect of cases which do not reach a court or tribunal and which are settled by the parties either on the basis of a realistic assessment of their chances of success or after bargaining.

Access to social goods is all important if the theory is to be reflected in the experience of individuals. In the same way that, just because all are free to go to court, few can afford to without legal aid, not everyone can make a return on their equal life chances. In working towards equality of opportunity, we must address the power structures that prevent equality of opportunity. This links back to the need to establish methods towards social justice provision generally and an enlargement of individual citizen's access to democracy. The understanding of power relations and the hypercomplexity of social power is a prerequisite of enabling the citizen to access social goods. Simply winning electoral power will not, of itself, be enough to communicate opportunity to those who have been dispossessed in the UK.

To compare the legal context with the notion of equality of opportunity in the secondary education sphere, some public schools will typically provide avenues to highly paid employment which state schools will not, even if the standard of teaching and facilities are effectively identical. However, apart from some difference in quality between lawyers, legal aid enables access to any lawyer which the citizen chooses and therefore equalizes the very poor with the very rich in court in terms of their representation. The shortcoming of legal aid is that it is not uniformly available, such that some people are advantaged by it and others disadvantaged by it. Legal aid operates as a mechanism for social justice for the worst off in society but as an engine of inequality at the same time.

It is suggested that satisfaction of the principle of equality of access is the only one that is possible without conflicting with the total responsibility of the courts for the substantive distribution of remedies to legal disputes. Equality of access is not provided by the English legal system as currently organized. These issues, and the Blair administration's proposals to meet them, are considered below.

POWER

It's the characteristic of our Western societies that the language of power is law, not magic, religion, or anything else.

Michel Foucault[41]

Law as the language of power

As Foucault maintains, the language of law is at the centre of the discourse of power in Western society. For the individual, it is in the arena of law that questions of rights and power are decided. Where there is no access to law, there is no power. Without power there are no effective rights and no real obligations. The issue of access is dominated by the lawyers themselves and by political decisions as to the availability of public resources. To quote Foucault, 'it is as if even the word of the law could no longer be authorised, in our society, except by a discourse of truth'.[42] That discourse of truth, for our purposes, occurs each time the justice system resolves a dispute, or denies access to such a process of dispute resolution, through the operation of its own acquired legitimacy.

The theory of power is explored most interestingly in the work of Foucault. Interesting in the sense that his 'small lives' theory of power as operating in all social and individual interactions, approximates most closely with the manner in which an accessible justice system operates for individual citizens. Whereas some dismiss Foucault's conception of omnipresent power relations as being too broad to be meaningful, its breadth enables the development of an understanding of how power is experienced by individuals. Foucault is concerned to offer us a technique, not a general theory nor a deconstruction of a meta-narrative.

Some things are only the way that they are because people say that they are the way that they are. For example, contracts are only legally enforceable because people say that they are enforceable. Property law only operates in the way that it does because people say that it does. Foucault's interest in 'les choses dites', is that once they become language, they become fact. Once law accepts them into the lexicon, they begin to exist in the world. This is a discourse which asserts the truth of such contracts and such property relations. Denial of access to that discourse is, in itself, an expression of power.

Power and the argument for reform

Foucault is a theorist of hyper-complexity in power relations. Power is creative, in his analysis. Through devolved power, individuals can become more creative in their own lives. By making law accessible through a reformed justice system, citizens can create their own lives. However, the role of law, in Foucault's analysis, is as a historic manifestation of monarchical power exercised under the code of law – 'the legal system itself was merely a way of exerting violence'.[43] The use of law, while not always a means of exerting violence, is certainly a mechanism for exerting control – sometimes through force.

There has been a disintegration of the liberal democratic model of democracy-through-law. Five elements coalesce: a crisis in the legitimacy of social institutions like Parliament; hyper-complexity in social relations which makes it impossible for central government to control by decree; the emergence of closed social systems abstracting to themselves arenas of social power; a greater need for communicative action to advance the life-world of alienated individual citizens; and a need for a new means of analysing these splintered power relations. Together the resolution of these elements forms one part of the solution of both individual needs and the generation of social discourse. The resolution of these issues is vital to generate effective and equal access to social justice. Essential to the creation of a just society.

Perhaps what Foucault gives us is a sense that our metaphysical attachment to democracy and human rights and the Westminster model of Parliament, is essentially bogus. That there is a fundamentally different take on our proud rationality and our models. Perhaps we need to disturb the old through the generation of a radically different justice system so that the new can begin to be born. The criticisms of the new politics of the third way is that it does not seem like the old, that is does not celebrate our desire for progress that is a logically structured processus. We are in fact at a time when (as Gramsci identified in his own time) the old had not yet died so that the new can be born.

Constitutional power

> I do not accept that there is a constitutional right of access to a free court system, anymore than I could accept that before the National Health Service was set up in 1948 . . . a 'constitutional' right to free medical services was being denied, although we all recognise that the health of the nation makes a high call on scarce public resources.
>
> Lord Irvine[44]

The other aspect of law discussed above in outline, is its constitutional role. Through law, the individual becomes as powerful as the state. Both are subject to law and both are theoretically capable of calling on it to affirm their rights. The practice is more complicated. As considered throughout the discussion thus far, the practice of the law is about the content of rights. In the constitutional sense, access to legal and quasi-legal services is about the implementation of constitutional norms. Lord Irvine's words quoted above, show a limited acceptance of the constitutional role of *access*.

95

This ignorance of that context is all the more surprising given that the skeletal reforms[45], outlined below, refer constantly to the talisman of 'access to justice' as an apologia for dangerous abrogation of the individual's right to approach a lawyer for advice without consideration of the size or nature of the claim. Irvine talks in the language of 1960s human rights activism without concern for the possibility of putting those rights to work. His happy elision of the constitutional right to free healthcare, long a part of the political consensus in the UK, with the language of cost-cutting and public resources, is indicative of his blithe acceptance of broader cost management at the expense of core civil and political rights. Legal aid will not grow into the welfare state mould at a time of such confused ideological focus.

HEGEMONY

From power to control

Taking the role of the legal system in terms of the exercise of power, is then the role of the legal system as part of a hegemonic concentration of social power. Hegemony, in Gramsci's account of it, is the exercise of power by one class over another, with the consent of that other.[46] Consent is organized but not necessarily imposed by force. Thus it is with law. Those who are not able to access law are nevertheless subject to it. By agreeing to be subject to the rule of law, those who are disenfranchised from the system are both oppressed and content. This theme is mirrored in Chomsky[47] in his discussion of the illusions which are fostered in the population to ensure their continued support for institutions necessary to the promulgation of society. Among these illusions are respect for law, even though law is not always accessible to those who are encouraged to believe in it.

For Gramsci this discussion is addressed to the proletariat eventually taking power from the ruling class. This book uses the idea as part of the movement towards empowering people without the overthrow of political power. At that level it is social democratic (or 'welfare state-ist'), rather than truly socialist.

Praxis – steps in law reform

To use the Marxist jargon, implicit in the New Labour programme, there is a need to understand the means by which the revolution which brings power to the people is to be effected. It is contended that the programme of reform set out in Part V, *Models for Reform*, is a central part of achieving that revolution in the locus of power. As part of the broader pledge to reform the constitution so that power is exercised closer to those who are affected by it, Blair seeks to give power and influence to ordinary people where previously it had not existed. The Marxist undertow of this programme has gone unnoticed – primarily because it is obscured by policy to do with the economy which borrows expressly from monetarist economics and neoclassical endogenous growth theory. It is also hidden because the detail of the constitutional reform proposals has been slow to emerge. The enormity of the change that is to be made to social structures would, however, be too easy to overlook.

Praxis, in terms of the legal system, involves the opening up of access to all citizens to discuss and dispute the content of their rights between each other, with corporations and with government. While this stops short of overthrow of the entire polity, it does constitute an important reallocation of responsibility for the legal system to political agencies which are electorally accountable to the population. This is put to work in the proposed Ministry of Justice. It is also observable in the mooted reform of legal aid by means of locally-based political priorities for the legal aid budget. Power is thus devolved to local government. A balance is made possible between the needs of individuals and the broader political commitments of government.

New law, new Britain

In mirror image of Blair's call for New Labour to deliver a new Britain, a new justice system will make it possible for individuals to exercise their autonomy and for communities to shape their personality. The legal system is the most entrenched of the social institutions which the Labour Party must face down. In Part V, some of the initial steps towards that goal are marked out.

COMMUNITY

The importance of community

The issue of community is becoming more and more important for the Labour movement. Ever greater reliance is placed upon the ideal of community by political scientists of both the left and right wings of the political spectrum.[48] In the British context, however, this ideal contains a number of dangers. Indeed, while the ideal commands a portion of the political *Zeitgeist* in the 1990s, it remains a dangerous ideal on which to base a political strategy: primarily because it is a concept with an uncertain meaning. Communities are potentially dangerous and prejudiced arenas in which individuals are oppressed and discriminated against, as well as contexts in which groups can nurture their individual members and achieve common goals. The history of Northern Ireland is an abject lesson in the potential for communities to foster hatred and violence between identifiable communities or within geographic areas. The radical centrist approach to community is generally enthusiastic, drawing on modern American communitarianism as well as classically socialist conceptions of collective power in some instances.

The meaning of 'community'

In the historical context, the notion of community is orientated primarily around the geographic locus. Communities are areas of people of similar class and occupation. A community is best identified by the things which bind it together. The best example of a British community is probably the coal communities found in Wales and north-east England, where people lived in terraced housing ranged around the coal face. Education, shopping and leisure was carried on within that geographic area in predominantly similar ways. The sense of a cohesive 'community' has been broken down by the development of communication, transportation systems and by the collapse of support for the family as an institution. It is not obvious how society as a whole will now come to conceive of new communities: unless we are certain of this, it remains a shifting sand on which to build a reformist programme.

The root of the word 'community' is 'commune': the need to communicate and to come together. Among the most obvious anthropological observations is the drive among human beings to come together and form groups. At the centre of this grouping is the advent of language. The traditional community on the nineteenth-century model, has begun to splinter. The nuclear family is increasingly an anachronism. Community now depends upon understanding the ways in which human beings as citizens in the late twentieth and early twenty-first centuries will come together. Community is becoming a more fluid concept, based around the idea of freeing individuals' choices and thus liberating the ways in which people conceive of their own communities.

The question is, therefore, what does community mean in the modern context? Have the old myths of community been destabilized? Are communities said to exist in a physical space, or do they function in a virtual space in which people share an activity or a characteristic? In what sense is the Internet a 'community' or do communities require face-to-face interaction? The difficult question for today's society is the possibility of a community being forged without face-to-face interaction. It is difficult to conceive of a community which does not involve personal relations. Yet the growth in support groups for people who share medical conditions or who can only communicate their shared interests by telephone, are examples of voluntary ways in which people are relating to one another without necessarily coming into physical contact with each other.

The resulting question is whether the Internet, or other public electronic mail systems, could lead to the building of new-style communities. This example is more useful to us than it might at first appear. While the Internet is currently a fashionable communication tool, it is just another technological advance like the television or the telephone was before it. To make it possible for the individual to participate in this community, the technology must be available and affordable to all those who wish. The Internet offers potential for the forging of community on this basis or it offers the possibility of control by the corporations who own the phone lines and the machinery. A political stratagem built on making community building possible, must consider the means of allowing access between people. Communities will only build themselves if, first, the people want to build a community and, second, the opportunity to join the community can be accessed.

The broader conception of community, encourages us to think of cultural politics rather than geographic community politics. The underpinning problem is how to build a viable political programme on the basis of cultural politics. The notion of community is being replaced with something which more closely resembles cultural groupings. If a community can be established on the basis of groups of people who share common interests and attributes rather than the luggage of the traditional model, then that is a cultural link. In the tradition of libertarian socialist values, the pre-eminence of human rights makes it more difficult to enforce normative beliefs about the direction which society should take if the political structure is orientated around free-moving cultural currents.

One of the new cultural groupings is the 'Eastenders community'. This idea pursues the notion that a community will generate itself around shared points of cultural reference. A soap opera watched by millions becomes a form of community that is orientated around the shared reference points of those watching. In the post-modern arena, this form of community is every bit as valid as one which lives, works and shops together. There are other cultural meeting points: music, fashion, sport, shopping, media association, advertising, information superhighway, and dance 'rave' culture. Law fits into this pattern as one arena in which this cultural context can be shaped and developed.

Courting communitarianism

On the left, the most important work has been done thus far in the marriage of social democracy and American communitarianism. However, this is a dangerous marriage. Social democracy continues to emphasize the role of rights whereas communitarianism is concerned with the imposition of responsibility. The limitation of communitarianism is that it is an American conception, centred on the need for individual action in the absence of a welfare state. In the American context, welfare is the remedial safety net stretched out for the underclass. The core danger in American communitarianism is that it permits of a sufficiently broad interpretation to accommodate the thought of Murray within the language of active communities as well as the more liberal thought of Etzioni. While both Etzioni and Murray have much to say about the family structure – a great deal that is similar in a communitarian context – Murray advocates the bell curve theory of educational abilities based on racial, genetic differences.

For the radical centrist position, there is a dilemma in seeking to balance the language of responsibility with the traditional notion of rights creation. In Etzioni's model, communitarianism emphasizes responsibility to the exclusion of rights.[49] This programme holds within it the danger of failure to regenerate civic life – one of the core aspirations of the European left in the wake of the monetarist experiment. The intention is that by imposing responsibilities, you also impose correlative rights on behalf of others. The communitarian thought process does not account for this shift in the power balance. It is pointless imposing responsibility without also creating rights which enable the individual or community to live up to those normative claims. It is pointless to require obligations without creating a viable legal system in which those obligations can be moulded and put to work. Where the communitarians fail is in the lack of principle or political philosophy to underpin their normative claims. The rhetoric of the communitarian movement is typically pitched at the level of complexity of newspaper editorials.

The communitarian movement and autonomy

Etzioni's notion of culture revolves around the imposition of moral claims that are shared by the communitarians. There are two main objections to this approach. First, it cannot demand the support of the entire population because it deals in morals that society cannot share in their entirety. Second, it offends the principle of autonomy of moral choices which I have outlined above.

The splintering of society is the subject of the philosophy of ethics as well as politics and sociology. MacIntyre (1981) argues that modern society has moved away from a coherent social order which gave a sense of value and identity in traditional societies.[50] Rather than a cohesive social structure, contemporary society is made up of individuals, each pursuing their distinct desires and preferences. The picture of the individual and society that MacIntyre paints holds water as an account of the way modern society has evolved. MacIntyre uses this insight to take the Aristotelian tradition of the 'virtues' as a model for communitarian values with which to criticize modernity.

Walzer objects to the loss of self in the welter of fluid cultural communities:

> If we are necessarily and essentially social beings, then modern society cannot be understood as the mere negation – fragmentation, destruction, loss – of community. If the idea of the unencumbered self is a mythical creation of false theory, it cannot give a true picture of the self in contemporary society ... we are in fact persons and we are in fact bound together. The liberal ideology of separatism cannot take personhood and bondedness away from us. What it does take away is the *sense* of personhood and bondedness.[51]

Taylor blames the breakdown of society on liberal individualism. However, separation and divorce are all a part of modern life: therefore, it is not a deterioration of society, rather it is a difference in its structure. This is the view taken by Rorty, who defends what he calls 'postmodernist bourgeois liberalism', and by Rawls in his 'political not metaphysical' account of justice. Modern liberal society, they argue, is already a 'community' of autonomous individuals. As Sayers explains:

> social relations based on private property and market exchange – *is* fragmenting and destructive: not of community or society *as such*, but rather of a particular form of society, namely traditional society. Such relative autonomy is a real feature of the modern self.

The question then arises as to whether modernity itself is a negative thing in the communitarian conception:

> Both [views of communitarianism] portray the impact of modernity as negative. They lament the destruction or the

danger of destruction of the traditional forms of community, and oppose the value of community to that of individual autonomy as if these were exclusive of each other. However, if contemporary society is not simply the negation of community but rather a different form of it, then it cannot validly be criticised by appeal to the abstract notion of community as such ... The transition to modernity has not been an entirely negative process. The destruction of traditional social relations has occurred through their replacement by new and different ones. What Communitarianism portrays as a process of mere loss can also be seen as the creation of the autonomy of the self and an individual identity relatively independent of family and social position.

If the radical centrist position is to embrace the idea of autonomy, it must ensure that the way it treats communities reflects a commitment to individual autonomy. The only sensible link between autonomy for the individual and fairness for society, is to allow communities to evolve without government interference except to the extent that it is entirely necessary. What is essential for the welfare state socialist is that politics is able to create the norms around which that municipal and communal growth will operate. Perhaps this radical centrist politics is to be built on a contract between personal autonomy and community: the question then is whether or not community here should be defined as 'a system of culturally-linked individuals'?

Social justice in a changed world

Where is social justice to be generated in this maelstrom? The new right failed to meet this hyper-complexity issue by disempowering many organizations without creating a sufficiently enforceable social contract in its place. The theories of justice must work in a number of different spheres. Justice must operate in terms of economic life chances, in terms of political power and in terms of reparation for claims (legal or otherwise). The system of justice provision must be regenerated. The Rawlsian conception of justice is based upon the notion of a contract which is generated in the ideal speech situation of a new society being formed.[52] Its inhabitants are placed behind a veil of ignorance, ignorant that is of their role in that society once the veil is removed. Rawls's argument is that, if a society is formed in such a situation, the citizens would choose the structure of their society to reflect a more perfect notion of social justice than ever evolves in a market capitalist system.

While there are many possible critiques of this idealistic analysis of social justice, what is important to realize is that it is an exercise in theory building in the grand European style. Rather than focusing too closely on the detail, what is relevant is the use to which this theory building can be put. By discovering what we mean by a 'just' society, we can plan policy (or its presentation) to realize that end goal as closely as is possible within the political environment of the time. Without the theory, the realization of the goal is impossible. What Rawls offers is the notion of society in which justice approximates to equality of economic power. What we may choose to use as our lodestar of justice might be different.

The idea of fairness[53] might offer a closer approximation to equality of life chances. This end goal enables us to begin a debate about efficient welfare provision that is targeted at those with specific need or provided on a universal basis. The central tenet of a social contract is one which we may need to generate in policy on a new constitutional settlement, or to resolve conflict in Northern Ireland, but not in terms of regulation of the financial markets. The social contract might be a useful framework in which to present ideas of citizenship and inclusion in the radical centrist project. A positivist framework of rights provision will depend upon a sense of inclusion in this project on behalf of the population.

To build a project based on social justice, as part of a project of social regeneration, issues of poverty and welfare provision must be addressed at the same time as facing the issues of the new agenda. The welfare state socialists' ordinary values are central to a conception of social justice which people can understand even if they do not immediately accept all the potential consequences. To build a social contract, one must have agreement but before you can have agreement you must have identification between people as to the core societal problems which that context will seek to address. In modern Britain, the power imbalance between have and have-not must be redressed, if not by changing economic relations *per se*, then by realigning the political symmetry of those goals. Law has a role to play in this development. Social justice will stem, in part, from the notion of community in the radical centrist project. It will only work in tandem with broader equality of outcome.

Stakeholder democracy

Another modish expression of these ideas of empowering citizens within communities is 'stakeholding'. The principle behind stakeholding is that it enables individual citizens to have a stake in society. By analogy with shareholders in companies, if you feel you own part of something, you are able to contribute to it more purposively. The act of giving a stake to individuals is an act of devolving political power to individuals. In Hutton's analysis this stakeholding concept is applicable to constitutional reform rather than simply to economic structures. Indeed Hutton's core point is that the obsolescence of the British constitution is itself a drain on the efficiency of the economy.[54]

The legal system distances many people from access to their rights through delay, cost and over-complexity of rules and procedures. This much is developed in Part IV, *Components of Delivery*. There is no longer a clear class demarcation. Security has become one of the more important benchmarks of class. The middle class is now a broad band of people who are not poor enough to be on benefit but not rich enough to be free of financial worry.

Communication and social systems

The discussion moves from community to communication. The common stem 'commune' is particularly apposite in the context of a society going through great upheaval. As we enter the millennium, there is societal, institutional and existential *Angst*. Change is happening too fast for our social mores to accommodate it. Therefore, 'law' becomes essential to operate as the forum in which critical disputes or requirement for advice can be satisfied. It is by reference to 'the law' and polity that this commune can operate.

Communication and law

On the understanding of the justice system that is being developed here, law is the means by which the polity translates its decisions to the broader world. On some analyses, this operates by means of handing the reins from politicians to lawyers in the administration of justice. There are three key issues tied up in the debate about communication and social systems. At an ideological level, this issue centres on the debate between Habermas and Luhmann. The correlation of this debate with Giddens's theory of structuration is picked up below. The issues relate, first, to the nature of law as a means of communication as considered by Habermas; second, the social role of law as means by which citizens in democratic society communicate between one another and with social institutions about the development of their interaction; and, third, the nature of social systems in effective social communication.

Systems theory maintains at one level that society is too hyper-complex for communicative action to work. Systems theory should not be the *correct* analysis – as it cannot conceive adequately of the individual or of communications outwith systems (for example, tribunals or arbitration, not courts – the privatisation of law in this context does not, perhaps, constitute a system) as considered below. Habermas is right to put communication at the centre. There must be structures within which individuals, groups and society more broadly can reach towards answers in a changing world. Our newly complex politics requires these communicative capabilities to function effectively.

The social role of law as communicative action

We have got law the wrong way round. It is not something to be worshipped. Rather, it is a tool with which the life world should be developed.[55] There is a colonization of the life-world by law. Law subsumes human transactions, actions and reactions. It offers an analysis of those human activities and then carries through the means of controlling them. The language of law operates as a means of conceptualizing human behaviour. That things are said and analysed in a particular way, renders those things into truth. The justice system operates as a means of communication.

To enter into this discussion requires that the individual be able to access the justice system in the first place. The barrier to this appears to be the analysis of the justice system as a closed social system which is able to control that debate. In this theory of autopoietic social systems, the individual does not appear to occupy a place within this schemata. While there is a narrow difference in political terms between Habermas and systems theorists like Luhmann, the impact of their difference in analysis will be all-important for the individual.

Autopoiesis and law

The underpinnings of autopoiesis as a conception of law is best summarized by Teubner:

> 'the autopoiesis of consciousness' is a radical attempt to reformulate the individual's consciousness and his capacity for self-reflection in a systems-theoretical way. The objection that systems theory marginalises the human individual for society, that it treats individuals as 'blind agents', as dolls, without which the game could not go on, is without foundation.[56]

Where the view based on individual autonomy is weak is in the understanding of the way in which the moral decisions of the individual are translated into a social construct. The autopoietic view has the edge in that it sees the role of the social institution as conducting these discussions as part of a self-reflexive process. The two attitudes both contain elements which make claims to the identification of the nature of social system and to have located the ideal form of system. One of the fears held about systems theory[57] is that it is a systemic game, and that people are seen as little more than counters on the board of said game. In political terms, the competing claims are efficient communicative action on the one hand, and a fear that dehumanized systems will ignore the requirements of real people on the other.

This is the tension in the claim that the power to communicate lies only with the system, or – to use Luhmann's phrase – communications, not with the individual. The achievement of language is one of the few anthropological victories of life on this sordid little planet. To take the control and possibility of communication by language away from the agents and put it in the hands of the process (either the communication itself or the 'system') runs against the grain of the received, ordinary values of much of the audience. As Teubner puts the autopoietic argument:

> the human subject which is consigned to the social
> environment involves society to a considerable extent. On the
> one hand, the social constructs of 'persons' are absolutely
> essential for society to be able to constitute actions from
> communications by means of self-observation.

The participation of the individual is as part of the observing brief set out by the autopoiesists. The tension here is that if communications can communicate, what is to prevent them from observing at the same time? If individuals cannot communicate, how can they observe? And if they do observe, how can they communicate those observations except by other communications which in turn must be watched? At what point does the hyper-cycle simply implode under the weight of this logical self-penetration?

The solution is in the separation of the individual from the social. The fusing of individual and social, the anecdotal with the observed, the microcosmic with the macrocosmic, makes understanding either more complicated. The central claim for autopoiesis must be in its attempt to separate the two elements and consider each independently of the other.

> [Autopoiesis] breaks up the unity of the individual and
> society, and makes us view human thought and social
> communication as autonomous processes which reproduce
> themselves according to a logic of their own.

The political issue with 'processes which reproduce themselves according to a logic of their own' is that it is reminiscent of any definition of power which is outside the control of ordinary citizens. The fundamental question is whether a system developing its own rules is preferable to a society that enables individuals to select their own life choices while exercising autonomous control over social institutions. Arguing against the uninformed power conflict is the assertion that the role of the legal system is outside the aggregate influence of the lawyers' consciousnesses. The analysis of John Griffith, for example, is not enough to understand the legal system.[58] Rather, as Teubner has it, law is the product of an emergent reality, the inner dynamics of legal communications.

This removal of the locus of consideration of legal norms to the system avoids the consideration of their relationship to individuals. The effect of legal norms, their impact and their power is on individuals at their end. It is the individual who is locked up, loses access to her children, or who loses a house. The reason for legal norms being applied is because of the behaviour of individuals creating the need for a legal norm. The effect of legal norms being applied is their effect on the lives of human beings. Talking then of the systemic legal norm is to look at that part of the process which occurs between the behaviour of, and the impact on, the individual. It returns us to the question of how communication is effected in a way that differs from Ingrams' analysis of liberal-democratic rights creation.

CONNEXITY

Beyond law and politics: Connexity and social justice

While the legal system remains inaccessible for most people, society is changing profoundly. One impact on the legal system in the changed world is the growth of what Mulgan calls 'connexity'.[59] In his terms, despite this growing interdependence, institutions like the legal system are failing to connect with individuals by not providing them with access to remedies. As the world changes in this way, individuals are less able to protect their rights, to impose obligations on others or to forge new identities and connections. The growth of inter-connectedness and the increased concentration on human rights raise the following sorts of problems:

> [T]he clearest sign of all of the heightening tension between freedom and interdependence is that in much of the world today the most pressing problems on the public agenda are not poverty or material shortage (although these remain acute

107

for large minorities), but rather the disorders of freedom: the troubles that result directly from having too many freedoms that are abused rather than constructively used.[60]

Having freedoms, but being unable to protect or advance them, is bound up with the growth of dispossession and disaffection in 1990s Britain. The modern legal system[61] makes little allowance for inequalities of bargaining power and the impossibility for most people of accessing legal advice. This is at root a political question, calling for a need to examine the possibility of social justice and equality without the possibility of recourse to law.

Law is, in theory, the great leveller. Only in the context of law is an individual as equal in power to any other individual.[62] Where the legal system denies access, then that ability to be equal is lost. Therefore, access to justice is not simply about law or about legal procedural rules, it is about rectifying the denial of social justice. It is about the provision or denial of basic civil liberties. In Mulgan's terms, a 'weakness infuses liberal politics which imagines the individual as a self-sufficient entity, not formed by society, and owing nothing to it, but rather heroic in his or her isolation, and defined by a series of claims that can be made on society'.[63] That is true of the legal system. Concentration is poured on to the creation of models for codes of rights and obligations with little attention being paid to the manner in which those rights can possibly be protected. The individual is not self-sufficient. Access to law or to justice is necessary to achieve or create self-sufficiency.

The further problem for the legal system is the extent to which it is a closed system. In the power equation quoted from Foucault (p. 15) – that in Western societies power is discussed in the language of law rather than magic or religion – the individual who cannot enter the closed system of the law is denied power. Where power is discussed in the language of law, not being able to enter that discussion is a denial of power. As Teubner argues,

> 'Legal reality' . . . is a social, not a psychic construct . . . it is
> the product of communications. And among social constructs,
> it is a highly selective one, since it has come into existence
> with an autonomous social system, the hypercyclically
> constituted legal system.[64]

The law seals itself from other discourses about politics and constitution. Yet, it is through law that constitutional reform must be put into action.

Speed and politics

It is a commonplace that there has been a growth in communication – what is less clear is whether more is being communicated or whether there is a useful quality of information being exchanged. Within this information society, law still operates as an important means of communication between citizens. The legitimacy leant by law to discussions of social rights plays a part in shaping the language of morality. Through cross-border means of communication, techniques of expanding law have become global. The proliferation of human rights rhetoric in formerly non-democratic states is testament to this. Law is used more and more broadly by pressure groups as well as by individuals.

The collapse of the communist bloc in eastern Europe in the late 1980s and 1990s was fuelled by the increased speed of communication. The dissemination of samizdat newspapers in the former Soviet Union and Czechoslovakia (a network of photocopied and faxed newsheets) communicated advances and news of events instantaneously. Technology has been able to change the world radically in this way. There is an immediacy of ideas which geographic space had previously slowed. Speed itself has become a part of the political structure by requiring action and reaction far more rapidly than before. As Mulgan puts it, 'freedom has expanded beyond any historical precedent at just the time that the world has become more interdependent and interconnected'.[65] He goes on to say that,

> As a phenomenon, and as a way of looking at the world, connexity is forcing itself on to public consciousness through everything from global warming and the Internet, to ever more intensive arguments about the virtues and vices of free trade.[66]

Will speed and greater communication cause the state to end or simply challenge it, through law and other media? In Mulgan's opinion, for a government to succeed in cultivating responsibility it must understand the plurality of society: 'A state which has too much power may infantilise its citizens.'[67] The mantra is that it is better for a decision to be made locally to its effect – this it seems, must depend upon the nature of the decision. Mulgan focuses on the Latin root of the word 'communicate', *communicare*, to share. His ideal government would be on which was:

> sensitive to their own capacities and those of their citizens to strike the right balance between their overall responsibilities, and the freedom of citizens to exercise responsibilities for themselves ... reversing the tendency of politics to

disempower people by drawing responsibility away from them, reducing their power to a post hoc acceptance or rejection.[68]

Perhaps familiarity breeds contempt in an anti-political age, as Mulgan has pointed out elsewhere.[69] Perhaps it is an accessible system of justice which makes this possible. The reliance on 'voluntarism' unfortunately seems set to disappoint in a politically apathetic age. Mulgan urges us towards less compulsion from government. Through law we allow others to shape their own truth, their own discourse and their own communications. In this analysis, the Third Way is about community, whereas traditional socialism is about central control. In liberal democracies, absolute values have become very unfashionable. The important point is that government is in fact about control and not about the slightly fey term 'governance'. Communities will create their own hypercyclical rules – rules give rise to mechanisms of appeal whereas prejudice gives rise to violence, mistrust and antipathy.

Autonomy in connexity

The preceding creates a complex problem for the issue of the level of autonomy to be expected of citizens and to be exploited by them through the justice system. One of the clearest analyses of this position is in Ingrams' *A Political Theory of Rights*, which looks at the understanding of what constitutes a 'human right', what their moral claims are, and how they should be conceived of politically. Her initial position is that the classical view of individual rights sees them as goods which are 'owned' in some way by individuals on the basis that they are human.

Ingrams prefers to see rights as being created and protected through the filter of subjective political and moral belief which in turn undermines any claim to their objective existence as inalienable rights. The concentration on 'autonomy' is considered to be the better understanding of the conception of rights, based on a Kantian position about the value of the human being which is involved in a social contractual interaction. She then develops her position to take a stand related to Habermas's 'social conversation' of developing consensus about rights. The foundations of her position deserve some analysis to understand the qualities that are imputed to the individual in this area.

[The reigning conception of rights] demystifies rights by
showing them as logically ties to certain normative
descriptions of ourselves. In the Lockian world what we must

do to discover rights is to recapitulate the conception of persons as self-owners.

Rights are embedded in normative theories about the world. They do not grow out of objectively existing criteria.

The 1990s obsession with human rights does not command universal assent. MacIntyre, for example, derides belief in rights as at 'one with belief in witches and in unicorns'. Etzioni interestingly calls for a 'moratorium on rights' while the focus is trained instead on 'responsibility'. The 1990s American communitarian line echoes perhaps a more traditional socialist message of the individual as moral agent. Rather than being centred solely on personal gain and the role of personal achievement for self-selected, the individual in Ingrams' and Held's analyses, is necessarily involved in and concerned by the social ramifications of their choices. As Ingrams has it:

> Apparent ontological disputes turn out to be misleading ways of canvassing the merits and demerits of different conceptions of persons ... conceptions that favour certain traits such as separateness and independence may be regarded by some people as less revealing of human nature or less attractive morally, than ones which identify traits such as sociability and connectedness.

The consideration of the person, in this analysis, must take account of the public aspect to the individual. Essentially, this position is the foundation of Rawls's and much of liberal democracy's consideration of the individual. The sole level of majority consensus in democratic societies is that there is some point at which the choices exercised by the individual interact with the social.

The criticism that can be levelled against the liberal democratic analysis is the reliance on rationality in the individual agent. What is not accounted for is selfishness or barefaced irrationality. In the selection of moral questions, there is much scope for the selection of purportedly 'irrational' (or perhaps more accurately, 'non-mainstream') moral choices. The liberal democratic view is therefore centred on the requirement of moral pluralism. If individuals are to have autonomy, they must be free to make their own life choices. The theory is that considering a person to be an end in him- or herself, is to respect his/her distinctive capacity to create and pursue his/her own aims and projects. This freedom depends upon the ability of individuals to hold different opinions as to the good life. Herein lies the essential difficulty: how to marry the idea of moral pluralism with social, or group, action.

The autonomic viewpoint throws its concentration on the individual as the *fons et origio* of its conception of social structures. In the rightist, libertarian stance, Nozick (1974) formulates a similar position with reference to the autonomous subject as 'a being able to formulate long-term plans for its life'. Similarly, in Raz's conception of 'significant autonomy', the concept requires the ability to 'adopt personal projects, develop relationships, and accept commitment to causes through which their personal integrity and sense of dignity and self-respect are made concrete'.[70] Ingrams's structure of autonomy focuses more explicitly on a Kantian position. The basic elements are: that autonomy defines freedom negatively as belonging to rational will 'being able to work independently of *determination* by alien causes'. From here springs the more useful positive concept of freedom where individuals choose self-imposed laws. 'What else then can freedom of the will be but autonomy – that is, the property which will has of being a law unto itself.'[71] The primacy of the system and the availability of communication replaces self-determining will where the power to communicate and choose is abstracted to the system.

The problem with the systems-theoretical conception of the individual, in, among others, Luhmann, is that this central relationship is obfuscated. The restraint that might be offered by a freely communicating system is that the choice is taken away from communication between individuals and located in choices selected and elected by the autopoietic communication. As Rawls has it: 'acting autonomously is acting from principles that we would consent to as free and equal rational beings'. The autopoietic view, naïvely stated, suggests that the individual is served by an autopoietic transfer of inputs from the outside world to the system and the communicative outputs of that system. The individual's position is protected and enhanced by this osmotic discourse. The purist autonomic position would suggest that this removes the power from the individual. However, the social implications of the individual maintaining control over moral and political choices are that there could never be meaningful consensus. Ingrams, for example, moves explicitly towards the position held by Habermas that the difficulties of resolving these disputes can only be solved through an ongoing discourse which aims for the 'ideal speech situation'.

The result is an uncomfortable compromise of the basic assertion that it is the individual who makes the choices: the individual has to choose *à la carte* instead.

Choice is represented by the role given to consent. The idea
of independent validity is captured in the thought of
principles that any free and equal rational being would
endorse.[72]

Is autonomy to be tied up in the idea of choice in a way that is necessarily linked to consent? Logically, consent does not presuppose the exercise of choice. The two may be linked in some circumstances but consenting to a state of affairs cannot be equivalent to the exercise of free choice. To consent to something, in a social context, requires choice from a menu rather than choice from all the possibilities which the individual can conceive of. The issue of how free any individual is to choose is a question of politics. However, this does not remove the underlying question: What is the relationship between choice and consent to a list of choices? Autonomy, in its ordinary use would indicate a general freedom to choose. Closing down the options to a menu of consent necessarily implies compromise.

Any political programme must provide a menu at some point: even if it is simply a selection between frameworks in which comparatively free choice is to be exercised. In Ingrams's analysis, the exercise of autonomy necessarily involves the potential for the compromise of entirely free choice. In this way Kant moves towards the social contract position, where individuals are held to be morally autonomous but are also held to have consented to an agreed collection of moral (and other) choices.

> Our own will, provided it were to act only under the
> condition of being able to make universal law by means of its
> maxims – this ideal will which can be ours is the proper
> object of reverence; and the dignity of man consists precisely
> in his capacity to make universal law, although only on
> condition of being himself also subject to the law he makes.

So how to permit the individual to grow within the social in this justice system? Law must fight against systemic imposition of norms and standards. Imposition of such norms must be explicitly political if the justice system is to function effectively. Otherwise, the role of the justice system must be to permit individuals to communicate their aspirations for their own life-choices to the outside world.

COMPLEXITY AND CHAOS

There is a need to be careful in using scientific concepts to support social scientific points. Therefore, it should be made clear that what follows is meant to be primarily a metaphor but one which develops into a confident assertion that perhaps there is literal validity in that metaphor. The science that is to be misused are the two modish concepts of chaos and complexity. Their metaphorical use is in the pursuit of the idea of hyper-complexity advanced in this Part. The thing called 'society' (itself a term whose content is at issue) is an ever more tangled web requiring a different politics to reflect and appeal to the various collections of aspirations contained within it. A proliferation of power centres and social systems outwith the direct control of central government, but theoretically subject to the rule of law, generates a comparative level of chaos. 'Chaos', not in terms of anarchy or sedition, but rather in the sense of an amalgamation of numerous actions and reactions, actors and systems, generating socially observable but frequently inexplicable phenomena. Included in this category are phenomena like the growth of single issue politics and protest which has united the working and middle classes; the mawkish display of national mourning following the death of Diana, Princess of Wales; and an intensifying lack of respect for politicians and political institutions.

As with the development of quantum physics, it is possible to identify simple events arising from an accumulation of unrelated episodes. Examples given are the well-known butterfly flapping its wings in Beijing and beginning a chain reaction which causes rain in New York; or the dripping tap that, despite the maintenance of a steady flow of water, lets water fall at occasionally irregular intervals as a result of random and chaotic factors outwith the control of the scientist-observer.[73]

In terms of law, and other social phenomena, it is useful to consider the role of chaos as generating events which cannot be readily explained in the Cartesian affection for cause and effect. Capra uses this metaphorical trick to explain a post-Cartesian, Zen account of social relations and the need to adopt holistic approaches to everything from medicine to social relations.[74] Law is an important device to meet this chaos. Rather than continue to allow this chaotic generation of events, the justice system provides a means for individual, chaotically-arising disputes to be addressed and resolved. Law is a force for order at this level. Rather than a build up of unresolved issues leading to large-scale upheavals, individual issues can be addressed with the comparatively scalpel precision of dispute resolution, as opposed to the drawn-out and blunt instrument of political change. Constitutional reform more generally is usefully seen as a means of permitting chaotic episodes to be addressed where individual dispute resolution cannot cater for issues which exist on a larger scale.

The theory of complexity is then a useful understanding of how a reactive, responsive justice system can operate in the context of a hyper-complex society. In scientific terms, complexity considers the way in which simple phenomena can lead to complex results. One frequent starting analogy is the simple phenomenon of wind leading a complex and unpredictable pattern of waves crashing on to land. Complexity is said to indicate the natural tendency for physical and biological systems to take this complexity and nevertheless produce regular patterns from it. In short, a tendency for plants and animals to generate order out of chaos.

The generation of common law perhaps responds to this metaphor. A complex and largely unpredictable mass of litigation comes to court and leads to a complex web of judicial decisions. However, those decisions are not entirely responsive solely to the dispute brought before the tribunal but rather by reference to an overarching structure of decided caselaw. A semblance of order is thus made of the chaos.

The models for reform considered in Part V, attempt to create structures which permit for these chaotic episodes to come to resolution and thus reduce complexity to harmonious social interaction. The purpose of the models advanced in this book are to meet need and hyper-complex social phenomena with responsive and democratically accountable structures which bring 'law' closer to 'the people' – thus making the justice system an engine for democratic renewal. Chaos and complexity indicate a necessary drive, none the less, towards order. That is better created and disseminated centrally than given over to accidental evolution.

From chaos, via complexity, to order – a useful metaphor.

CONCLUSION

The foregoing discussion aims to isolate some of the core themes of a political project with which to approach the reform of the justice system. The ideas begin with a fundamental assertion that law is the language in which democratic societies conduct the discourse both about the content of their core values and their application (or at times enforcement). Law is the medium through which power is exercised. Therefore, the starting premise for any discussion of law in a democratic context is that all citizens must enjoy equality in the power to create that law and in their access to it. Liberty can only come from equality: before law all must be equal. Without equality, there is a defect in our liberty. Some become more free than others. Those others are therefore repressed. It is important for the left that their adherence to equality as the core value is the necessary foundation of democracy through law.

The welfare state demands universal access that is capable of inequality only as a result of democratic, political decisions and not by virtue of disparities in economic power. That there is some level of inequality to satisfy individual need is a position accepted by

115

Bevan – it stands to reason. So the nature of equality is a matter at issue. Its resolution must be a political decision as to entitlement to social goods distributed through a welfare state. For law to operate on a principle of equality of access, it must be capable of responding to need. That is, advice agencies, courts, legal advice through legal aid, must all facilitate equality of access to those social goods which are allocated to them by the welfare state. The decision as to eligibility must be made close to the locus of its application as a means of enabling communities to generate themselves and as a means of protecting individuals against the potentially harmful nature of some communities. This requires 'the law' to operate as a public service and not as a self-generating locus of power for the economically advantaged, or for its own agents.

From this discussion of the various political attitudes to legal affairs policy, the discussion of political project, and the theoretical background to the new politics, it is important to consider the structure of the components of the justice system as currently organized. The approach taken is to consider the English system and then to draw comparison with other jurisdictions. From there, a series of models for reform are constructed, building on the analysis in this Part.

The core theme of this discussion has been to place equality of access at the centre of the debate about the creation of a viable justice system in the UK. Within the context of law there is therefore an apparent conflict between individual autonomy and communal pro-vision. The importance of permitting the generation of individual rights is placed in the context of individuals recognizing a level of social responsibility, which permits access to publicly funded legal services to enter a conversation about the content of those rights and responsibilities. Community remains a key radical centrist value which aims to promote equality by promoting inclusion in that community and access to the social goods which that community shares. The greater danger is identified as being in social constructs, such as the legal system, which exist as autopoietic systems creating their own norms and means of discourse. The place of the individual in relation to social systems on this level is considered to be more problematic than the promotion of inclusive community. There is a line in relation to these systems between the communicative action favoured by Habermas and the stylized forms of systemic commu-nication discussed by Luhmann and Teubner. The former permits of a means of discourse which promotes rights and responsibilities, whereas the other casts the individual in the role of the object of that discourse. The difference between these two positions is an imbalance in the power of the system as opposed to that of the individual citizen.

The following sections, culminating in *Models for Reform*, aim to map out the precise structures which will permit this individual autonomy, promote equality and reduce systemic hazing of the discourse about our rights.

NOTES AND REFERENCES

1 J.-P. Sartre, *Critique of Pure Reason*, (London, Verso, 1994).

2 Rawls, *A Theory of Justice* (Oxford, Oxford University Press, 1972).

3 Luhmann, *The Differentiation of Society*, (New York, Columbia University Press, 1982).

4 MacCormick, 'Legal Right and Social Democracy', *Legal Right and Social Democracy* (Oxford, Clarendon Press, 1982), pp. 1–17.

5 MacCormick, *ibid.*, p. 2.

6 Hume, *Enquiries Concerning Human Understanding and Concerning the Principles of Morals*, in Selby-Bigge and Nidditch (eds) (Oxford, 1975).

7 Hayek, *Law, Legislation and Liberty – The Mirage of Social Justice (Vol. 2)* (London, 1976).

8 Aside from a more difficult argument about the political machinations which cause some people to benefit from those legal rules and other people who do not benefit: that is, any right for A imposes obligations on B not to interfere with A's right, thus advantaging A in comparison to B.

9 MacCormick, *op. cit.*, p. 8.

10 Prodigy, *The Jilted Generation* (XL Recordings, 1995).

11 See Cohen, 'Labour and Social Justice', *New Left Review*, Vol. 207, Sept/Oct 1994.

12 *Ibid.*

13 See, for a full exposition of this idea, Elliott, *Labourism and the English Genius* (London, Verso, 1995).

14 See J. Habermas, *New Left Review*, Vol. 183, 1990.

15 J. Habermas, *The Philosophical Discourse of Modernity* (Cambridge, Polity Press, 1987).

16 Not least is the proximity of communicative action to the systems theories proposed by Parsons, and pursued by Luhmann, while being reviled by luminaries of the new left like Anthony Giddens. Discussing these issues in a new political language is essential if the centring of 'discourse' as part of the debate is not to be mistaken for a displacement of the unfashionable 'individual' from populist political discussion.

17 A political project, in the populist and the theoretical sense, needs to use both the tools of post-structuralism to dissemble the myths of past ideologies and also understand the work done by critical theory in suggesting new methods of

enlightenment for the citizen. There has been, for too long, a separation on the left between its thinkers, its political actors/activists, and its natural electorate. The new right re-created conservatism when it married the active and intellectual parts of its personnel in the 1970s. That the results of this new ideology caused such economic and social disaster is due to the redundancy of the ideas from the outset and not to the programme itself.

18 See Mandel, *Late Capitalism* (London, Verso, 1989).
19 See in respect of this change, A. Giddens, *The Third Way*, (Cambridge, Polity Press, 1998) Luhmann, *The Differentiation of Society*, (New York, Columbia University Press, 1982).
20 M. Foucault, *The History of Sexuality* (London, Penguin, 1981).
21 See, Gavyn Davies, the *Independent*.
22 See, New Media/Mediaologies.
23 P. Virilio, *Speed and Politics* (New York, Semiotext(e), 1988).
24 *Ibid.*
25 *Ibid.*
26 See, Taylor and Saarinen, *Imagologies: Media Philosophy* (London, Routledge, 1994).
27 See, Mandel, *Late Capitalism* (London, Verso, 1988).
28 As derived perhaps from R. Nozick, *Anarchy, State and Utopia* (Oxford, Blackwell, 1974).
29 Brown, *Fairness*, John Smith Memorial Lecture.
30 A. Giddens, *The Third Way* (Cambridge, Polity Press, 1998).
31 T. Blair, *The Third Way*, Fabian Pamphlet 588, (London, The Fabian Society, 1998).
32 R. Nozick, *Anarchy, State and Utopia*, *op. cit.*, p. 49.
33 Rawls, *A Theory of Justice*, (Oxford, Oxford University Press, 1972), p. 4.
34 Held, 'Inequalities of Power, Problems of Democracy', in Miliband (ed.), *Reinventing the Left* (London, Polity Press, 1994), p. 48.
35 A. Giddens, *The Third Way* (Cambridge, Polity Press, 1998), p. 161.
36 Rawls, *A Theory of Justice*, *op. cit.*
37 Held, 'Inequalities of Power, Problems of Democracy', *op. cit.*, p. 58.
38 For a very good account, see Daniel, 'Socialists and Equality', in Franklin (ed.), *Equality* (London, IPPR, 1997), pp. 11–28.
39 T. Blair, *New Britain* (London, Fourth Estate, 1996), esp. p. 100 *et seq.*
40 See Parekh, 'Equality in a Multicultural Society', in Franklin (ed.), *Equality* (London, IPPR, 1997), pp. 123–55.
41 M. Foucault, *Power/Knowledge: Selected Interviews and Other Writings 1972–1977*, ed. C. Gordon (London, Routledge, 1980) p. 201.
42 M. Foucault, *The Order of Discourse* [1971], in R. Young (ed.), *Untying the Text: A Post-Structuralist Reader* (London, Routledge, 1981), p. 55.
43 M. Foucault, *The History of Sexuality, Volume 1* (London, Penguin, 1978), p. 88.
44 In a speech to the Lord Mayor's dinner for Her Majesty's judges, 23 July 1997.
45 'Skeletal' at the time of writing.
46 Gramsci, *Prison Notebooks*.
47 N. Chomsky, *Necessary Illusions* (London, Pluto Press, 1989).

48 See, T. Blair, *The Third Way*, Fabian Pamphlet 588 (London, The Fabian Society, 1998); A. Giddens, *Beyond Left and Right*, (Cambridge, Polity Press, 1993).
49 Etzioni, *The Spirit of Community*.
50 MacIntyre, *After Virtue*, (Oxford, Duckworth, 1981).
51 Walzer, 'The Communitarianism Critique of Liberalism', *Political Theory*, Vol. 18, 1990, p. 10.
52 See, Rawls, *A Theory of Justice* (Oxford, Oxford University Press, 1972), and *Political Liberalism* (New York, Columbia University Press, 1993).
53 See, Brown, *Fairness, op. cit.*
54 Hutton, *The State We're In*, (London, Jonathan Cape, 1995).
55 Outhwaite, *Habermas – A Critical Introduction* (Cambridge, Polity Press, 1994), pp. 86–7.
56 Teubner, *The Law as an Autopoietic System*, (Oxford, Oxford University Press, 1994).
57 See, for example, A. Giddens, *The Third Way*, (Cambridge, Polity Press, 1998).
58 J. Griffith, *The Politics of the Judiciary*, (5th edn., London, Fontana Press, 1997).
59 Mulgan, *Connexity: How to Live in a Connected World* (London, Chatto & Windus, 1997).
60 *Ibid.*, p. 5.
61 The better appellation is, probably, a 'postmodern legal system'. As with Jameson's definition of the term 'post-modern', our legal system is constantly self-referential, it pastiches old codes of dress and language and draws for new ideas on old texts and habits of thought (see, generally, F. Jameson, *Postmodernism, or the Cultural Logic of Late Capitalism* [London, Verso, 1989]).
62 See, for example, the recent McLibel litigation in which two individuals were able to defend an action brought by the megalithic McDonald's corporation, converting it into the longest trial in English legal history to date.
63 Mulgan, *Connexity* (London, Chatto & Windus, 1997), p. 9.
64 Teubner, *Law as an Autopoietic System* (Oxford, Blackwell, 1993), p. 45.
65 Mulgan, *Connexity* (Chatto & Windus, 1997), p. 1.
66 *Ibid.*, p. 3.
67 *Ibid.*, p. 226.
68 *Ibid.*, p. 229.
69 Mulgan, *Politics in an Anti-political Age* (Cambridge, Polity Press, 1994).
70 Raz, *The Morality of Freedom*.
71 Kant, *The Groundwork Metaphysic of Morals*.
72 Ingram, *A Theory of Rights*, (Oxford, Clarendon Press, 1994).
73 Gleick, *Chaos* (London, Heinemann, 1989).
74 Capra, *The Turning Point* (New York, Simon & Schuster, 1982).

Part III

Publicly Funded Legal Services

4

The Development of Legal Aid

I am a big supporter of the Labour Party but I think that what they
are doing to legal aid is shocking.   *Ben Elton*[1]

The aim of Part III is to consider the manner in which legal services
are currently provided through publicly funded means. Much has
been said in previous chapters about the manner in which different
theoretical stances conceive of access to the justice system, but so far
there has been little empirical discussion of the nature of the
principal means of providing such services: the legal aid scheme. The
provision of legal aid in 1949 is identified as the primary means by
which access to law for citizens is currently provided.[2]

Defects in the system

The core political issue remains the cost of providing legal and other
representation to the public, although preceding chapters have
outlined the broader constitutional and ideological importance of the
approach to legal affairs policy. Access to justice was not a core policy
of the Conservative administrations under Thatcher and Major. The
real problem is one of rising cost and limited access to justice.

On 1 April 1993, the then Lord Chancellor, Lord Mackay,
removed the entitlement to civil legal aid for about 14 million
people by altering the income threshold. Yet, at the same time, the
cost of the legal aid budget to the Lord Chancellor's Department was
£1.1 billion in 1993, a rise of over 21 per cent compared to 1992.
Legal aid expenditure was increasing amid the Major government's
attempts to control public expenditure. However, the spiralling
legal aid budget was causing more systemic problems than that. It
had risen from £570 million in 1989/90 to £1,100 million in
1992/93. Criminal legal aid had decreased as a proportion of the total
legal aid budget, falling from 58 per cent of the total budget in

1989/90 to 46 per cent in 1992/93. The cause of the realignment in proportions of the legal aid budget was the growth of civil legal aid applied to family law matters. Legal aid for matrimonial work is rising and accounted for 30 per cent of the total budget in 1992/93.

What emerges from this thumb-nail assessment of the Major administration's policy is the demonstration of two simple points. The first is that the Conservatives failed to realize their own ideological goal of controlling public spending on legal services from 1979 to their eventual loss of power in 1997. The second is that, when in 1993 the Major administration sought to advance its policy on legal aid spending, it did so by crude cost cutting, rather than an ideologically driven approach to policy. This is indicative of the myopia which characterized Conservative policy on justice affairs during this period. While matrimonial legal aid was proving to be the engine for much of the increase in legal aid spending, the Conservatives decided simply to change the threshold for eligibility, rather than seek to restructure the system in a way which would have satisfied their other ideological goal of liberating people while also controlling public spending.

At no point was there evidence of a serious, systematic attempt to address these issues in policy terms. Rather, the legal system over which the Labour government inherited control in May 1997 was in very great difficulty indeed. Behind the rhetoric of the Conservatives, who relied on their Courts Charter to represent a convincing justice affairs policy, lay a very different reality. Indicators of the severity of the problem included: long waiting times for criminal trials, particularly for those held in custody; repeated failures to meet targets and timescales set by the Courts Charter, while at the same time mothballing courts in order to save money; stringent eligibility criteria (consistent with income support thresholds) for legal aid, severely restricting access to justice; a massive court closure programme, reducing still further access to justice; and the introduction of a policy of bringing lesser charges by the Crown Prosecution Service in order to reduce unit costs by keeping cases in the lower courts.

It is important to rehearse some of the arguments surrounding the decline of the legal system and, in particular, legal aid. At a time when court charges and civil legal fees were soaring, legal aid eligibility was cut as part of the removal of 14 million people from legal aid eligibility in 1993 (considered above), despite a more than 600 per cent increase in public expenditure on the total legal aid budget between 1979 and 1997. The Conservative-run court system was characterized by waste, delay and inaccessibility.[3] The only two sectors of society who are at present able to access the justice system are the very wealthy or those on income support. The majority of British citizens, typically those who are in work or who have only modest savings, are unable to gain access to legal advice under such a scheme.

This problem was an intractable one for successive Conservative governments in the 1980s and early 1990s, as the difficulty of accessing the court system developed into a chronic problem for citizens. It was this state of crisis which the Labour Party identified, and in response outlined new policy in *Access to Justice*.[4] The keynote to Labour policy was an understanding that a legal system which is inaccessible to the great majority of its citizens fuels feelings of social alienation and disrespect for the law. Yet the reinforcement of the rule of law and a proper balancing of citizens' mutual rights and responsibilities was identified as being necessary to underpin civic life and to regenerate local communities.

In the final analysis, the law is neither comprehensible nor accessible to all of Britain's citizens, whereas it ought to be a means by which the aspirations of individuals, families and whole communities are realizable. A democratic socialist administration must be committed to making people more aware of their rights and responsibilities and to empowering them to assert those rights and to enforce the responsibilities of others to them. The implications of this commitment to the best interests of the citizen has enormous resource implications. Both the legal system and the legal aid scheme that funds it to the tune of £1.7 billion annually, are reliant on lawyers and expensive court-based litigation. The crisis in the provision of legal services requires a change in the scheme by which services are provided from central government, to reflect the needs of local communities. What is clear is that there will be no new money to spend on legal aid. Therefore, there is a need for a more fundamental refocusing of the structure of publicly funded legal services.

Some of the elements which must be developed to achieve this refocusing include the structures set out in Part V, *Models for Reform*. For example, the legal aid franchising scheme, considered below, must be reformed and extended to control the cost of access to justice and to set high standards for the quality of services provided by franchise-holders. The proposed community legal service will also build on the work of local law centres and Citizens' Advice Bureaux to provide a comprehensive network of independent outlets for publicly funded legal services. It is this extra dimension which will be essential to the development of a feasible legal affairs strategy.

Outwith the strict remit of legal aid policy, there is also a political recognition of the need to refer the fee structures, training and procedures of the Bar and the Law Society to independent review. The Labour Party had formerly intended to refer the issue to the Monopolies and Mergers Commission to ensure that the interests of the consumer of legal services are not infringed by current practices.[5] In the reform of the legal profession, there is an identified need to introduce direct access to the Bar and multidisciplinary partnerships. The judiciary are increasingly in the spotlight. The powers of the judges are great and, with the development of administrative law, becoming greater.[6] However, in the light of recent revelations as to miscarriages of justice,[7] this necessitates some reforms if public confidence is to be strengthened, not least in the broadening of appointments to include more solicitors and academic lawyers.

THE GENESIS OF LEGAL AID

The history of legal aid is typically described as having passed through three stages:[8] the period from 1949 to 1989 when the system was administered by the Law Society, the period from 1989 to 1995 after the Legal Aid Act 1988, and finally the period from 1995 onwards which was expected to herald a new approach in Conservative government policy. These categorizations were made before the 1997 General Election, and therefore the third category should be replaced with the mooted reforms of the New Labour government, including the Access to Justice Bill 1999 and the modernization of the legal system legislation.

The following discussion will follow that of the Legal Action Group[9] in assessing legal aid as encompassing not only alterations in that administrative system but also the development of law centres.

The welfare state settlement

The legal aid system was initially devised to provide a post-war settlement for the many thousands of claims brought in the wake of the loss of life in the Second World War. These claims related to probate and matrimonial matters which were administered by a reduced population of lawyers. To meet this demand the legal aid system was created by the Attlee government to ensure that there should be no want of access. The Labour Party has committed itself to honouring the principles contained in the Legal Aid and Advice Act 1949:

> to make legal aid and advice more readily available for
> persons of small or moderate means, to enable the cost of

legal aid or advice for such persons to be defrayed wholly or partly out of moneys provided by Parliament.[10]

The statement of the purpose behind the legislation continued: 'No one will be financially unable to prosecute a just and reasonable claim or defend a legal right'. Two points arise from this purposive statement in the legislation. First, assistance is to be made 'more available' for people who have 'small or moderate' means. Therefore, it was accepted that legal assistance was beyond most ordinary families where their means in the austerity of late 1940s Britain were modest. The inclusiveness of this statement contrasts with the restriction of modern legal aid eligibility only to those reliant on benefits.

Second, the cost of such assistance was to be 'defrayed' by Parliament. From the outset the most appropriate system was one which gave authority to the Law Society to administer the legal aid system using public funds. This is in contradistinction to the model of the National Health Service created in 1948 which provided medical care which was free at point of use to all citizens by means of the mass employment of medical professionals. The legal profession managed to retain exclusive competence to its sphere of influence at a time when governmental policy favoured the nationalization of private institutions which impacted on social welfare or the economy. In the consideration of the proposals for a national legal service in Part V, it is important to bear in mind the attitude which precluded such an institution even at the high tide of nationalization.[11]

The administration of the fund by the solicitors' profession for fifty years was a coup. Without meaning to imply any biased attitude to legal aid allocation or policy, the political influence of the profession over the constitutional freedoms of the British citizen in the control of legal aid payments to solicitors constituted an important role for a non-governmental organization in the use of public funds. Smith accounts for the creation of a full legal aid scheme as being based in part on the Law Society's concern that solicitors would otherwise have found it difficult to rebuild their practices after the war.[12]

The composition of the legal aid scheme administered by the Law Society, under the responsibility of the Lord Chancellor and an advisory committee, was promoted by the Rushcliffe Committee. The primary features of the scheme outlined in the Rushcliffe Report, other than in relation to executive control, were that the scheme be available for those of modest means (and not simply the poor), that it cover private client work, that there be a means test for eligibility, and that public money be used to pay solicitors' and barristers' fees directly. The means test remains important in the context of the notion of equality in relation to the justice system, moving away from the universality principle, which underpinned the welfare state structure.

The legal aid scheme has expanded greatly since its creation. Important extensions of the scheme include the duty solicitor scheme under the Police and Criminal Evidence Act 1984, and the general advice and assistance scheme (the 'green form' scheme).

Introducing law centres

As Smith refers to in his account of the creation of the legal aid scheme, there was little specific focus on the needs of the poor within the scheme.[13] That is not to say that the poor were excluded. Rather, the Attlee administration favoured those of modest means as well as the poor by including within the scheme all of a solicitors' private client business. There had been a proposal from the Poor Man's Lawyer Association that there be a focus of public funds on rent restriction, employment compensation and a broad range of small claims: all of which fell outwith the usual run of the solicitors' practice. At the time of writing, industrial tribunal work, social security tribunal work and proceedings before coroners' courts are not eligible for legal aid. The Access to Justice Bill provides for the Legal Services Commission to divide those services for which public assistance will be available. This may be extended to include tribunal representation.

In this way the law relating specifically to the affairs of the disadvantaged is being sidelined from legal practice. A number of points lead to this conclusion. First, lawyers will not undertake work for which their clients will be unable to pay unless there is legal aid available. Where there is no legal aid, there is no legal advice. In many tribunals there is an effective bar on legal representation by the express denial of legal aid. This point is explored further in *Alternative Dispute Resolution*. Second, where there is no legal community advising regularly in an area, the procedural and substantive norms which are created are non-legal norms which results in a difficulty for citizens to acquire advice as to procedure and likelihood of success in an area where there is no code of available law. In short, an absence of lawyers means that tribunals do not proceed with procedural predictability nor substantive certainty. Instead there is discretion in the tribunal which may operate in one way or in another, within the confines of administrative law as an appellate jurisdiction. Third, a lack of legal population of some aspects of social life means a lack of legal scholarship of the kind that is lavished on commercial and tax law issues where there are teeming hordes of publications, advisers, lawyers and case law.

In all of these respects the poor are badly served by the legal system because legal aid is not made available. One potential saving grace is the law centre, a concept explored in greater detail in Part IV. Its role as Smith's second stage in the development of legal aid is important, however. The law centre comes closest to the form of legal aid preferred by the advocates of a national legal service or a legal aid scheme focused solely on issues of law relating to the poor. In 1977 the first law centre opened in North Kensington to provide advisory services in relation to issues relating to the poor: in short, areas not including crime, matrimonial law, wills and probate, personal injury or conveyancing (being the staples of solicitors' practice). Other issues were dealt with by private practitioners under the legal aid scheme. The law centre offers a community-based advisory service dedicated to specific forms of work relating to the law of social exclusion.

The law centre model in the Netherlands was born out of the university based advice systems in the 1970s. This sounds suitably Dutch, and in contrast to a profession-led British system. However, there is much to link the two given that the English legal aid and law centre structure is supported in many instances by motivated practitioners who are prepared to commit themselves to taking on particular forms of work at low profit margins.[14] The genesis of the law centre movement, fuelled by the American experience, was begun by work done by lawyers attached to the Labour Party.[15] The importance of the law centre development to publicly funded legal services is that is plugs the gap which is not met by a judi-care system which relies on private practice. To return to the discussion of the existence of a market in legal services, further proof that market forces are inappropriate for the organization of the justice system is evident from the non-availability of legal aid in a number of contexts which are particularly significant for those on benefits and for the working poor.

An emerging Ministry of Justice

The proposal for a specific form of Ministry of Justice is considered in Part V, *Models for Reform*, whereas this section is specifically aimed at the isolation of a department of government which has come, ever more, to constitute a single ministry with responsibility for the justice system. As considered in *Models for Reform*, there is a long way to go before the whole of the justice system is satisfactorily subsumed within a single department. However, it is possible to identify a small department gaining momentum and moving beyond being caught within the confines of the Lord Chancellor's medieval role as head of the judiciary towards becoming a department headed by an elected member of Cabinet – present there because of some administrative power rather than as a legacy of his membership of the Star Chamber and the Privy Council. For the development of justice in the UK concomitant with the growing enthusiasm for human rights and access to justice for the disadvantaged, it is essential that such a function emerges from the grounds of a constitution ensnared by the ceremonies of the Middle Ages. The Lord Chancellor must be able to speak up for justice policy in the same way that the Chancellor of the Exchequer and the President of the Board of Trade are able to speak for economic interests and industry. The inappropriateness of the office of Lord Chancellor to fulfill this particular role is examined in greater detail within the discussion of the Ministry of Justice.

The creation of the Legal Aid Board in 1989 under the provisions of the Legal Aid Act 1988 ensured that there was a single civil service bureaucracy responsible for legal aid, rather than the practitioner-led Law Society. As considered below, the merging of responsibility for the whole of the legal aid budget in the Lord Chancellor, ending the division between criminal and civil legal aid in administrative terms, offered a first glimmer of an emerging responsibility for legal affairs policy in a single department. Furthermore, it offered a ballast to the professions' control of this area through the Law Society, introducing political and bureaucratic governance for the first time. The further development is the creation of a single ministry with overall responsibility for justice policy. The dimension which had eluded past Lord Chancellors was the power to confront the legal professions and to relax their grip on all of the practicalities of administering justice through legal aid, court-based litigation and access to membership of the advisory professions. Lord Irvine, Lord Chancellor at the time of writing, has expressed exactly such ambitions for the Lord Chancellor's Department:

> The ambition of any Labour Lord Chancellor must be to
> restore legal aid to the status of a public social service which
> is so highly regarded for its economy and efficiency in
> securing access to justice that, with the support of the public,
> it can compete for scarce resources with the most highly
> regarded services such as health.[16]

The Courts and Legal Services Act 1990

Under section 17 of the 1990 Act, the statutory objective is identified as 'making provision for new or better ways of providing such services and a wider choice of persons providing them, while maintaining the proper and efficient administration of justice'. This legislation, however, was directed most clearly at cost-cutting. For the first time, conditional fee arrangements between solicitor and client were made legally enforceable. Importantly, it began the process of eroding the exclusive rights of audience enjoyed by the Bar in English and Welsh courts by extending the people able to be granted such rights by the Law Society and the General Council of the Bar. This erosion was a quid pro quo for the solicitors given that exclusive rights in solicitors to conduct property conveyancing work were also removed.

The Lord Chancellor's Advisory Committee on Legal Education and Conduct was created under the 1990 Act[17] to advise the Lord Chancellor in relation to legal education and the training of the profession. Within its express statutory remit is the comparison of working practices in other member states of the European Union. This important policy adjunct to the role of the Lord Chancellor as a Cabinet minister should have contained the ability for English and Welsh justice affairs policy to reach beyond the historical constraints and ceremonies of the English legal community. As a further development of this break with the complete domination of legal services by the English legal profession and judiciary, the office of Legal Services Ombudsman was introduced to pursue complaints in relation to the activities of lawyers under the 1990 Act.[18] Its significance is the creation of an office outside the control of either of the professions' lobbying organizations (the Law Society and the Bar Council) with power to investigate complaints connected to matters arising under the 1990 Act. This Advisory Committee will be abolished in 1999.

The 1990 Act constituted the beginnings of a fundamental cultural shift in the administration of the legal system and in the organization of the legal profession. For the lay person it is difficult to see how these changes would translate themselves into anything more than cosmetic alterations. The 1990 Act itself did not advance alternative dispute resolution methods by any significant measure, nor did it remove all of the restrictive practices which make up the legal profession's control of dispute resolution and the distribution of the legal aid fund.[19] The creation of an Ombudsman was a fashionable political development of administrative law principles to empower citizens to make complaints to a non-judicial person. However, the Ombudsman remains without effective sanctions or staffing capabilities to match the power of the professions over the lives of ordinary citizens.

Targeting need and striking the balance

Legal Aid – Targeting Need was the Conservative government's penultimate consultation paper for the reform of legal services before the 1997 General Election.[20] The central message in this consultation paper was to:

> introduce a system of block contracts covering the type,
> quality, volume and price of services to be provided ...
> improve the targeting of funds towards areas of need,
> particularly where suppliers can provide high quality advice
> at less cost than the present court based approach.

The Green Paper trumpeted 'A New Approach'.[21] As considered in relation to the cost management approach, there is a trend in legal affairs policy to focus on the cost-cutting element in the role of the Lord Chancellor's Department. *Targeting Need* personified this approach precisely. References to 'price', 'supplier', 'incentives for suppliers', 'discipline for setting priorities' and 'high quality', all match the consumerist approach which has come to infest issues of constitutional politics. This invective against the politics of consumerism and cost management is not myopia to the problems of administering public services on finite budgets, rather, it is born out of a frustration at the inability of the cost-cutters to succeed in their goal in the absence of any understanding as to what they hope to achieve at the end in ideological terms.[22] Without an understanding of the principle, there can be no successful targeting of those resources. The refusal of the Major administration to accept that there was such a thing as social need made it doubly complicated to target it in a Green Paper on legal aid. There are seeds of this continuing focus on cost in isolation from political priorities in *Justice at the Right Price*, Lord Irvine's consultation paper on these issues, considered in Part IV, *Components of Delivery*.[23]

The preceding discussion is not to say that there was *no* mention of access to justice in the Green Paper. In tune with the times, paragraph 1.1 read simply: 'The aim of the Government is to improve access to justice'. However, the next paragraph continued by outlining one necessary part of this as being that the 'administration of justice is efficient, effective and affordable'. There is no discussion of the nature of the rights of citizens in this context, nor of the manner in which access to justice is to be made meaningful in relation to a disempowered, disadvantaged populace seeking to resolve disputes regarding their employment, families or liberties.

The Green Paper made a number of encouraging noises to do with the advancement of alternative dispute resolution without producing any concrete mechanisms by which non-court based structures would be developed. Rather than pursue the logic of greater individual freedoms into the realms of deconstructing the power monopolies of the legal profession and creating a range of forums in which citizens could air their disputes, the successive Conservative administrations focused on the need to reduce the cost of antiquated justice procedures to the Exchequer. Ironically, the maintenance of a structural status quo, subjected to occasional tinkering in an effort to oil its wheels and reduce its cost, failed to achieve the larger political targets of an empowered citizenry able to make their own way in a see-saw economy.

The Major administration's plans for the legal system were intellectually hidebound by its focus on consumer charters and complaints procedures. These placed the onus for efficient services on the individual to protest rather than on the state to provide a suitable service from the outset. In a situation in which advice services are a priori in difficulty, it is illogical to organize service quality around the principle that it is for the unadvised citizen to challenge the actions of the public body. While empowerment to protest is an essential totem in the rolling development of democratic societies, there is a concomitant need to protect the ability of individual citizens to protest with equal access to the system which controls the resolution of their disputes. That level of equality of opportunity is essential in the democratic context. The detailed content of *Targeting Need* is examined below in relation to block contracts (pp. 142–5).

Lord Mackay, the then Lord Chancellor, also published a White Paper called *Striking the Balance*[24] which, in Smith's view, 'provides evidence that the high point of state support for publicly funded legal services for the poor has passed'.[25] *Striking the Balance* was concerned to manage the cost of legal aid – containing three separate leaflets with its main text to reassure legal aid users, non-legal aid users and taxpayers that the reforms would be in all of their interests. The White Paper set out similar aims to *Targeting Need* but shed much of the rhetorical references to access to justice – choosing to focus instead on the need for value for money from legal aid and the need for greater simplification of the law to enable citizens to protect themselves. Smith identifies in this a movement away from providing more legal aid to the public and towards raising court fees to cover court costs, introducing Lord Woolf's proposals for reform of civil procedure, and freezing the total legal aid budget. Indeed, in the general drift of policy within the Lord Chancellor's Department (regardless of government) and in the justice system bureaucracies, this would appear to sound the death knell for a legal aid system subsidized from public funds on the 1949 model.

THE ADMINISTRATION OF LEGAL AID AS A WELFARE BENEFIT

We have considered the status of legal aid and the legal system as a welfare benefit[26] in considering the public service ethos, which is currently missing from the administration of justice as something other than a public service in line with mainstream local government and other such communal, locally-based activities. There is a division both in legislative terms and in administrative terms between criminal legal aid and civil legal aid. It is a division which is instinctive rather than reasoned, and superficially attractive rather than logically impenetrable.

Two points emerge from the preceding discussion: first, that legal aid on the 1949 model is on the decline and, second, the Lord Chancellor's Department has begun to emerge as a fuller department of state than hitherto in the last decade.

The make-up of legal provision

It is worth examining in some detail the current availability of legal aid. There are four contexts to consider: the 'green form' scheme, assistance by way of representation ('ABWOR'), criminal legal aid and civil legal aid.

Green form legal aid is the most innovative of the reforms in the Legal Aid Act 1974, enabling solicitors to give up to two hours advice without the need for the legal aid certificate from the Legal Aid Board's area director. The scheme permits the lawyer to give advice to the lay client or to take any action (other than court or tribunal representation of the client) which assists the client in respect of that advice (such as writing a letter before action). The green form scheme is subject to a means test which the solicitor administers at the first consultation, requiring that the client's disposable capital be £1,000 or less and that his/her income be £80 per week or less.

The ABWOR scheme extended the green form scheme in 1979 to enable lawyers to represent the client in court. The proceedings in which this scheme is available include most magistrates' courts work, or cases where the hearing is on the same day as the consultation, or exceptionally in county court proceedings, and before mental health tribunals. The solicitor is required to obtain the prior consent of the Legal Aid Board although there is no limit on the fees which can be recovered under this scheme. The ABWOR scheme involves both a means test and a merits test in many circumstances, except duty solicitor schemes and hearings before mental health tribunals.

It is only if a client's disposable income is less than £72 per week that there is no contribution required from the client.

Criminal legal aid is available in three main formats: advice and assistance in police stations, duty solicitor schemes before magistrates' courts, and legal aid in criminal trials. The availability of advice and assistance in police stations is an important right to help the citizen defend her liberties while in policy custody after arrest or while helping the police with their inquiries. The duty solicitor scheme was the first to be created in 1982 following the Report of the Royal Commission on Legal Services.[27] The Legal Aid Board now controls the duty solicitor scheme by allocating entitlement to some solicitors to provide this service. For criminal practitioners, making it on to the duty solicitor roster for a given area is an important source of business, aside from private client (or 'own client') work. The duty scheme provides a lawyer for those who cannot afford one to represent them in criminal trials. The assistance scheme moves one step further by paying solicitors to attend at police stations and give advice to individuals there, and claim their fees from the legal aid fund to a limit of £90. The assistance scheme requires solicitors to be on-call twenty-four hours during their allotted periods. Typically, for the solicitor, attendance at the police station will lead to work to be done at trial or after attendance at the police station.[28]

Criminal legal aid at trial is generally made available on application to the court during hearings. Rarely is it refused. The application in magistrates' courts is made to the court itself, or to the justices' clerk. In the former case, the view of the clerk is usually taken by the bench. Refusal is based on an assessment that an award of legal aid would be contrary to justice or that the defendant's means are outwith eligibility for legal aid. In some cases, legal aid must be granted on a merits basis (as in cases involving serious offences such as murder) whereas in other cases there is a means test before it is made available.[29]

Civil legal aid is available in line with both a means test and a merits test for the client. This is a 'judicare' system: one in which the essential lawyer–client relationship subsists between the solicitor and the client, but with the cost of the lawyer's fees being met by the state rather than by the client. The merits test requires the applicant to have a reasonable prospect in the case.[30] The means test is pitched (at the time of writing) at a capital base of £6,750 or less and a disposable income of £7,777 or less. At that level there is a requirement to make some contribution to the cost of legal aid. Legal aid is only provided without charge (at the time of writing) if the disposable capital base of the applicant is £3,000 or less and if the disposable income of the applicant is £2,625 or less. There is also liability to a statutory charge under which the Legal Aid Board will recoup some of the funds disbursed in meeting lawyers' fees. Civil legal aid is unavailable in most tribunals (i.e., not courts) and in defamation cases.

The context of criminal legal aid

Responsibility for criminal legal aid was passed to the Lord Chancellor in 1980 in the wake of the Report of the Royal Commission on Legal Services.[31] This was an important development in that it moved the system one step closer to the creation of an all-encompassing Ministry of Justice, rather than having responsibility for legal aid divided between the Home Office and the Lord Chancellor's Department, although still under the stewardship (then) of the Law Society.

It is a truism about criminal legal aid that its availability is an inviolable part of a constitutional settlement which ensures that no citizen can be convicted of a crime without a fair trial. A fair trial requires adequate advice and representation for the defendant. This means that if an individual is unable to pay for representation, then a lawyer must be paid for by the state. In fact, the individual is able to choose the solicitor which she wants to represent her and have that person's fee paid by the state. Similarly, the solicitor will usually recommend a particular barrister to conduct the advocacy function of Crown Court trials (and some magistrates' court work) and have that barrister paid for by the state. Guidelines restrict the arbitrary use of Queen's Counsel and junior barristers for the same case, unless such doubling up can be justified in the particular case. In short, the defendant has the complete freedom to choose her legal team, knowing that her choices will be subsidized by the state through criminal legal aid.

The English legal system uses salaried lawyers employed by the state (through the Crown Prosecution Service) to conduct the prosecution of such trials. Proponents of the national legal service would be required to argue for the creation of a public defender's office to conduct the defence in criminal trials. The argument against such a structure points to the inefficiencies of the CPS in bringing trials and raises the concern that such inefficiency would be brought to bear on the liberties of individuals. The inertia of bureaucracy would discourage the type of investigation and imaginative legal argument which occurs in the private sector. The argument is a reversal of the division between the free market approach and the welfare state approach considered in Part I. The affection of socialists for human rights militates away from the use of state socialist structures for criminal defence. It indicates a suspicion on the left with bureaucratic institutions in democratic societies which have been deployed by right-wing governments or manipulated more successfully by commercial, corporate entities through highly-paid lawyers, since the Second World War. The leftist position favours self-help in this context.[32] Ideologically, the positions are impossible to reconcile. The socialist position is necessarily compromised once it accepts that there are situations in which the individual's interests are not best served by social or municipal structures.

The reason for this tortured abnegation of principle is the understanding that there is something more essential about the rights which are at stake in relation to criminal cases, as compared to civil litigation, considered below. The ability of the individual to receive legal advice is predicated on the notion that what is at stake is the liberty of the individual from the coercive power of the state. The latter view would see the enforcement of criminal law as a claim brought by the rest of society to deal with the actions of an individual which are found to breach the compact reached on the social level between citizens. The post-modern view of the state as something to be deconstructed as an engine of oppression is made to apply to all forms of social power rather than simply to bourgeois government, in Marxist terms.

Another model of criminal law, in relation to petty offences such as theft and road traffic offences, is that citizens other than the accused are acting together against the defendant to punish a failure to observe the communal code against taking another's property or endangering others by driving too fast. The confusion for post-modernism is separating out the substantive rules as to property (which might be argued are oppressive of the dispossessed) from procedural justice in which the collective will is imposed on particular individuals who choose not to comply with it. On this model, there is something to be said for using a public defender's office in relation to petty offences where the role of the tribunal is to find facts, rather than to referee an adversarial contest.

The context of civil legal aid

Civil legal aid is available on the basis of means-tested eligibility for forms of advice or representation which fall within the established categories. Outwith the categories are forms of representation which appear before tribunals, rather than courts, in the main. Thus advice to do with employment law will not attract legal aid for legal representation before an industrial tribunal but it will be available where that representation raises a specific point of law which is heard by a court.

With reference to civil legal aid there is a merits test under which the lawyer is required to attest to the likelihood of success if the action is pursued (or defended). This test is deemed necessary to prevent public funds paying for vexatious or hopeless litigation. It is worth comparing this with the merits test for criminal legal aid where it is enough that the case falls within a number of categories of serious offence, even if there is little likelihood of acquittal. It should be ceded that withdrawal of legal aid in such circumstances should happen because that would create bureaucratic problems, making it impossible for some defendants to defend themselves. What is more difficult to justify is a failure to accept that some forms of civil justice, such as homelessness, ought to be deemed to satisfy the merits test as of right. The disaggregation of civil legal aid in this way is important to ensure that justice is applied in all cases.

Having compared and contrasted current approaches to criminal and civil legal aid, it is important to examine some of the developments in the dissemination of legal aid in recent policy by the Major administration and the Blair administration.

Budgeting

There are many savings which could be made in the more efficient running of the legal aid system from central offices. The Lord Chancellor's Department has failed to make up the lack of civil legal aid with the excess in the criminal legal aid budget which has not been used in the last accounting year. The use of private pensions (rather than state provided pensions) for judges will cut the LCD budget by much of the amount of the judicial pensions bill. More flexible use of resources will enable the legal aid budget to be expanded simply by their better use.

FRANCHISING

The biggest break away from the 1949 model of the legal aid system occurred with the introduction of franchising, a system which is intended by both the Parties to develop into block contracting (considered below). Franchising differs from the classic model of legal aid in that it is no longer automatically available to all solicitors and barristers on the basis that their clients are eligible. For the first time, a solicitor will also have to qualify to enable her to claim for legal aid. In time, the system can expect to be extended to include barristers as well. A lawyer is required to obtain a franchise from the

Legal Aid Board to continue to be able to claim legal aid fees.

The basis for receiving a franchise is the Legal Aid Board's satisfaction that the solicitor is able to manage a series of case files adequately. It is a certificate which indicates the solicitor's administrative capabilities, rather than a measurement of her legal competence. The franchise does operate as a form of quality assessment mark for the citizen but not in the sense that the citizen would want. Citizens would prefer to know that the solicitor is a lawyer who knows about the law, is able to give suitable advice, and is a competent litigator. That the solicitor can organize a filing system does not correlate with these concerns.

The intention is that franchises can in the future be offered to non-lawyer advice agencies. There has, however, been some criticism of this proposal.[33] The concern is that franchising will not acquire core funding from franchised work, it will only be an add-on to their general advisory function. Further, franchising continues to operate on the model of lawyer-led advice services, a structure which is not suitable for non-lawyer agencies in all circumstances. The result of these reservations is either that funding of advice agencies must be altered or that franchising is perhaps not the best method of distributing legal aid money.

The longer term possibility for the franchising scheme is that, once all solicitors have a franchise contract with the Legal Aid Board, the Board will be able to control the level of fees paid to solicitors. In cost management terms, this means that the legal aid budget can be reduced simply by freezing or even reducing the fees paid to solicitors by changing the tariff. Therefore, it is a system with great bureaucratic appeal. What is surprising is that it has not been given a veneer of political attractiveness by presenting the bureaucratic merits of the system as being a mechanism by which central government is able to control the behaviour of solicitors, particularly at a time when complaints against the profession are on the increase. Franchising could, and should, be developed to award contracts only to firms which satisfy the Board that they are competent lawyers, in line with the concerns that citizens have about lawyers' capabilities. As part of a movement towards the reform of the legal profession, franchising offers great possibilities.

The drift in practice has been towards the franchising of legal aid services to specific law firms. These law firms are paid fees directly from the Legal Aid Board. The cost of legal aid can be monitored by a dialogue between the two parties as to the line between cost-effectiveness for the firm and for the Legal Aid Board. Significantly, because the firms are selected according to industry recognized criteria of efficiency and standard of service, it would be possible for the Ministry of Justice and the Legal Aid Board to monitor the quality of service for the client. As important as client service is the ability to examine the needs of the lawyers.

Much of the legal aid work is at present carried out by a dedicated band of law firms which often operate on very small profit-loss margins. To ensure that the resources of these lawyers are maximized, the political body overseeing justice policy needs to be able to respond to their needs. Such responsiveness becomes possible under a franchise system because these disempowered lawyers who support these areas of practice can conduct a dialogue with the legal aid funding bodies and with central government. The end result will be an improvement in the legal service offered.

The current system of franchising is a trend which should be in place within the next few years. It is expected that solicitors' firms wishing to do legal aid work will be required to obtain a franchise. The benefit of the franchise system is therefore that the quality of work performed by the legal practice is capable of being monitored by the Legal Aid Board to ensure that the representation which is received by the ordinary litigant is of a sufficient standard. The further advantage is that it enables the Legal Aid Board to exercise greater control over the rates charged by legal practices and thereby actively manage the size of the legal aid budget.

Franchising constitutes both a partial alternative to the current system of legal aid funding and a means of controlling expenditure. The result would be that by maintaining the level of the legal aid budget, more representation could be provided for more people than at the moment.

The important difference between the Labour and Conservative approaches is that the Labour Party is committed to the improvement of the quality of justice as a priority. The Major government mooted the introduction of competitive tendering for legal aid franchises, which has attracted the condemnation of the Labour Party and all of the profession's governing bodies. The accent cannot be solely on reducing cost: rather it must emphasize the importance of quality of service.

THE STRUCTURE OF THE ACCESS TO JUSTICE BILL 1999

The Access to Justice Bill 1999 creates a new body, the Legal Services Commission, in place of the old Legal Aid Board. The Commission is charged with responsibility for the public provision of legal advice and assistance in both civil and criminal contexts. The new Commission is charged with responsibility for administering the legal aid budget through the Community Legal Service ('CLS') for civil legal aid and through the Criminal Defence Service ('CDS') for criminal legal aid (cl. 2). The Commission itself will be comprised of between seven and twelve members appointed by the Lord Chancellor for their expertise in legal training and so forth.

The Lord Chancellor's Advisory Committee of Education and Training is to be abolished. It is replaced by The Legal Services Consultative Panel which will have responsibility for similar functions to the old Advisory Committee in relation to education and training (cl. 31, introducing s. 18A of the Courts and Legal Services Act 1990). Recommendations made by the new Panel are to be published by the Lord Chancellor.

In relation to the CLS and the CDS there is still a lack of publicly available pilot information as to the manner in which either of these schemes is to work. The risk is therefore that the work of these two new bodies, charged with subtly different tasks from their predecessors, will be done without the benefit of piloting. As pointed out in Part IV *Components of Delivery* below there are a number of issues to do with the democratic accountability of these organizations which will be responsible for making funds for legal advice and assistance available on a local basis. Similarly, there is nothing contained in the legislation which will enable the CLS or the CDS to decide the types of case for which public assistance ought to be made available: compounding the problems for those bodies in determining how to decide between the mixed priorities of the family law budget and the industrial tribunal budget.

The Commission is given a broad financial remit (in cl. 4) to do anything which is 'necessary or appropriate for, or for facilitating, the discharge of its functions, or is incidental or conducive to the discharge of its functions'. Expressly within cl. 4 is the possibility for entering into contracts with other persons to carry out some of these tasks on a delegated basis, or to make loans or grants to other persons to enable them to carry out some of the Commission's own functions. Of particular concern is the ability of the Commission to 'invest money'. This moves far beyond the welfare state model of a government agency into the realms of quasi-governmental bodies which are not even required to spend the whole of their budget on their core functions, but are able to invest some of that money (on the terms of the legislation) otherwise than in providing the public service for which they were created. Given the difficulties with the remit of the CDS and CLS, it is suggested that this breadth of fiscal competence is unfortunate.

The other important progression, considered in relation to the Community Legal Service in Part V *Models for Reform* is the acceptance in the legislation (at cl. 7(5)) that there can be disaggregation of legal aid such that public moneys are applied to different forms of advice and assistance at different levels depending on political priorities. Within this remit, the Commission is required to set out a Code (in cl. 9) in relation to the manner in which public funds are to be made available and as to the operation of the Community Legal Service. The Code will also be required to consider issues such as the suitability of funding family disputes mediation from public funds and the means by which applications for funding are to be made. What is also made plain is that applications for funding may require the citizen to incur a fee to the Commission akin to the contributions required to be made as part of the old legal aid structure.

BLOCK CONTRACTS

Block contracts differ only slightly from franchising. The block contract is a franchise awarded to a solicitors' firm which entitles it to claim against the legal aid fund for its fees. The principal difference is one of bureaucratic organization. The block contract system aims to create a group of monopoly providers of particular kinds of legal service, in relation to specific legal subject areas, for identified geographic regions. The franchise holders will be restricted in number, although it is not clear at present, how restricted that number will be under any of the published schemes of block contracting.[34] For each type of work (for example, matrimonial, housing or crime) there will be an allocated legal aid budget for each financial year. Only the franchised firms will be able to claim against that money: claims will be made to sub-budgets which are allocated to their use in the financial year. Central government will then be required to maintain 'slush' funds to massage away any over-rigidity in the system.

The aim of these schemes are principally to control the cost of the legal aid budget by allocating only the amount of money which government is prepared to spend on legal aid in each area in any financial year. The other advantage, as with franchising, is being able to control the standard of advisory work. In *Targeting Need*,[35] the first formal proposals for block contracting were presented. The core change is set out in the Introduction:

> At present, any qualified person can supply legally aided services. Under the new scheme, only suppliers meeting certain quality standards would be able to do so.[36]

The main policy initiative is to introduce block contracting, organized according to political selection of the distribution of contracts between types of case, subject to Parliamentary scrutiny. Added to that would be encouragement for the advice agencies other than lawyers to provide advisory and representative services in an effort to create some form of market rigour, albeit market rigour in relation to bidding for public money. The impulse for this change, as set out in the Green Paper, is not to do with the undemocratic nature of an 'increasingly criticised' legal aid system (criticized, apparently, for its rising cost and decreasing coverage[37]), but rather the fact that it 'does not encourage value for money from suppliers or control their expenditure effectively'.[38]

In relation to 'very high cost cases', the Green Paper had suggested that compulsory competitive tendering should be used to encourage service providers to bid for the right to receive specific contracts for particular forms of litigation. Ironically, this strategy would seem to suggest that the litigant's power to select an advisor from the (supposed) marketplace would be hampered by restricting the litigant to the contracted lawyer if the litigant was unable to meet the legal fee from his/her own resources.

The thinking behind block contracting is straightforward: legal aid expenditure is too high because lawyers cost too much; legal aid spending is rising because lawyers' increased fees are causing the inflation. It is the same thinking which informs Lord Irvine's proposals for conditional fees. Wall has expressed doubts about the assumption that lawyers' fees are behind the rise in legal aid spending.[39] In his analysis the increase must be also attributed to increased inflation caused by the state and an increased demand for legal services from the public. This latter point is shared by Smith.[40] The former analysis, that is state induced inflation, refers to the cost of government policy which causes more litigation and procedural rules that then lengthen cases or otherwise raise the cost of litigation through inefficiency. This analysis tends towards the thesis advanced in this book, that only an integrated reform of justice policy can both increase the democratic capital of the justice system and reduce the pro rata cost of producing the current amount of justice services.

More generally, the drawbacks with the block contracting proposals are numerous. Principally, the complaint is that there will be no ability for citizens to receive advice if the budget is used in any given financial year. The proponents of the system argue that there is always a centrally held budget which would make good any shortfalls of this type. However, the system would appear to be at the mercy of a rash of claims to do with a particular area – such as a repeat of the asbestosis litigation in the 1980s.

The bigger problem is with the creation of a class of law firms which are the only ones entitled to claim against the legal aid fund.

Any remaining vestige of market forces contained in the legal system will disappear once monopolistic providers emerge. The effect of block contracting will be to drive firms without contracts into bankruptcy on the basis that they will not be able to earn legal aid fees. Small firms with a viable client base and some local goodwill will find themselves merged into larger firms which have block contracts. This will have the effect of reducing choice, resulting in a legal system where the same few solicitors' firms conduct all work of a particular type in a particular region. It will also reduce locally available advice in many rural areas that are currently serviced by small solicitors' firms which are unlikely to win block contracts. Furthermore, where there is a risk of spending all of the allocated budget in any financial year, those firms will be encouraged by their own financial well-being to hold progress on particular cases over until the next financial year. The net loser will be the citizen.

The principal shortcoming in the block contract idea is that it is a bureaucratic answer to a problem rather than a structured political solution to the problems inherent in the English legal system. Block contracting assumes that legal aid is necessarily the best model for providing solely legal services to the public. It avoids the more systemic questions about the needs of citizens to receive advice and representation in a number of different forums and contexts – many of which are not currently the preserve of lawyers. The strength of the bigger provincial legal firms will be enhanced, as will that of the specialist Bar. What is not clear is how the citizen will benefit, aside from a promised reduction in public spending.

The Labour government has committed itself to franchising funded out of block contracts but has expressly disavowed compulsory competitive tendering as a means of achieving this. The complaint with compulsory competitive tendering is that it encourages the awarding of contracts to the lowest bidder rather than to the highest quality service provider. The line between the two policies is therefore a narrow one, but one which might yet make all the difference to the citizen who receives advice from an advisor selected for a contract on grounds of competence rather than one selected on grounds purely of low cost.

What remains to be considered is how this block contracting system will differ in real terms from a drift towards a form of national legal service in which a selected group of law firms and other advisors make the bulk of their income from budgets allocated by the state. Ironically, if a hypothetical national legal service created in 1949 had been privatized it would presumably occupy a similar model. Formerly state employed lawyers would be organized as private sector lawyers subject to governmental regulation of their continued ability to claim government money to pay for their practices.

The approach taken by Lord Irvine is considered in the next section.

LORD IRVINE'S LEGAL AID REFORM PROPOSALS

Introduction

Lord Irvine has clung to his mission statement of providing effective justice at low cost by removing a large number of cases from the legal aid net. In short, any case where financial damages are sought will be excluded from legal aid provision, subject to exceptions that are being pressured on Lord Irvine by the profession[41] and trade unions but which have been difficult to identify in the preparatory stages of the law reform legislation. The conditional fee idea was launched in *Access to Justice with Conditional Fees*.[42] The aim is to enable people to get to court, having reached a conditional fee arrangement with their lawyer, in situations where legal aid would or would not have been available.

At the time of writing it is impossible to assess the likely future impact of the proposals on the justice system. However, in Part V, *Models for Reform*, we consider a series of structures which, it is suggested, will be necessary for the Blair administration to achieve its political and ideological goals in this area. In the remaining sections of Part III we analyse the task facing the Lord Chancellor's Department and the various policy approaches which are currently being implemented in the operation of legal affairs policy.

The most important development in the context of legal aid policy is the plan to remove cases involving money judgments from the legal aid net altogether.[43] Instead of being entitled to claim from the legal aid fund, the litigant will be required to enter into a conditional fee arrangement with a solicitor such that the solicitor will only receive a contractually agreed fee if the litigation is successful. The general issue of conditional fees is considered in more detail in Part V. In this section, the proposals for conditional fees put forward by Lord Irvine will be examined in detail below immediately after consideration of the breakdown of legal aid eligibility in 1998 before the implementation of Labour's proposed reforms and the structure of franchising. It is important to remember that conditional fees form Labour government policy but not Labour Party policy. The proposals for conditional fees have been developed (fairly rapidly) in the period since the 1997 General Election victory.

The proposals are fivefold: the introduction of conditional fees to replace civil legal aid in damages claims; the introduction of legal insurance as part of conditional fee arrangements; the introduction of block contracting through community legal services; the introduction of a Legal Services Commission for civil and criminal matters; and a tougher merits test. Conditional fees, legal insurance and the block contracting proposals are considered here. The detail of community legal service structures are considered in Part V.

Conditional fees – not legal aid

Conditional fees are the 'no-win, no-fee' arrangements practised by American lawyers under the title 'contingency fees'. The client negotiates a fee with the solicitor which constitutes a percentage of any winnings which the litigant might receive. If there are no winnings, the lawyer receives no fee. The purpose behind this reform, as stated by Lord Irvine, is to increase access to justice for citizens by ensuring that they are able to receive advice from solicitors regardless of their means: that is, their own wealth is not a pre-condition to receiving legal advice.

One thorny aspect of this policy is the insurance policies required to act as a safety net where there is no public money provided to do so. Security for the fee will be achieved by the acquisition of an insurance policy which will pay a fee in the event that there is no victory in court. Lord Irvine is not disheartened by the lack of any such commercial insurance arrangement at the time of publication of the policy. He has said that the cost of insurance premiums will not operate as a barrier to entry in obtaining conditional fee arrangements on the model which he envisages. The figure given for premiums necessary for medical negligence cases has been reported as being as high as £15,000 but Lord Irvine has confided to the House of Lords that, 'I am told that cover has more often been provided at much lower sums – in the region of £3,000'.[44]

It is important to examine what this means. As a prerequisite to entering into a lawful conditional fee arrangement, the litigant or the solicitor will be required to pay £3,000 to an insurance company by way of a premium to insure against the risk of losing the case. A premium of £3,000 will operate as a very effective barrier to entry for most ordinary litigants who cannot be advised that they have a very good chance of winning. Furthermore, the litigant would have to be assured that she had very good chances of winning significantly more than £3,000, such that the premium would be recovered. A solicitor paying for such insurance on a one-off or an ongoing basis will be similarly discouraged by a small amount of claim. For either side, this is not an investment in any meaningful sense. An investment generally suggests the acquisition of some asset which can be turned to account in future. The acquisition of insurance in this context merely constitutes another expense which will deter those with perfectly viable claims, albeit for modest amounts. In short, the requirement that there be insurance premiums acquired commercially places an unacceptable level of financial risk on the potential litigant which can be expected to deter the bringing of litigation in the first place.

The final issue with the conditional fee proposals raised by Lord Irvine is the imposition on lawyers in private practice to become entrepreneurial deal-makers rather than simply legal advisors. Having begun to put lawyers through the mill of franchising, with its attendant mountains of time-consuming paper work, and the promised development of a similarly bureaucratic block contracting system, the requirement that lawyers negotiate deals with clients adds a new dimension to the complexity of even high street litigation. The practitioner will be required to keep a careful and inexpert eye on the number of cases undertaken which have a risk that no fee will be paid despite investing expensive overheads in litigating them.

A number of new financial management tasks also present themselves. Acquiring insurance for such a portfolio of litigation will be a complex task in itself. Negotiating bank facilities for overdrafts will become even more difficult as the identification of receivables becomes an even more hazardous process than hitherto. Under the legal aid scheme it was possible to receive money on account. In a conditional fee arrangement, everything hinges on the judgment at the end of the proceedings. The cash flow implications mean that all of the receivables are collected at the end of the case. It is therefore perfectly possible that law firms will go into insolvency where they undertake a number of conditional fee cases which take too long to settle and therefore cause those firms to become unable to pay their creditors while waiting for fee income. The result for the litigant will be further interruption and delay. These are issues which Lord Irvine's proposals have so far failed to deal with.

Lawyers also face several professional conduct issues, aside from the economic difficulties. In advising a client there are the problems of explaining the likelihood of success and failure, and of the best means for the individual litigant to proceed. On top of that process is the need to explain the structure of fee arrangements to the lay client, and the many imponderables of success and failure. The potential for liability in respect of a client who latterly claims not to have understood the difficult arrangements, and the many permutations of settlement, is immense.

And all that is before confronting the thorny issue of money.

The money problem

The policy grew out of the Middleton Review considered in Part I. Lord Irvine is sensitive to the criticism that the policy pursues Middleton's cost-cutting zeal at the expense of other issues. In a speech to the House of Lords he said:

> Let me refute the assertion that our proposals for reform are Treasury-driven to cut the legal aid budget. This is wrong. We do not intend either to increase or reduce the cost of legal aid in real terms. We plan to spend not one penny less than the last Government planned to do. But we also plan to take control of the legal aid budget.[45]

The difficulty with this assertion is that, at the time of the publication of the proposals, there were no exceptions from the principle that all claims for money damages would be subject to conditional fee arrangements in place of civil legal aid. Some concessions have been wrung from the Lord Chancellor subsequently. For example, housing cases are expressly excluded from the conditional fee scheme. The principle behind the exception being that housing cases will not have sufficient money at stake to make it possible to organize them on the basis of 'no-win, no fee'. A further concession is to examine the possibility of concessionary slush funds to be used in particular cases of hardship. This general undertaking to create a discretionary form of social fund does not equate to a legal aid structure capable of being monitored and properly managed.

However, having accepted the principle that there will be cases in which solicitors will not be prepared to enter into a conditional fee arrangement because of the likely size of the award, it is difficult to see why it should not be applied to all cases in which solicitors are not enticed by the amount of money at stake to risk taking on the case. The answer is that, since the introduction of the legality of 'no-win, no-fee' cases in the 1990 Act, there has been a disappointingly low take-up rate: disappointing in the sense that it has not produced a sufficient reduction in the take up of civil legal aid.

One regular complaint about the nature of conditional fees is that they give a lawyer too large a stake in the conduct of the litigation, such that the lawyer is likely to press for victory at a higher amount than settlement for a lesser amount. Lord Irvine's view is that this has not been borne out by the experience of conditional fees since their introduction in 1995.

The issue of conditional fee arrangements is revisited in Part V,

Models for Reform, as part of an integrated approach to the restructuring of legal aid.

Rethinking block contracting

With regard to the level of the legal aid budget, a commitment has been made to freeze it at current levels. Ensuring the budget remains static is to be achieved through the use of block contracting:

> We plan to spend not one penny less than the last
> Government planned to do. But we also plan to take control
> of the legal aid budget. We plan to by buying services from
> lawyers through the mechanism of block contracts. Lawyers
> will be asked to contract for work at fixed prices. Our
> intention is that block contracting should be used to take
> control of both civil legal aid and criminal legal aid.[46]

The central argument in favour of a fixed fee, block contract system is that lawyers are simply paid too much at present from the legal aid fund, therefore block contracting will introduce a discipline which bolts them to fixed income for particular forms of work. The administration of the block contracting scheme will be as follows:

> Regional Legal Services Committees will involve local people
> in drawing up plans which will match services to the needs of
> a particular area and determine how they can best be
> delivered. This chimes with the Government's wider
> objective of returning power to the community.

The principle of community control of budgets, as observed in Ontario and New South Wales below, still leaves a number of issues as to the manner in which local boards will be required to comply with national standards, the selection of the people who will constitute those boards, and what form of appeal (if any) local people will have against the decisions of that body. These issues are pursued in Part V. It is important to note that there is, at the time of writing, no specific model created for this development.

Drawbacks in the proposals

As considered at length in Part II, the policy papers issued by the LCD since the 1997 General Election have confused styles of rhetoric. In *Access to Justice with Conditional Fees* (1998) there is no mention of providing a higher quality of service through the use of block contracts, rather the only discussion is of lower price. The presentation of this policy as a single thread of cost-cutting does rather give the lie to the occasional bluster that there are more wholesome concerns behind the reform proposals.

The real concern with conditional fee arrangements is that they distort the parties' analysis of the merits of the case by introducing a new dimension, that is the commercial agreement as to fees which the parties have reached with their lawyers. For the legal profession this will necessarily develop ambulance chasing as law firms seek out those cases which seem likely to generate sufficient damages awards and thereby suitable fees as a proportion of those damages awards. The further problem is the challenge raised by the losing party as to the size of the fee agreed by the victor and her lawyer. The operation of the indemnity costs rule will merely exacerbate the effect of this awkward development. Similarly, the current proposals suggest that defendants may continue to receive legal aid,[47] thus putting greater pressure on the plaintiff to settle where she is operating on a conditional fee with her lawyer while the defendant is having her legal fees paid from public funds. There will be reduced equality between litigants if the scheme is allowed to operate on this basis.

The real problem is that, at the time of the publication of the proposals, precious little research has been done as to the manner in which conditional fee arrangements will operate in practice as a replacement for civil legal aid.

COMPARISON WITH OTHER JURISDICTIONS

Having considered some of the principal pillars of the English system of publicly funded legal services, it might be useful to compare some of the main themes with systems in other jurisdictions. The preceding discussion will be extended into the construction of a new model for the English justice system, together with an analysis of the means by which these publicly funded legal services are delivered to citizens. The perspective offered by other jurisdictions will be of some utility in this development.[48]

The Netherlands

Of the civil code jurisdictions in the European Union, the Netherlands has a system which is closest to the English legal aid model administered by its Ministry of Justice. The equivalent to about only one half of total legal aid expenditure in England and Wales was spent in the Netherlands per capita of the population.[49] Much of the reason for this can be attributed to the lower cost of the Dutch inquisitorial criminal justice system which reduces the need for expensive, adversarial court-based proceedings. Eligibility levels, linked to wage control legislation, are generally higher than in England and Wales. Legal aid money is used to fund both private sector lawyers providing legal advice and representation and also law centres, called Buros voor Rechtshulp. The Buros act as a form of law centre, free at point of use, which give advice to citizens on social welfare law cases. Importantly, they also act as a referral point for such legal advice in some cases.

The genesis of the Buros can be found in the university based initiatives of the 1970s that provided free advice. As with the English experience, a network of advice centres grew out of the initiatives of individual lawyers dedicated to the provision of socially useful advisory work. There is a different culture among the Dutch legal profession, a fact highlighted by the Legal Action Group, with the bulk of practitioners undertaking some legally aided work – unlike the English profession where it is left to a particular cadre of lawyers who undertake principally that work alongside other high street advisory work. Unlike the English law centre network, Buros operate as independent foundations, receiving funding from the Ministry of Justice, providing a service to their local communities without any formal links with that community. As with the English legal system, there is a history of difficulty in employees of Buros being able to represent their clients in court on parity with fully qualified advocates, due to professional association rules on salaried employment.

Canada

There is a distinction between the Anglo-Canadian and Francophile traditions of different legal jurisdictions within Canada. Ontario and Quebec approach legal services in different manners in accordance with their common law and civilian traditions respectively.[50] In Ontario there is a mixed system of private practitioner legal aid, as in England, and legal advice centres. Funding comes from the state federal governments. Another interesting use of funding, mirrored in Australia, is the collecting of interest made on client accounts from law firms. This amounts approximately to half of the funding provided by each of the state and federal governments.

In accordance with much policy in North America, a levy is raised from practitioners as a condition of retaining their practising certificates, and this is put towards the costs of maintaining the legal aid bureaucracy. As with regional devolution in community legal service and block contracting schemes in England, legal aid is distributed by local area boards in accordance with state-wide criteria. This grants a large amount of autonomy for local boards to focus legal aid spending on local priorities.

The legal advice services (or 'clinics') are administered in part by the Law Society together with officials of the Attorney General's department. The legal advice clinics operate on a local basis to supplement those areas of legal practice which are not covered by the formal legal aid scheme. The distinction in role offers the possibility for private practice and public advice agency to offer, between them, a comprehensive advisory service to citizens as part of an integrated justice system. In accordance with North American public service practice, the clinics operate under guidelines set out in mission statements. This is in contrast to the legal system in England (aside from law centres and Citizens' Advice Bureaux) which operates in a manner that is insulated from other public service cultures.

In Quebec, the political will of the early 1970s to create a structure within which legal aid could be offered on an American model led to the creation of the Commission des Services Juridiques. The legal profession succeeded in preventing the politicians going the extra stride and creating a public legal advisory service. The Commission organizes the regional legal aid boards (known as 'community legal services') which in turn supervise local legal aid offices. This is a bureaucratic structure which contrasts to Ontario's autonomous local control and has led to some complaint in Quebec as to the accountability of the central administration.[51] The principal development in Quebec has been to provide education to the public and in universities, as well as providing advice to the public. The importance of developing public legal education in England is taken up in Part V.

America

The American, Canadian and Australian jurisdictions are more advanced in the use of a multitude of legal and quasi-legal agencies to develop access to justice programmes. The marketplace for information and computer-based technology in the USA is more advanced than in the UK generally, as considered in Part V.[52] Of particular interest is the ability of Americans to access legal information and legal services on the Internet and through other such advice agencies, without the need for advice from qualified lawyers at all stages of the process. The greatest feature of the US legal system is the large number of lawyers, the aggressive marketing techniques used by lawyers, and the development of legal aid systems in the absence of a welfare state.

Australia

The most progressive of the Australian jurisdictions is New South Wales. Many of the Australian developments are considered in detail in Part V in the context of the introduction of a law foundation and the broader use of information technology to access advice agency services. Australian legal aid is administered across Australia but with effective control being delegated to legal aid commissions for each of the states. The boards of these state-based legal aid commissions are composed of a mixture of practitioners and lay people giving some representation to lay interests at a more local level. The legal aid commissions have a broad remit covering the administration of legal aid budgets in their area, as well as running public education initiatives and local legal advice centres. In New South Wales a network of Community Justice Centres provide advice for citizens in a number of specific contexts.[53] It is an important feature of the state-based commissions, mirrored in the proposals for a community legal service in England set out in Part V, that there is great autonomy for the legal aid commissions in the way they spend their budgets and the local priorities that are set for legal aid use.

WHAT IS LEGAL AID?

At the heart of this book is the nature of legal aid. It is typically at the core of the debate about resolving defects in the justice system that the discussion of legal aid emerges. While it is the contention of this book that legal aid is not the sole means of measuring the success of the justice system, and that a more integrated reform is necessary, there can be no real doubt that legal aid forms an important part of the system. The issue is then as to the nature of legal aid itself. As explored above, it is easy to consider the availability of legal aid as being coterminous with the availability of justice. This misconception is a result of understanding legal aid as being a welfare state benefit. As discussed, while the current legal aid scheme was introduced at the same time as the Attlee government's welfare state programme, it did not correlate with the model used for the NHS. This issue is pursued in relation to the national legal service proposal considered in Part V.

Legal aid is a payment by the state to lawyers in the private sector in return for their providing of advice or representation to eligible citizens. What it is not is a purchase of justice, *per se*. Expenditure on legal aid does not equate with acquisition of justice. That said, it is perfectly proper to examine the manner in which legal aid is currently provided to consider whether or not there is a more efficient method of providing justice for the same use of money.

Legal aid is currently based on centrally organized bureaucratic principles. The Legal Aid Board assumed the responsibilities formerly discharged by the Law Society (before the passage of the Courts and Legal Services Act) to distribute the legal aid budget across England and Wales by refereeing the claims for legal aid made by lawyers in private practice. Franchising offers a move away from a system which was created with the lawyers' convenience uppermost in the legislative mind: it is an important cultural step. The size of the legal aid budget has led to the urgency for reform which principled analysis of the British constitution had long required.

English legal aid, in comparison with structures in other jurisdictions discussed above, is centralized and unresponsive to the local priorities of the communities which it is supposed to serve. The legal aid structure escaped the welfare state net by not being provided through a national legal service structured along the lines of the NHS. Instead it remained outwith effective political control being organized through the Law Society. The creeping establishment of the Lord Chancellor's Department as a department of state with full political control over justice policy is a welcome democratization of this state of affairs. However, it has yet to go far enough. Legal aid remains a bureaucratic edifice belonging to an age before the generation of a public service ethos in local government and the growing expectation among citizens that they are entitled to suitable levels of service and attention from public services such as courts and legal aid.

Aside from its public sector implications, legal aid has an effect on the economic business of lawyering and in the distribution of communal goods. It also runs contrary to the logic of much of the substantive law affecting remedies generally and damages awards in particular. Legal aid constitutes a redistributive interruption in the ordinary logic of the legal system. The indemnity costs rule, that a costs award will follow the victor in litigation, is considered to be a candidate for reform to equalize the use of legal aid with litigation that is not legally aided. Similarly, legal aid gives power to a litigant over one who is not legally aided. Once a certificate for legal aid is granted, the litigant has (in theory) a claim over the whole of the legal aid fund, which will typically give her bargaining power over an unaided counterparty who is required to meet legal fees from her own resources. Legally aided clients are less likely to settle because they do not bear as great a risk of being forced to meet the costs of the litigation personally. Altering this balance of power is routinely advanced as an important means of equalizing opportunities between litigants.

The problem with legal aid – and a proposal

What is rarely acknowledged by lawyers in considering the legal aid bill is that legal aid is a payment of money from central taxation directly into lawyers' pockets. The question whether or not the legal aid bill is too high, is really a question about whether or not too much money is being paid to lawyers. The point was made in Chapter 1 that there is no such thing as a market in legal services. Restrictive practices in the legal system, nothing less than an informal cartel formed by professional expectations, maintains standard fees at a high rate which has led to the current high level of the total legal aid bill.

The question therefore arises: why is legal aid to be provided in this way? Should legal aid seek to provide the whole of the fee to the lawyer as it does currently? An alternative system would be one which identifies the standard amount of money which would be required by a litigant to defray the cost of litigation. The legal aid fund would provide payment for a standard amount of money which the Legal Aid Board considers appropriate for that type of case. By capping the amount of money available for particular types of case, lawyers would have to make the decision whether to offer their services for this amount or whether to price themselves out of the market for legal aid. The litigant would then have greater scope to acquire representation in the legal marketplace. The litigant would be able to seek further amounts of legal aid where it could be demonstrated that the case contained complications which took it out of the ordinary run of cases.[54]

There is no reason why all of the cases which are currently paid for by legal aid and which are undertaken solely by barristers and solicitors should be able to continue. Voluntary agencies and advice agencies should be able to provide these services and make claims on the legal aid fund where they can demonstrate the necessary competence.[55]

There is typically a distinction made between criminal legal aid and civil legal aid in this context. The constitutional argument is made that criminal legal aid concerns basic human rights, the right to freedom of person and the right to a trial, whereas civil litigation concerns less precious subjects. That there is a possible conceptual distinction is beyond question. Whether the distinction is always real is another matter. The ability to defend yourself against an action to repossess your home is of more significance than the ability to defend a road traffic offence.

Where the conceptual difficulty arises more significantly is not in this *horizontal* measurement of availability of legal aid into broad income categories. What appears to be more useful is to divide this issue into *vertical* differences between types of case. Where public resources are being used, there ought to be some public recognition that some types of case are of greater utility than others. Group actions for medical negligence are of greater social utility than the failure of City fraud trials.

The argument runs: why should a centre left administration allow millions of pounds to be used by the apparently wealthy when other taxpaying individuals are not able to bring actions against their employers using legal aid? The solution would be to take the politically courageous decision to deny legal aid to the apparently wealthy (who receive it simply on the grounds that their lawyers and accountants can demonstrate that they have ostensibly no assets) and decide instead that other types of litigation are politically more important.

This approach has two immediate problems on its face. First, it cuts against the principle of greater equality by introducing inequality in the form of bars to publicly funded legal services. Second, civil libertarians would be concerned that politics is being brought explicitly into the arena of justice. The answer to the first concern is the simple assertion that the current barriers to publicly funded legal services are hidden because they rely on the bulk of the population having income or capital above very parsimonious eligibility levels. That means the bulk of the population cannot afford to go to law. Making the law more equal means taking advantage away from those who are currently 'more equal' than the ordinary individual.

The response to the second concern is that the system currently advantages the well-off to the detriment of the less well-off: that is already a question of political power. Introducing politics to the situation expressly has the advantage of making legal aid provision more transparent and accountable. A political decision to focus resources in South Wales on housing disputes and social welfare claims would be unpopular with those who would seek to use the system to fund the whole of their defence in white-collar fraud trials – but that is in the nature of politics.

For example, one third of the total legal aid budget (civil and criminal legal aid combined) is spent on matrimonial disputes. That is an annual amount of about £500 million paid to lawyers to conduct private divorce proceedings. This expenditure of legal aid on matrimonial disputes fails to recognize that in many situations the courts are not the best place to decide family disputes and that lawyers are not the best people to give advice or to reach these decisions. It also avoids the difficult question of whether or not we wish to use large amounts of public money to fund private matrimonial disputes rather than investing in families by means of mediation or counselling services. Putting concern for social justice at the centre of policy is the only way to ensure that public money in the legal system is applied primarily to ends which are socially just.

A constitutional issue

What is important is to realize that legal aid does not of itself equal 'justice'. As said, legal aid is merely a payment of taxpayers' money directly to lawyers' bank accounts. It is the lawyers who claim the amount which they are owed: the system is demand-led. The fee paid results from some minimal haggling with the Legal Aid Board. It is the lawyer who measures and evaluates the work that is done. The lawyer accounts for an amount of time spent on preparation, conference, research, travel and representation. Legal aid occupies a talismanic role for those who debate law reform but it is only one way in which justice can be provided by the public purse. It does not constitute a welfare state benefit, strictly defined. Therefore, it need not be defended stoically by the left. Perhaps, instead, there are other structures which could complement the provision of legal aid to provide more effective justice services for the citizenry.

The legal aid system is required to facilitate a more community-based attitude to the justice system. As considered above, in relation to Part II, *Theories of Social Change*, there is a need for a closer correlation between the courts system and the forms of advice and the services offered by local government. As local government comes to appreciate the need to be more accountable and responsive to the demands of local communities, local justice as the forum in which citizens resolve disputes as to the nature and content of their rights, must become more responsive to their needs.

Similarly, the constitutional importance of access to justice, and in particular legal advice and representation, must be recognized as part of the need for equality between individual citizens and other persons as to their fundamental rights. Without a legal system which makes itself available more broadly to the full range of social and individual concerns that make up a democracy and its polity, the very nature of that democracy as a social endeavour founded on the principle of the rule of law is untenable. The absence of equality both of opportunity and outcome in the context of *access* to justice constitutes an unacceptable mismatch of social power leading to an hegemonic oppression of the legally enfranchised over the others. Citizens are ciphers – before the law they have no individuality or diversity, all should be equal in substance, in procedure and in access.

Legal aid is the principal means in the English legal system of resolving this constitutional dilemma. It is a system used in a number of jurisdictions in subtly different forms. Part IV considers the different agencies and agents responsible for the delivery of justice services and legal aid.

NOTES AND REFERENCES

1 Stand-up comedian and writer, interviewed on *Clive Anderson Talks Back*, BBC1, 15 November 1997.
2 Current at time of writing.
3 As identified by the Woolf Report, Lord Woolf, *Access to Justice – Final Report* (HMSO, 1996).
4 Labour Party, *Access to Justice* (London, Labour Party, 1995); see Appendix.
5 *Ibid.*
6 Lord Irvine, *Public Law*.
7 For example, the recent details regarding the overly zealous conduct of Lord Goddard in the trial, conviction and execution of Derek Bentley.
8 There is a slight division in approach between the Legal Action Group, Smith *et al.*, *A Strategy for Justice* (London, Legal Action Group, 1992), p. 3, *et seq.*; and Zander, *Cases and Materials on the English Legal System* (7th edn., London, Butterworths, 1996), p. 440.
9 Smith *et al.*, *A Strategy for Justice* (London, Legal Action Group, 1992).
10 The 1949 Act was repealed by the Legal Aid Act 1974, which in turn was repealed by the Legal Aid Act 1988.
11 The Rushcliffe Report did recommend a salaried advice service as part of the legal aid scheme created in 1949 but this recommendation was not implemented.
12 Smith *et al.*, *A Strategy for Justice* (London, Legal Action Group, 1992), p. 4.
13 *Ibid.*
14 *Ibid.*
15 *Justice for All* (Society of Labour Lawyers, 1968).
16 Lord Irvine, 'The Legal System and Law Reform under Labour', in Bean (ed.), *Law Reform for All*, (Blackstone Press, 1996), p. 6.
17 Section 19 of the 1990 Act.
18 Section 21 of the 1990 Act.
19 The discussion of alternative dispute resolution was held over until the *Targeting Need* Green Paper in 1995.
20 Lord Chancellor's Department, *Legal Aid – Targeting Need* (Lord Chancellor's Department, May 1995, Cm. 2854).
21 *Ibid.*, p. 21.
22 For a survey of the objections to this Green Paper, see Goriely, 'The Government's Legal Aid Reforms', in Zuckerman and Cranston (eds), *Reform of Civil Procedure*, (Oxford, Clarendon Press, 1995), p. 347, *et seq.*

23 Lord Chancellor's Department, *Justice at the Right Price*, A Consultation Paper (Lord Chancellor's Department, 1998), www.open.gov.uk/lcd/consult.civ-just/fast/htm.
24 Lord Chancellor's Department, *Striking the Balance: The Future of Legal Aid in England and Wales* (1996), Cm. 3305.
25 Smith, 'Legal Aid on an Ebbing Tide', *Journal of Law and Society*, Vol. 23, (1996), p. 570.
26 In Part I, *Rethinking Justice Provision*, this is a theme which is taken up in Part V, *Models for Reform*.
27 Report of the Royal Commission on Legal Services (1979), Cm. 7648.
28 The numerous defects in this system have been considered in a number of sources: Baldwin, *The Conduct of Police Investigations*, (HMSO 1992), pp. 25–52; Sanders and Bridges, (1990) New L.J. p. 85; Ingram, *The English Legal Process* (London, Blackstone Press, 1998), p. 75.
29 Sections 21 and 22 of the Legal Aid Act 1988, set out the criteria for the merits and the means tests.
30 Section 15 of the Legal Aid Act 1988.
31 Report of the Royal Commission on Legal Services (1979), Cm. 7648.
32 A. Giddens, *Beyond Left and Right* (Cambridge, Polity Press, 1993).
33 See, for example, Smith *et al.*, *A Strategy for Justice* (London, Legal Action Group, 1992), p. 22.
34 Lord Chancellor's Department, *Legal Aid – Targeting Need* (Lord Chancellor's Department, May 1995), Cm. 2854.
35 *Ibid.*; also Lord Chancellor's Department, *Access to Justice with Conditional Fees* (Lord Chancellor's Department, March 1998).
36 Lord Chancellor's Department, *Legal Aid – Targeting Need* (Lord Chancellor's Department, May 1995), p. ix.
37 *Ibid.*, pp. 12–14.
38 *Ibid.*, p. viii.
39 Wall, 'Legal Aid, Social Policy, and the Architecture of Criminal Justice: The Supplier Induced Inflation Thesis and Legal Aid Policy', *Journal of Law and Society*, Vol. 23, (1996), p. 549.
40 Smith, 'Legal Aid and Justice', in Bean (ed.), *Law Reform for All* (Blackstone Press, 1996), p. 43.
41 Such as the Bar Council's labyrinthine proposal for a Contingency Legal Aid Fund to provide relief for cases which go awry due to a conditional fee arrangement.
42 Lord Chancellor's Department, *Access to Justice with Conditional Fees* (HMSO, March 1998); www.open.gov.uk/lcd/consult/leg-aid/lacon.htm.
43 *Ibid.*
44 Lord Irvine, in a speech to the House of Lords, 9 December 1997; www.open.gov/lcd/speeches/1997/adjn-deb.htm.
45 *Ibid.*
46 *Ibid.*
47 Lord Chancellor's Department, *Access to Justice with Conditional Fees* (HMSO, March 1998); www.open.gov.uk/lcd/consult/leg-aid/lacon.htm.
48 An excellent survey of publicly funded legal services in other jurisdictions is

provided in, Smith *et al.*, *A Strategy for Justice* (London, Legal Action Group, 1992), p. 75, *et seq.*

49 Figures taken from Smith *et al.*, *ibid.*

50 *Ibid.*

51 *Ibid.*, p. 88.

52 See such web-sites as Legal Tech (www.legaltechshow.com) and the digital lawyer products (www.digital-lawyer.com), for the range of computer-based applications aimed specifically at lawyers in those jurisdictions.

53 For details, see the Community Justice Centres website at www.nsw.gov.au.

54 This system has more in common with the German 'legal insurance' system. As discussed, it might be that control of fees through quality assured franchising would reach the goals of increased access at lower cost.

55 The competence referred to is considered below (pp. 138 ff.) in connection with franchising and the quality of service provision.

Part IV

Components of Delivery

5

Litigation and Dispute Resolution

Now there's no justice, you've only yourself that you can trust in.
Paul Weller, Wild Wood[1]

The aim of Part IV is to consider the means by which advice, representation and decision-making are controlled in the justice system as it is currently comprised. The discussion begins at the end, perhaps, with an analysis of the Woolf Report into the workings of the civil justice system. The advantage of starting here is the opportunity it affords to consider the complaints which are regularly made about the way in which the legal system operates – particularly in relation to cost and delay in respect of procedural rules. It then moves to consider the voguish debate about the need for alternative means of resolving disputes. The discussion moves beyond the standard forms of ADR such as tribunals, mediation and arbitration, into the broader range of 'private' means of dispute resolution, such as financial markets rule-books, conciliation services, counselling and local authority appeals procedures. There is an analysis of the composition and status of the legal profession and the judiciary, with an eye to situations in which change might lend greater acceptability to the way in which they use public funds. Finally, the role of advice agencies is considered to show up the possibilities for increased use of ADR while considering the restricted utility of the legal professions in many circumstances.

Part IV's title, *Components of Delivery*, harks back to the necessity of considering the means by which the legal system operates as part of the justice system alongside other personnel and systems. The term 'delivery' returns to the central discussion of the need for standards of social justice to be treated as realizable goals requiring suitable systems to achieve them. By considering the nature and adequacy of these bodies, attention will then move on to Part V, *Models for Reform*, which sets out structures which should build on a restructured justice system to ensure efficient and effective delivery systems for social justice.

ACCESS AND PROCEDURAL RULES – THE WOOLF REPORT

The archetypal lawyer's discourse about the reform of the system is set out in Lord Woolf's investigation into the civil justice system, culminating in a Report called *Access to Justice*.[2] Lord Woolf's proposals do not offer a panacea, rather they move towards a form of legal system which is concerned with equality and fairness between citizens.

The three giants: cost, delay and complexity

Lord Woolf's fundamental aim is 'to improve access to justice by reducing inequalities, cost, delay, and complexity of civil litigation and to introduce greater certainty as to timescales and costs'.[3] There are also a tranche of specific objectives within that broader remit. Lord Woolf has expressed the opinion that the system of civil justice ought to be 'accessible, efficient and just'.[4] He described the current system as being 'expensive, slow, uncertain and unequal'.[5] The last identified problem is interesting. It has hints of the statement of aims of the Legal Action Group: that there be 'equal access to justice for all'.[6] In Lord Woolf's opinion, people are not afforded an equal opportunity of justice if the system operates to deter them from seeking or obtaining access to justice.

The easy criticism of Woolf is that his strictly procedural reforms alone are unlikely to make any more litigants come to law. The problem for litigants is often not the concern about the delay involved in litigation, but rather the cost of paying for the first consultation with a lawyer. This is a subject in which there is a lack of academic research.[7] Anecdote and supposition often replace hard data. The legal profession is generally identified as being, at one and the same time, the root cause of the current malaise and the main threat to the success of Lord Woolf's reforms.[8] The blame for cost, delay and complexity is lain at the feet of a self-serving profession that benefits from a labyrinthine set of procedures which it controls.

Control is said to be exercised in two ways in this context: first, knowledge, and, second, manipulation. Only lawyers understand how the system works and therefore it is within the power of lawyers alone to use their knowledge to simplify litigation. Further, lawyers use fabled 'tricks of the trade' to drag litigation out. Seeking exhaustive discovery, asking complex interrogatories, pursuing end-less interlocutory applications, making payments into court, and so forth, are the frequent weapons used by lawyers to increase their fees and increase the bargaining power of their clients.

The underpinnings of the Woolf Report

There are two key goals underpinning the Woolf reforms: getting cases out of the courts system; and ensuring that cases coming within the system are conducted in a 'proportionate' way.[9] The draft Rules of the Supreme Court, prepared by Lord Woolf, will require that a case be dealt with 'justly'. The aim of case management is to achieve a just result where the rules do not otherwise provide for it. For example, if the rules do not provide for a set timescale or a set cost for the litigation, then the court will be given the discretion to impose such directions to ensure that the case is dealt with justly. The rules should also have the effect that litigation is a last resort.

Lord Woolf has proposed that there be three streams of litigation within the new civil court structure: small claims, fast-track claims, and case-flow managed claims. He has identified the following as the core of his proposed reforms: 'a fundamental transfer in the responsi-bility for the management of civil litigation from the litigants and their legal advisors to the courts'.[10] Caseflow management in the civil courts is the linchpin of Lord Woolf's proposals.

At the lowest tier of the new structure Lord Woolf has proposed to raise the limit (from £1,000 to £3,000) for claims to be taken into the 'lawyer-free zone' of the Small Claims Court. Simple procedures should be imposed for small claims (thus the enlargement of the Small Claims Court jurisdiction). An intermediate level of procedure should be imposed for intermediate cases, and so forth. Speed of decision is greater, without the stress of an elongated, lawyeristic process. The principle of 'proportionality' looms large in the Woolf Report. It is assumed that cases will be bracketed into economic significance on the basis that those of little cash worth are rarely in need of complex legal solutions. Cases which are of greater sig-nificance, in spite of their value, would be capable of court-based remedy in the usual way. The amount of expense, time and complex-ity involved in a case should be in proportion to its importance.

The proposed fast-track procedure will introduce a fixed fee for cases worth between £3,000 and £10,000. The aim is that the litigant will know a range of essential information: the upside and downside of the cost, the timescale for the litigation; and the exact procedural requirements which the litigant must satisfy. It aims to introduce – to use Lord Woolf's expression – 'no frills litigation'. The fast-track litigation will revolve around fixed directions for the conduct of proceedings. The aim is to prevent lawyers from being able to delay the process by operating outside the deadlines or applying for overly lengthy timetables. This is intended to introduce greater equality for litigants by preventing some litigants from oppressing their counterparties by allowing costs to increase by means of delaying proceedings. For more affluent litigants this is a common tactic to force counterparties to settle for less than otherwise they might, given the risk of receiving a lower award or being forced to pay the other side's costs.

The third limb of the new system, caseflow management, constitutes, in the terms that Woolf proposes, a radical alteration in civil procedure. There are two basic possibilities for the manner of change: first, impose existing rules more strictly, or second, remove current elective procedures altogether and impose strict formats for preparing litigation. Supporters of Lord Woolf's reforms point to one example of judicial case management which has led to practical benefits in the litigation over the Lloyds of London insurance market. By using 'high-powered judges' it was possible to break up the very complex litigation into 'manageable portions'. This enabled test cases to be brought for different stages of the litigation. Had it not been for this innovative form of judicial case management, in the words of Lord Woolf, 'Lloyds would have bitten the dust ... it has been a huge earner for this country'.[11]

While the system at present enables lawyers great leeway in the way in which a case is pleaded, one possible reform would be to introduce standard forms of pleadings instead. Similarly, settlement conferences could be made obligatory to force the parties to consider the possibilities of settling their dispute rather than coming to court. Stages in the process like interrogatories and discovery could be put on a strictly timetabled footing and prevented from being dragged out.

Uniformity or disaggregation of different types of case?

Soloman and Somerflot in the USA set out the essential elements for the efficient operation of caseflow management: judicial commitment and leadership; court consultation with the legal profession; court supervision of case progress; the use of standards and goals; listing for credible dates; and strict control of adjournments. It is a truism that judges are only in control of the parts of litigation which appear in court in front of them. They do not control which cases come to court nor whether the parties manage to settle the case before trial. Case management is a system which enables the conduct of litigation according to a predetermined timetable in accordance with selected procedures. Therefore, there will not be total uniformity after all – rather a menu system of applying procedures. What is not clear is whether this uniformity will always be just. While the draft procedural rules contain a power for the court to do justice, it is not clear that that will enable the court to ignore the new timetables in all cases. The example of personal injury litigation, considered on p. 169, suggests that rigid timetables will require litigants to incur greater costs than is the case at present.

THE CASE AGAINST THE WOOLF REPORT

Does size matter?

One regrettable feature of the Woolf Report is that the importance of a case is not necessarily to be measured by reference to its significance to the parties but rather by reference to its cash value. A claim for payment of social security benefit will generally be small compared to a breach of contract claim between commercial parties. The potential impact of Lord Woolf's proposals is that social welfare law claims would be de-prioritized at the expense of the interests of commercial parties. The notion of equal access to justice for all becomes a difficult goal to achieve if the system ranks claims on the basis of cash sums.

The very fact that a litigant will be required to rebut a presumption of lack of importance merely underlines the fact that those of restricted means are being relegated in the juridical scheme of things, at the expense of high-cash commercial litigation. Broadening the scope of access to justice is not served by erecting barriers to entry in this way. It is the regulation of the mundane cases which are the measure of a legal system's egalitarianism, despite Lord Woolf's nod to the need to remove inequality.

There are difficulties with involving the trial judge and counsel at trial in the earlier stages of the litigation process. The first problem is a logistical one, requiring the same personnel to be present at all stages. It is likely that it will be more difficult to organize judicial time and counsels' time to coalesce. Similarly, Lord Woolf's suggestion that judges and masters work together in teams creates greater management and logistical problems. The programme of multi-track interlocutory management hearings, it is suggested by the available empirical evidence, often operate to lengthen litigation rather than to shorten it. The more substantive problem is the question of the impartiality of the trial judge having heard interlocutory applications and hearings to do with settlement of the dispute. When the matter comes on for trial, the judge will already have been exposed to many of the substantive issues.

The chief opponent of the Woolf proposals is Michael Zander. He argues that at present more than 50 per cent of cases settle without court order.[13] Therefore, the introduction of judges into the decision of these cases is more likely to impede settlement than to hasten it.[14] The general thrust of these arguments is picked up in the following discussion.

Resources and the implementation of caseflow management

For caseflow management to work efficiently, there needs to be sufficient resources at the courts to manage the increased flow of paperwork and bureaucracy. As with all bureaucratic systems, ways of conducting procedure emerge over time. Other countries use the caseflow management technique have allowed it to evolve over time. In the English system, it will require a radical change in culture in the short-term. The alteration will also require the availability of court staff trained in the operation of the new system. There will need to be education for judges and a growth in experience for litigators.

The costs profile of litigation will be altered by the introduction of caseflow management. Lawyers will be required to take on tasks which they were not required to perform in the past. Therefore, there is an increase in cost built into the early operation of the system. Over time, the expectation of the Woolf Report is that more cases will settle, and therefore there will be a net reduction in the cost to the legal aid system and the Lord Chancellor's Departmental budget. What is not clear is how the new procedural rules will be enforced. At one level, much of the proposed change could be enforced by the rigid application of existing procedures set out in the rules of the Supreme Court and the County Court Rules. The insistence on rigid adherence to new rules will probably require enforcement by sanction, rather consensual development of a new way of undertaking litigation.

Too much judicial control – justice or process?

The issue is between judicial control of litigation and party control of litigation. Is it an interference by the judges to set down timetables for the conduct of litigation? The answer to this question might depend on a more fundamental view of the role of the civil legal system. There are two competing views. In Lord Woolf's opinion, involving judges at an earlier stage will increase the likelihood of the issues being defined sooner and the parties reaching settlement. According to Zander this will increase the cost of litigation by requiring parties and lawyers to attend court sooner in cases which would probably settle in any event.

It is not surprising that Lord Woolf takes the approach that he does. His remit was couched in terms of resolving a crisis in the management of the civil justice system. Reducing the impact of the three giants of cost, delay and complexity were his fundamental goals. In treating a legal system as an economic machine there is a reduced emphasis on the system as a system of justice. The quality and nature of the needs of the litigant are reduced at the expense of the overriding imperative to process as many units as possible. Litigation is seen in terms of numbers of case fed through the procedures rather than individual disputes between citizens or groups. The social role of law is the key question here. While there is no denying the extent of the crisis of feasibility facing the English legal process at present, there is a great danger of ignoring the true purpose of that same system.

THE CASE FOR DISAGGREGATION

The argument propounded in this section is that, as part of administering the legal system as an element within the welfare state, there is also a need to make distinctions between different types of case. Some forms of litigation require particular types of procedural rule. One such example is personal injury litigation.

Personal injury claims and fixed fees

There has been a large amount of research conducted by Nottingham Trent University for the Association for Personal Injury Lawyers (APIL) in the county court which disagrees with research carried out by Genn for Lord Woolf on High Court cases. APIL's findings are as follows:[15]

- There are large disparities in fees for similar types of work.
- The average profit cost for personal injury cases exceeds Woolf's maximum standard fee.
- A greater percentage of cost is incurred before the issue of proceedings than Woolf thinks right.
- Costs are concentrated on client conference (29 per cent), correspondence (22 per cent) and documents (30 per cent).

What is not clear is whether these lawyers would lower their fees, work more quickly or less efficiently if subjected to fixed fees.

169

The approach taken by the Woolf Report is to concentrate on 'proportionality' – that is the disparity between the level of cost and the size of the ultimate award. Woolf believes that altering court procedures will not solve the problem by itself. Therefore, Woolf proposes a 'staged fixed fee' to reduce costs and encourage shortening of litigation. The main questions are whether the quality of work will be affected by using less experienced lawyers more; whether fixed fees will mean overpaying lawyers in many circumstances; and whether the answer is better taxation of the system and closer judicial management under existing procedural rules.

The impact of this research on conditional fees

There is an impact on conditional fee arrangements. The research finds that there is a basic minimum amount of work which is required to be done before any personal injury claim can be brought. Therefore, contingency fees for claims of a small amount will lose a higher proportion of the award to base level fees. If the aim is to make it easier for small claims to be brought by private individuals, the following problem arises. Where there is always a level of fee of, say, £1,000 incurred, if the claim is for £2,000, at least half the award will go on lawyers' fees. Where the claim is for £10,000, the proportion lost to basic lawyers' fees is proportionately less.

Genn's research for the Woolf Report demonstrates that there are a number of cases in which costs exceed the size of the award. There is a real risk that some people will lose all of their award in paying their lawyers' fees. The percentages of total claims where costs exceeded the award were as follows: Genn, 40 per cent; APIL, 21 per cent. The judicial award is supposed to replace the plaintiff's lost income and cost of medical treatment in many cases. Therefore, not having the award passed to the plaintiff net of the lawyers' fees could in some instances lead to real hardship. There are great dangers in this media-friendly area that poverty-stricken litigants will be seen to have been fleeced by their lawyers under conditional fee arrangements. There is a dearth of research and of pilot projects into how this system can work. The risk is, therefore, that lawyers will be seen to have been over-compensated while the victims of personal injuries will be seen to have been short-changed.

Front-loading fees

The personal injury lawyer generally seeks to advise a client from the outset as to the potential success or failure of a claim. This process will, however, often take some time while the evidence (including expert reports) are amassed. The nature of personal injury work is the high level of professional fees, legal and non-legal, that are involved. The criticism which APIL raises at the Woolf proposals is that they will require personal injury lawyers to incur most of these fees at an early stage in order to meet the pre-trial requirements of the new rules. Both for pre-trial review and pre-trial conference, most of the evidence will need to be gathered in advance. It is unlikely that settlement will be reached before this time, as is often the case at present. Therefore, the cost of litigation will actually increase. For cases on fast-track, there will not often be too many fees to be met out of the standard cost award maximum.

THE PROBLEMS WITH THE WOOLF REPORT: CONCLUSION

The primary complaint is that the Woolf reforms will be extremely expensive to implement. To alter the present system would require an enormous amount of bureaucratic tinkering and the re-training of many staff. The political problem is that the Woolf package will not solve problems of cost and delay within four to five years. Rather, the reforms will add cost in areas like personal injury litigation. The comparisons that are made with the German system by Woolf, overlook the fact that Germany has many more judges and courts than England and Wales. Woolf offers only a partial solution on its own terms: it says nothing about legal aid and the more complex issues of access to justice, as required by the remit handed out at the beginning. There is a greater need to reform the fundamental workings of the system to achieve the full range of problems identified in the Report.

Importantly, Woolf requires that costs are front-loaded. This would mean that there is greater litigation cost at an earlier stage than is currently the case. The issue must be whether Woolf's reforms will result in cases ending sooner or will it simply prolong cases which would otherwise settle. Woolf concentrates on the size of claim in deciding which form of justice. The political impact is that cases not involving large amounts of money will be perceived as receiving second-class justice.

As noted earlier, more than 50 per cent of cases settle without court order, making it unnecessary to force those cases to go to court. Instead, more judicial involvement will impede settlement in circumstances in which judges have no training in management (or even case management). Judicial case management poses logistical problems in terms of personnel. In terms of combating delay, interlocutory management hearings lengthen litigation, while in

171

democratic terms there is a loss of impartiality of a trial judge hearing interlocutory applications. The Rosenburg study into the broader use of pre-trial conferences in the USA, demonstrated that cases were elongated as a result. It is the litigants who will suffer this increase in cost and the courts system which will continue to choke.

The proposal for the Small Claims Courts procedure also presents a number of problems. It will not save money for ordinary citizens bringing successful litigation although it may save costs for institutional litigators who are typically the defendants in consumer complaints brought by individual citizens. As to the fast-track system, even Michael Zuckerman (who conducted some of Woolf's research) has expressed doubts that it will lead to cheaper justice.[16]

If the preceding discussion has been critical of Lord Woolf's reforms this is because there are a number of serious problems of detail with them. However, the thrust that there must be reform of civil litigation to reduce cost and delay is beyond question. The broad approach of Lord Woolf's enormous Report is to be applauded as a result. What is least satisfying about the Report is the fact that Lord Woolf was prevented from addressing the broader issues of access to justice and the impact of legal aid. The result is that it is impossible to integrate the reforms into the more general issues raised in this book, nor to examine the disaggregated structure suggested above.

ALTERNATIVE DISPUTE RESOLUTION

A false prophet?

Alternative dispute resolution (ADR) is frequently seen as the panacea that will solve the problems of the legal system. The attraction is the removal of law, lawyers and judges from the equation. All of the elements which are seen to create cost, delay and complexity. Or so the theory goes. It has been accepted by Lord Irvine and Lord Woolf as a necessary part of the reform of the English legal system. While many are enthusiastic about it, it can be more difficult to define exactly what is meant by it.

The better term that is sometimes used is *appropriate* dispute resolution.[17] That is, courts are to be used in situations where they offer the best solution, arbitration will be used where it offers the best solution, and so on. Naturally, this method of dealing with the issue contains the seeds of its own jurisdictional dilemma: how do you decide which system of resolving disputes is appropriate? ADR is an imprecise term and covers a wide range, from mediation in divorce, to small claims courts, to industrial tribunals. In general, there is no legal aid funding for cases that appear before ADR forums. Therefore, the enhancement of para-legal training and the improvement of advice agency organization are vital if access to due process that is increased by ADR is to be translated into better access to justice. The benefits for the citizen are increased speed of justice, the removal of the pressures of a legalistic process, and a more flexible form of remedy. The benefits for the Ministry of Justice are a decreased cost of representation for the litigant and a removal of caseload from the courts system.

Other advantages of ADR are that, as a method, it promotes tailored remedies which do not produce the same levels of bitterness, tension or financial cost as courtroom litigation. By encouraging dispute resolution away from the courtroom, central budgets are reduced both in terms of court funding costs and delays. By encouraging disputes that are not usually litigated because of the costs of going to court, individuals become empowered. More people currently appear in front of tribunals than courts in England and Wales. In the area of family law, lawyers frequently complicate matters without having particular expertise in their resolution. In many cases, counselling and advice, rather than straightforward litigation, is the best way forward. A mediation process would answer many of the points at issue between the parties to a marriage breakdown, thus avoiding the polarizing influence of court-based litigation. Lawyers will have a part to play in mediation, but a very different role from their current one.

Former US Chief Justice, Warren Burger, has observed that most people expect lawyers to be 'reconcilers, not warriors: healers not hired guns'. Where law prevents access to viable solutions and remedies, it denies the litigants access not only to their rights but also to their own potential. ADR offers some capacity to think more constructively about the discharge of disputes without the need for the hazing effect of legal discourse.

ENCOURAGING THE EXPANSION AND INTEGRATION OF ADR

Alternative dispute resolution covers a wide range of tribunals set up to adjudicate disputes between citizens and organizations without the need for expensive court-based litigation. Society as a whole is involved on a day-to-day basis in the resolution of disputes: in the workplace, in the classroom, and in the provision of vital local services. Only a very small percentage of such cases ever reach a courtroom. To concentrate entirely on courts is to miss the vast range of disputes that our society must manage. The use of alternative means of resolving disputes is therefore of great importance to people's lives.

It is vital, for example, that industrial tribunals are accessible to all those in work who have claims about their employers. These can range from personnel disputes between a single employee and the employer, to the arbitration of larger workforce disputes to avoid or conciliate in industrial action. Access to tribunals to mediate in racial or sexual discrimination cases are also extremely important.

In looking at the justice system in the round, it is important to style institutions in a way which enables them to meet co-ordinated political and democratic goals together without overlap or waste of resources. The use of ADR as a means of breaking down the reliance on court-based procedures, or on lawyers rather than other professionals, ought to be to fulfill specific roles rather than simply to plug the gaps. Tribunals at present do not attract legal aid. The advice agency system should be able to attract legal aid funding for tribunal work where citizens require specialist advice. A decision must be made as to whether or not it is appropriate to have lawyers present at such hearings, rather than disallowing legal aid in cases of disputes which affect the poor more than the rest of society (such as social security and unemployment disputes).

ADR is used, among other things, by commercial organizations for arbitration proceedings, every bit as much as tribunals are required to hear certain cases by legislation in arrears such as unfair dismissal. What is important is to ensure that ADR is used where it is most appropriate but also that it is the courts who resolve disputes to do with important arrears of legislative policy. The increased use of arbitration by commercial entities constitutes a dangerous move towards the privatization of law by these markets which reduces the ability of the law to control them. ADR offers hope in many circumstances and risk in others. This underlines the necessity of centralizing authority for the operation of all such ADR forums in one government department so that a co-ordinated approach to their operation and administration can emerge. The following are some of the ADR forums currently in existence which an all-encompassing Ministry of Justice should co-ordinate:

- Mediation
- Arbitration in industrial and commercial disputes
- Conciliation services in industrial disputes
- Industrial tribunals
- Social Security tribunals
- Immigration appeal tribunals

It is not intended that the justice system be simply subject to ever more bureaucratization. Rather an increased amount of centralization would enable a greater politicization of the goals of the justice system so that they can be publicly discussed and considered in the broader context of the entire justice system. A new Ministry of Justice, discussed in *Models for Reform*, could ensure the sharing of premises to reduce cost, and the extension of the support functions to ensure that efficiencies of scale can be translated to the citizen with a palpable improvement in the quality of justice received.

NOTES AND REFERENCES

1 Paul Weller, 'Wild Wood' from *Wild Wood* (Island Records, 1995).

2 Lord Woolf, *Access to Justice – Final Report* (HMSO, July 1996).

3 *Ibid.*

4 Lord Woolf, speaking at the London School of Economics, 30 January 1997.

5 *Ibid.*

6 See, for example, Smith *et al.*, *A Strategy for Justice* (London, Legal Action Group, 1992).

7 See, for example, Cranston 'The Rational Study of Law' in Zuckerman and Cranston (eds), *Reform of Civil Procedure: Essays on Access to Justice* (Oxford, Clarendon Press, 1995), pp. 31–60.

8 See, for example, Zuckerman 'Reform in the Shadow of Lawyers' Interest' in *ibid.*, pp. 61–78.

9 The proportion referred to is the ratio between size of damages sought, and size of legal costs.

10 Lord Woolf, *Access to Justice – Interim Report* (HMSO, June 1995), p. 52.

11 This policy argument is echoed in his lordship's dissenting judgment in the House of Lords in *Westdeutsche Landesbank v. Islington L.B.C.* [1996] A.C. 669, where the complex rules of equitable proprietary claims and the law on derivatives were eschewed in favour of a robust, *realpolitik* approach. He favoured the need for English law to continue to claim the confidence of commercial people around the world so that London remained an important commercial centre.

12 Soloman and Somerflot, *Caseflow Management in the Trial Court: Now and for the Future* (American Bar Association, 1987).

13 *Judicial Statistics*, 1994, Table 3.4, p. 30. See, for example, the *Report of the Personal Injuries Litigation Procedure Working Party*, (the 'Cantley Committee'), Cmnd. 7476, 1979, para. 9.

14 M. Zander, 'Why Lord Woolf's Proposed Reforms of Civil Litigation Should be Rejected', in Zuckerman and Cranston (eds), *Reform of Civil Procedure – Essays on Access to Justice* (Oxford, Clarendon Press, 1995), pp. 79–97.

15 It should be noted that the APIL research is skewed by the following: (1) all statistics are from plaintiff files only, (2) the files have been re-costed as part of the survey, (3) the research has been conducted on untaxed bills.

16 Zuckerman, *op. cit.*

17 Legal Action Group, *Appropriate Dispute Resolution in the 1990's* (London, LAG Publications).

18 The Social Security Tribunal offers a workable blueprint for the way in which tribunal services should be organized by a Ministry of Justice. The work of the Independent Tribunal Service should also be promoted as part of this process.

6

The Legal Professions

Reform of the English legal system has failed up to now because of
the entrenched power of the lawyers' guilds.   *Max Weber*

Dealing with the lawyers

Change is possible, even in the most established bastions of the
English legal system. In February 1994, Richard Slowe, a solicitor in
the firm SJ Berwin & Co., appeared as Alan Steinfeld QC's junior. In
March 1995, Lord Steyn, Chair of the Lord Chancellor's Advisory
Committee, recommended that there should be common primary
education for the two halves of the profession. The Bar perhaps slid
into terminal decline.

The lawyer often stands as gatekeeper to the acquisition of rights
and obligations. Where the profession itself is distorted, there is a
problem of acquiring entry to the availability of suitable legal
remedies. There is as much a need for the lawyer to take up the
cudgels as there is a need for a litigant prepared to fight it. The
nature of the legal system is therefore an equally important part of
the notion of access to law.

In 1995, women accounted for only 6.6 per cent of QCs. In 1989,
less than 50 per cent of barristers' chambers had any ethnic minority
members.[1] At the same time, more than 50 per cent of all black
barristers practised from the same sixteen chambers, indicating a
concentration of the non-white Bar in particular chambers. By 1995
there were only six non-white QCs. As the Bar continues to be so
unrepresentative of the population, while retaining actual monopoly
of advocacy in the higher courts and many of the courts of first
instance, the issue for the operation of the British constitution must
be: how can you *represent* the community if you are *not representative of*
it?

The nature of the professions is at the heart of the debate about the

177

ability to access law. And yet, as Weber indicates, a great part of political problem with reforming this system is the entrenched power of the lawyers' representative bodies. The Law Society and the Bar Council are vocal and significant players in the arguments about the reform of the system. Under their patronage, reform is generally piecemeal and technical – primarily because the lawyers abstract to themselves the authority to talk about the workings of the legal system. Again this becomes a discourse about power in which the lawyers are the only ones who are able to speak because they control the means of expression.[2]

Lawyers and ever more legal aid

In June 1998 an extraordinary thing happened in the House of Lords. A committee of law lords was set up to examine the result of the legal aid taxation of barristers' fees stemming from a long and complex criminal trial. The arguments before that committee ran roughly as follows. For the Legal Aid Board it was said that the barristers were simply charging too much. Reading between the lines, the Board is probably under some pressure to rebuff the fees claimed by barristers for criminal law work in the face of criticism in the broadsheet press about a number of senior barristers commanding very large fees from the legal aid fund. Consequently, it is easy to see why a star chamber was convened to investigate the propriety of the claims which the barristers and their clerks were making on public funds.

For the barristers it was said that the fees were not excessive. In the words of Mandy Rice-Davies, 'they would say that, wouldn't they'? Their point of view was put most clearly by Michael Mansfield QC, probably the most newsworthy of the counsel at issue, in *The Observer*.[3] The central complaint was that headline rates of pay for barristers from the legal aid budget did not reflect an annual income. Instead, those amounts were the gross payment from which tax, clerks' fees and other business expenses were deducted. Furthermore, the fee paid reflected the work done on a case performed over more than one year in long cases, and was therefore not an annual income.

In simple terms, the barristers argue that the net sum which they keep is considerably less than the figures reported in the press. For example, the *Guardian* summed up the committee's enquiry with the by-line: 'Law Lords told of QC's claim for fee of £416 an hour', a reference to the claim made by 'leading left-wing barrister Michael Mansfield' who 'claimed £20,000 from legal aid for a week's preparation for a case and one day in court'.[4] Mansfield's complaint is, therefore, that his net earnings do not reflect that headline, gross figure. However, that is true of anyone earning under the PAYE system. Further, the other expenses are the expenses of running a business which provides advice work – principally the maintenance of premises, professional subscriptions, indemnity insurance, travel, and so forth. What this points out is that the life of the sole practitioner is an expensive one. It also reveals that there are economies of scale if costs can be shared within a corporate budget. This is partly why barristers form themselves into chambers: expenses can be shared. Therefore, at that level, barristers are no different from any other small business.

What is not so readily dismissed is the fact that barristers maintain the quaint, Edwardian system of clerks who manage a barrister's practice. The clerk is immensely powerful – a power which is derived solely from tradition. The barrister's gown has a small pocket, it looks like another obscure flap, on the back of the gown. The genesis of this sartorial whimsy was in the days when the gentleman barrister would represent others in court and the grateful client would drop some token of esteem into the pocket. The pocket is on the back of the gown so that the barrister would not know the size of the token. In time, because barristers thought themselves above sordid subjects like money, they used clerks to organize payment of their fees, as well as maintenance of the diary and other aspects of a barrister's practice. In the modern age that means that the clerk controls the barrister's access to the solicitor client-base. A new barrister in chambers is at the whim of a clerk and the work which is found. Historically, clerks worked on a percentage of the barrister's fee, with the result that in many chambers the clerk would be earning more than most of the barristers despite being untrained.

Therefore, much of the nature of the barrister's practice and the expenses of doing business are entirely the fault of the profession itself. Many chambers have switched to salaries for their clerks with a percentage top-up. In most chambers, a flat percentage is taken from the fee in any event, on top of the monthly contribution to the chambers' rents. In a drive to make the Bar seem more like a profession and less like a gentlemen's club, many chambers are retitling their clerks 'practice managers' and adopting a more corporate-like structure. However, the complaints about money are caused primarily by the way that the Bar continues to do business.

All of the above need not cause a problem; there is no real reason why a profession should not choose to adopt quaint business practices with their private clients if those clients are willing to accept the terms. However, there is a different context when it is public money that is being used to pay those fees and subsidize those business practices. The crux of the matter is that legal aid is paid to lawyers from central taxation. To make arguments about provision of liberties and essential freedoms is to avoid the simple fact that lawyers are paid far more than the public purse can bear. There does need to be a system of legal representation provided at public expense so that no-one is prevented from coming to law. However, it need not require exorbitant public expenditure.

Mansfield made the point in his own defence that 'justice should not depend on charity', on the basis that his practice required him to operate on an overdraft for twenty years of his thirty years in practice. Indeed the provision of campaigning lawyers like Mansfield, who are motivated to work for legal aid rates of pay and often to work without any payment at all (*pro bono*), is precisely the sort of commitment which society and the legal system require to ensure the rights of citizens are protected in the criminal justice system. Mansfield is correct when he says that it should not be a matter for charity, but that does not mean public funds should be drained even further to line lawyers' pockets: it should be a matter for the provision of justice as a part of the welfare state. As considered in Part II, the welfare state approach to justice is the most compelling intellectual and practical justification for the organization of publicly funded legal services. There is a need for a system that permits lawyers to work on efficient margins but which does not drain public funds to a damaging extent.

Mansfield's solutions to the problem faced by a profession frequently reliant on overdrafts, is to adopt a four-point plan:[5]

- An acceptable and reasonable fee must be agreed in advance.
- A proportion of that fee must be paid on or prior to the first day of trial.
- Regular and automatic interim payments during the trial should be made.
- Final and complete payment must be made within 28 days of the end of the hearing.

The aim of this plan is to relieve the burden of a profession which is forced to work in arrears, sometimes receiving fees years after the event. In truth much of the focus of interim payments during trial would relate only to those cases where the trial would be so lengthy as to require frequent payments. Pre-payment of a part of the fee presumes performance subsequently in accordance with the expected length of trial and would not account for early discharge of proceedings.

However, the plan does pick up the points made in the *Introduction* to this book, which are pursued in Part V. There is no reason why the amounts paid to the lawyer should not be fixed according to the type of work that is being done. The onus would be on the lawyer to justify any increment beyond the standard fee suggested for the type of work. While this varies from Mansfield's 'acceptable and reasonable fee', which hopes for a bi-party agreement on price, the standard fee proposal ensures that the Legal Aid Board is presented as the seller rather than the buyer. If lawyers wish to undertake legal aid work, they must buy fixed amounts of public money with their work. That is the only possible mechanism for controlling public spending on lawyers' fees while also pursuing the logic of franchising in terms of quality assurance.

Distinguishing between criminal and civil legal aid practitioners

There is precious little difference between the practitioners for the most part. Legal aid solicitors will tend to take any work which comes through the door – although some practitioners will have preferences and specialities. The distinction is between those who command high fees and those who charge lower fees. Conceptually there would appear to be a distinction between criminal and civil law rights. This issue was considered in relation to publicly funded legal services in Part III. There is an obvious attraction to the idea that crime relates to the human rights of the defendant and therefore is to be distinguished from civil actions – with a concomitant alteration in the way in which legal aid is delivered. However, it is difficult to see why rights to housing should be considered less important than road traffic charges.

In short, there is no justification for introducing two tiers of legal aid provision. The distinction between the two is a historic one between lines of administrative competence. However, the principle of fixed fees should be extended across all subject areas for which legal aid is available. Advice in relation to matrimonial proceedings should be capable of being provided on a fixed fee basis in the same way that fees in respect of time spent travelling and waiting can be fixed. As part of the movement towards alternative dispute resolution and the use of non-legal personnel to deal with non-legal issues, a fixed fee scheme would allow for the simultaneous creation of distinctions between those functions which public funds will meet from lawyers and non-lawyers. As considered below in relation to matrimonial disputes, for example, there is no reason why public funds should not pay for mediation and counselling services in many instances, at a fixed rate, and refuse to pay for legal representation. It would be for citizens to decide whether or not they wish to pay for legal representation and advice for issues which public funds are not considered appropriate.

Fixed fees or block contracts? The impact on the profession

Block contracts have a dimension which is generally little discussed in the context of legal aid funding. In a system which is focused on the provision of legal advice and representation by private practitioners, rather than by advice agencies or public sector bodies, the preservation of fairness is all important. As considered in the free market approach it is essential for a functioning market that there is sufficient competition between service providers. The impact of block contracts is a centralization of service provision in those firms that are able to demonstrate suitable expertise and administrative capabilities to provide the contracted service to an entire geographic region alongside other contract-holders. In short, a solicitors' profession in which the majority of firms are made up of one, two, three and four partner firms operating as generalists on high streets will not be able to survive the movement to block contracting. Generalists will not be able to charge the legal aid fund for fees related to work for which they have no contract.

Taking franchising as a model, the firms will be required to demonstrate a history of work in each subject area as well as file management competence. Therefore, small firms will be required to sell their goodwill to larger firms which hold contracts. In short, small firms will die out either through bankruptcy resulting from a sclerosis in legal aid fees, merger with similar firms, or takeover by established larger practices. The movement will be away from a large amount of competition to competition between only those providers which have block contracts. Consequently, citizens will have fewer solicitors' firms to choose between. It is likely that the same few firms will deal with all disputes of a certain type arising in their region. A system relying on market freedom to protect the freedoms of its citizens will clearly not have that effect. Block contracting is an unattractive measure in terms solely of advice provision.

THE JUDICIARY

This section examines the role of the judiciary as a public service and a need for greater accountability in terms of selection and decision-making. There is a huge constitutional element to the role of judges and their relationship to the dispensation of justice through court-based litigation, and in relation to the possibility of facilitating justice by avoiding the use of courts. The central complaint levelled at the Labour Party's programme of increasing citizens' rights through a written code is that it will put the fate of Labour's first taste of political power in twenty years in the hands of the judges. The danger with judges, as has been identified by Griffith[6] and tabloid newspapers alike, is that they are predominantly old, male, white and from public school and Oxbridge backgrounds. In short they are not the ideal people to be empowered to introduce the programme of a democratic socialist government.

The answers to this criticism are threefold. First, the approach identified by this book is that of using alternative dispute resolution which does not require judges. Instead, it uses professionals who are trained in the area of competence of the appropriate tribunal. Second, the system must alter the way in which judges are selected and trained. These alterations will have a palpable and immediate effect on the quality of decision-making that is made by the judiciary. The means of doing this are outlined below. Third, specialist courts must be created just as specialist tribunals are created to deal with particular types of case which are considered to be of special importance. Examples of this are cases which involve complex issues of technical fact, such as environmental pollution or city fraud. There are also other areas of litigation which may require the advice of specially convened commissions to advise ordinary courts because they consider areas of complex rights of citizens. For example, it is frequently suggested that courts applying the Human Rights Act 1999 should be supported by a Human Rights Commission. The central question is one of deciding those cases which require legal representation and those which are better served by a specially convened tribunal. These issues are considered below.

Judicial politics

The position of the judges in the legal system is both pivotal and difficult. There is a large amount of literature concerning the judges. The reaction of the tabloid press and the left-wing politicians is that judges are old and reactionary. The opinion of right-wing politicians in recent years is that the judges have begun to develop into a power bloc which is challenging the ability of the government to govern. In the debate about the constitution, many take the view that a Bill of Rights is a dangerous idea simply because it gives too much power over citizens' rights to the judges.

These are the difficult parts of the judges' role in the legal system. Clearly, the place of judges in the system is also central to the business of deciding guilt and innocence, deciding what the law means, and deciding who wins and who loses. These questions are most important in the area of political cases such as the *Spycatcher* litigation, the banning of trade unions at GCHQ Cheltenham and the spate of miscarriage of justice cases in the late 1980s and early 1990s. The power of the judges is made all the more significant because the holders of that power are unelected. The exercise of their duties is beyond public censure, apart from comment in the press.

Who are the judges?

The first question to ask is, who are the judges? Given that they have enormous powers over our liberty, our rights to employment, housing and access to children, judges occupy a place in our society that is central to economic, political and social life. The English legal system is a complicated mixture of legally qualified and unqualified individuals. Most concentration in law schools and in the press centres on the decisions and opinions of senior judges. All senior judges are former barristers who have been selected for judicial office.

Furthermore, there are only two women judges in the Supreme Court. There are currently no judges in the Supreme Court drawn from the ethnic minorities. While fewer cases progress to the higher courts, it is these courts which decide the issues of law which are then binding on the lower courts. Therefore, the opinions and decisions of the senior judiciary are important because of the effect that they have on the rest of the legal system. The question then arises: how well are judges able to officiate over cases involving problems which, for example, are unique to women and ethnic minorities, when few judges are drawn from these backgrounds?

House of Lords, Court of Appeal and High Court judges

The decisions of senior judges, apart from shaping the common law, also filter out into the attitudes of broader society by their coverage in the national media. As important individuals within British society, the opinions of senior judges expressed outside, as well as within, the courtroom have a profound effect on the formation of social policy. For example, when a senior judge such as the Lord Chief Justice makes a comment about law and order policy, his views are reported with effect at least equal to that of the Home Secretary and other politicians.[7] Do judges have equivalent amounts of expertise with reference to social policy in these areas? Should the opinions of judges be given more or less weight than those of politicians, sociologists and community groups?

The further question is, should judges be involved in this kind of political argument at all? The role of the judge is based on his or her much vaunted independence. Unlike judges in the American Supreme Court, for example, who are appointed by the President and by Congress after their political views have been vetted, English judges have historically sought to maintain a distance from the detail of politics.

It is difficult to see how the decisions of judges in court can be kept away from public discussion. It is probably beneficial that they are made public by the press and that most cases are conducted in open court where the public can see justice being done if they choose to. However, the more difficult question is how judges are supposed to draw the line between being commented on in the media and seeking to make their views known in the media beyond reports of their comments in court.

Should judges give press conferences after judgment to explain the reasons for their decisions? The risk is clearly that the law would then descend into a circus. Judicial press conferences would take on the style of the National Lottery results. And yet senior judges have agreed to be filmed for television documentaries and to be interviewed on current affairs programmes such as *Newsnight* more and more in recent years.

The selection of judges

It is important to consider the appointment of judges, the retirement of judges, and judicial pensions. The appointment of judges is currently a secretive system of patronage between senior barristers, existing judges and the Lord Chancellor's Office. The process must be made public. It must be remembered that the Lord Chancellor is a Cabinet Minister and therefore a politician. The Attorney-General and Solicitor-General, the Government's law officers, are also political appointments and both offices are held by career politicians. The appointment of English judges can be seen as a matter of political patronage. While the system is a classic British arrangement of informed appointment behind closed doors to achieve the best results, there are those who complain that it compounds the unelected power of judges by making the reasons for their appointment secret. There is no publication of criteria for the selection of judges. Nor is there any means of knowing why other people were not chosen. The secretive procedure is similar to that for the selection of Queen's Counsel.

Further, the criteria for choosing judges must be made known so that it can be reviewed and criticized. The aim of this process must be to stop short of the American system whereby judges are selected on the basis of their political convictions. It is not necessary to vet the politics of judges, rather they should undergo a course of continuing education to bring them up to date with developments in the law and changes in the social underpinnings of the cases that they hear.

In response, Labour in 1995 proposed the creation of a Judicial Appointments Commission which would make decisions on the selection of judges in a way that is open to public scrutiny. Lord Irvine has announced in newspaper interviews that the government's policy is to make no change to the mechanism of selecting judges, thus preserving his own powers of patronage over the judiciary.[8] Among his first appointments were the advancement to the House of Lords of Lord Justice Hobhouse (a commercial law judge)[9] and Sir Peter Millett (a Chancery judge and well-known defender of the rights of judges to keep secret their membership of masonic lodges). This means that they will be able to interpret and apply leading decisions on the new Human Rights legislation despite having no experience of the operation of those concepts.

The Commission proposed by the Labour Party is the only efficient means of securing a constitutionally valid means of processing judicial appointments. The Commission as envisaged would have been composed of lawyers and laypeople and would have published the criteria on which it would have made its decisions and also the reasons for individual decisions. Rather than politicizing the selection of judges on the American model, it would have recognized the need for openness in judicial appointments, so that reform was made possible.

In the model proposed by John Smith's leadership, the Minister of Justice would be empowered to create a Judicial Commission ('the Commission') which would have full competence in the selection and appointment of those who hold judicial offices and also oversee the training and servicing of the judiciary. The Commission would be structured in the following way:

(1) the Commission would have a President who would be a lawyer qualified by reference to the rules of the Bar Council or the Law Society as either a barrister or a solicitor in England and Wales or Scotland or Northern Ireland;
(2) the Commission would have a Vice President who would not have any legal qualifications;
(3) the remainder of the members of the Commission would be composed half by persons who would have legal qualifications and half by persons not so qualified.

The Commission would make judicial appointments at times when they are so instructed by the Minister of State with competence for the administration of justice. The Commission would be required to present written reasons for their appointments of all judicial officers to the Lord Chancellor and to a select committee of members of the House of Commons with similar competence in relation to justice affairs policy. The work of the Judicial Studies Board would be expanded to consider the way in which judges need to be trained to cope with an increase in litigation of a politically charged nature in a society that is taking ever-readier recourse to law.

This proposal would go some way towards restoring the public faith in the judiciary by creating greater confidence in the way that they are selected. The real work will be done by deconstructing the illusory barriers which pretend that the judges are divorced from political disputes. The critics of a written constitution fail to take account of the fact that if a Bill of Rights is not introduced, then the judges will continue to make political decisions, as they do at present, in cases which are at root political (even though they have been translated into legal language).

Constitutional courts

As a further essential reform, the introduction of specialist courts in some areas, notably in matters concerning civil liberties and the environment, will enhance the quality of judicial decision-making while enabling courts to become proactive in seeking expert advice on the cases before them. The Commission, the Advisory Committee and the Law Foundation[10] will all be able to input to the process of judicial reform going forward.

One of the most progressive ideas in this area is to create a Constitutional Court which would decide on all cases arising under the Bill of Rights on a referral basis, as the European Court of Justice does with European law currently. The court would be serviced by a Human Rights Committee which would provide advice and arguments. The Committee would also draft opinions on any case brought before the Constitutional Court, in the same way that the Advocates General provide opinions for the European Court of Justice. This will ensure that cases which currently go before the courts will be allowed to develop in a distinct stream of jurisprudence, enabling citizens to understand their rights more clearly and allowing the media to scrutinize the decisions of the courts more effectively.

The second strand in the critical argument is that systems of civil liberties have little to offer the citizen. The full proposed programme of reform for an incoming Labour government should go farther than simple reform of the judiciary. The creation of a Law Foundation would marshal private finance to run pilot schemes in the justice system and to work to improve the procedural inadequacies in the current means of bringing actions in law. The use of court buildings should be revolutionized to bring the broader use of alternative dispute resolution (tribunals, methods of mediation and arbitration) closer together, this would lower costs and improve the resources available for the provision of justice. Advice agencies must be given greater support to take up the slack left by reduced availability of legal aid. New technology, pioneered in the USA and Australia, which enables citizens to learn about their rights and commence actions before tribunals without the need of a lawyer, must be piloted in the UK.

It is in these ways that improved justice will be brought to the British citizen: justice of a higher quality but at no increased cost. To focus solely on judges as the primary objection to the most important aspect of social renewal is to miss the point that the whole system needs reform. It is essential that we don't stand in the way of reform for fear of altering one small corner of the whole. Judges will continue to make political decisions and therefore must be policed as they do so. It is only when a culture of rights protection is established that citizens can begin to cherish the rights that they hold. It is only in this climate and via a rejuvenated justice system that communities can begin to activate their rights and move towards the goal of national renewal.

The ideas which the bulk of lawyers on the left have been exploring for some time now, will take the sterile, law-obsessed debate about individual rights away from the antiquated discussion of the evils of judges and out into the communities. The real question is not, 'how to disable the judges?' but rather, 'how to enable the citizen to activate rights without being impeded by cost or administrative delay'?

In considering the judiciary as public servants, it is necessary that a judge vacates office when she attains the age of 65. Judges returning to case after retirement must be prevented. A proper flow of judicial talent must be created. The Minister of Justice should have the power to review the cost of judicial services and to consider pension schemes approved for the purposes of Chapter IV, Part XXIV, Income and Corporation Taxes Act 1988. This measure would not only ensure the level of pensions for judges and ensure that those lawyers who are attracted to the bench by the existence of pensions still apply, but it will allow for a large reduction in the budget.

The courts system

The Courts Services Agency (CSA)[11] exists to carry out the administrative and support work of the courts and general tribunals. It is therefore the CSA which is at the heart of the problem of administrative delay in the court system. While the operation of procedural rules, as considered above, also poses a large roadblock, it is the CSA which is responsible for the smooth administration of the remainder of the system. The CSA is part of the Next Step agencies programme introduced by the Conservative administrations to dismantle the civil service, replacing them with quasi-private sector organizations which were expected to be subject to market discipline in the discharge of their functions.

The CSA's report for 1997/98 shows that there were 25,404 outstanding cases in the Crown Court at the start of the year, up from 23,757 at the start of the previous year. The number of sittings was expected to rise to 90,800 days from 89,125 days in the previous year.

Much can be achieved by a re-examination of the way that the system works in practice and in the redrafting of many of the complex rules that it enforces. It is important to address the issue of making court procedures and practices simpler and more cost effective. By maintaining close contact with the profession and the day-to-day practices of the courts structure, it is possible to identify means of improving the treatment and the service that the law offers to its consumers from the moment they identify a legal problem to the time when they pursue a legal remedy. Class actions are one very good example. The litigation commenced by 15,000 Benzodiazepine tranquilliser addicts, in their case against the drugs manufacturers for failing to warn doctors or patients about harmful side effects, has been halted because of the unavailability of legal aid for the plaintiffs. It is also to re-examine the procedural rules which prevent such actions being brought and legal representation being excluded.

As considered below, the extension of the law centre system is vital to a process of increasing access by justice by being available for all citizens to help them understand whether or not the difficulties that they face with employers, benefits agencies or simply their neighbours have a legal solution. Labour will seek to bolster and co-ordinate the work done by law centres. By networking the resources that law centres and legal aid practitioner firms do, it will be possible to provide solutions for the users of this service more efficiently and effectively. In this area, increased use of the work of bodies like the Law Commission, and closer attention to the detailed proposals that they produce on substantive areas of law, are central to the better administration and use of justice in our society.

Legal training

The training of lawyers has become a vexed subject. The recent litigation brought against the Inns of Court School of Law, which trains barristers, alleging racism in 1992/3 and the threatened litigation in respect of irrational admissions procedures, has brought legal training into disrepute. There is a concentration at law schools in universities on commercial subjects to the detriment of lawyers who wish to practice in areas of crime or social security regulation.

Labour has proposed to implement a system of fused vocational training across the profession which will be made available at universities rather than solely at the old Colleges of Law for solicitors and the Inns of Court School of Law for barristers. This will enable a fairer system of legal education, so that the profession is infused with new blood and is better able to represent the population. A committee will need to be created to oversee the running of these courses and maintain standards so that people receive the best possible representation. The Legal Services Consultative Panel must be developed as part of the advisory network for the LCD to ensure that standards of representation are maintained and that the representativeness of the profession is enhanced. The proposals for a unified training course should be adopted and a number of certified institutions of higher education should be enabled to administer the vocational training courses. Access to these courses must also be broadened.

One trend in legal education which needs to be controlled is the concentration of law schools on commercial subjects, whereby it is possible to obtain funding for lecturers from large city law firms. This is very much to the detriment of the development of non-commercial areas of law. The other important point is the education of the public. The use of new technology is an essential tool in this respect. As are law centres that are free at point of use, thus enabling active education of the population as to their rights. An increase in para-legals and library facilities as part of the court structure will also open up access to legal knowledge.

There are observable trends in the profession generally which should be allowed to continue. Among these areas is the slow fusion of the two sides of the profession. It is suggested that the Bar will continue to contract until it becomes merely a specialist advisory profession which conducts advocacy for and alongside solicitors. The preservation of the independence of this area of the profession is a very real asset in the present justice system. Therefore, the drift towards multidisciplinary partnerships should be resisted while it is still commercially realistic for the Bar to stand on its own. The duties on advocate-solicitors in appearing before courts must be raised to emulate this code of independence.

One further point that needs consideration is whether Labour wishes to move towards the continental European system of a career judiciary. The advantages are that judges would receive training throughout their careers in not only the area of law in which they are required to give judgment, a requirement that does not exist at present, but also in the art of reaching decisions and balancing the needs of the parties. This would enable judges in stipendiary magistrates' courts and county courts to take a more active role in the search for the truth in litigation which is often hidden behind the 'all or nothing' approach of lawyers, and often fails to take account of the real objectives of the parties. By developing a career judiciary, these systemic problems could be removed and the judiciary could become more professional in the management of court business and in the delivery of judgments.

ADVICE AGENCIES

The law centre and Citizens' Advice Bureau perform a vital function in providing free legal advice to citizens. These bodies can identify legal problems to do with social security, housing, employment and other more general problems. This essential first point of call is under-funded and their scarce resources are disparate and uncoordinated.

Radical centrist policy requires a renewed focus on law centres and Citizens' Advice Bureaux which could be networked with the Law Foundation's monitoring and research functions so as to pool resources. It is of paramount importance that these bodies retain their independence and any tendency towards centralization is resisted. However, the importance of these agencies means that they must be able to share good working practices, personal expertise in particular areas of giving advice, as well as other resources. The growth of computer and telecommunicative technology makes it possible to link these organizations together in a way that will enhance their ability to give advice to the public and which will make the provision of justice for the citizen an achievable goal.

On a regional basis, it would be possible to co-ordinate the personnel and skill requirements of the system. On a national basis, expertise in areas of, for example, housing law or employment law, can be brought together to work on solutions for generic forms of problem faced by the law centre customer. The networking of these resources on a regional and national level should save on cost by reducing duplication of work and facilitating the advancement of shared thinking on problems.

Citizens' Advice Bureaux, law centres and other advice centres

The Citizens' Advice Bureau (CAB) network grew out of an initiative begun in 1938 between a number of government departments to provide advice to citizens in time of national emergency. The onset of the Second World War brought that eventuality to life. However, it was not until the late 1960s that the network was formerly organized under the banner of the National Association of Citizens' Advice Bureaux (NACAB). The creation of the legal aid scheme in 1949 meant that advice agencies were marginalized in contradistinction to advisory services provided by lawyers. The abortive proposal for a national legal service was the closest the welfare state came to acquiring a national advice structure. The Citizens' Advice Bureau network typically provides advice on a casework basis undertaken by a mixture of trained advisors and volunteers. The network is not able to provide legal advice in all or even many of its centres. Instead it relies for the most part on a referral system with local solicitors. The CAB specialities are casework involving local authority services and benefits and a number of consumer related complaints. The great advantage of the network is its ability to offer a more informal type of advice than lawyers in private practice.

The funding of Citizens' Advice Bureaux is a mixture of some central government money, local authority money and a great reliance on charitable funding and other private sector grants. Its central body, NACAB, receives a substantial grant from the Department of Trade and Industry, whereas individual Bureaux receive grants, in the main, from local government.

The law centre network is distinct from neighbourhood and local legal advice centres in that they employ salaried lawyers on a full-time basis (local centres operate by using local private practitioners on an occasional basis to run free advice clinics). The importance of law centres is in their ability to provide a legal advisory service which is free at the point of use to local communities.

In part the law centres appear to be a reinstatement of the national legal service of a cadre of lawyers retained to provide free legal advice. However, there are significant differences. Law centre funding is the main problem. Much of the funding comes from charitable and other grants. The Lord Chancellor's Department does not provide the core funding which law centres need. As a result, the centres have tended to open and close with little predictability as short-term political considerations have provided or removed their funding.

The relationship of law centres to the profession is an interesting one. There is a tendency for private practitioners to look down on advice agencies, charitable advice centres and law centres as being less professional than traditionally organized lawyers. However, the experience of clients appears to be that the informality of law centres is a great attraction and provides a more amenable service. In the beginning, the Law Society was unhappy at permitting law centres to practise law, before eventually agreeing to a compromise in which the centres restricted themselves to giving advice in areas outside the staples of private practice.

Aside from the two main sources of legal advice are centres which offer advice on housing disputes or consumer affairs. The growth of local authority complaints and appeals mechanisms in a number of areas has led to a greater need for advice services offered directly by local authorities to help citizens to negotiate their way through the legal protocol and procedures.

Integrated advisory services – a national advisory service

What is needed is a means of bringing together the disparate strands of community advice work, and in doing so straddle local authority advisory services, the general service offered by the Citizens' Advice Bureau network and the legal advice offered by private practitioners and law centres. What is unimportant is the vested interest of the legal profession and the many complications of local authority funding; these are secondary concerns to the interests of the citizen. What is important is the needs of the citizen. By putting the citizen at the heart of an advisory service organization, it is possible to restructure advisory services. The best way of doing this is to categorize the services which the citizen will use: governmental services, general legal advice, general non-legal advice.

In the first category the citizen requires specific advice about central government and local government services. This could range from establishing the means of access to a statutory ombudsman to understanding the method of complaint about a local authority decision. Local government must be required to create or fund centralized advice services which are able to direct the citizen between the various bodies and departments of central and local government. In many instances this will require the use of information technology and suitably trained advice workers who can explain how to access the relevant information.

The second category refers to issues to do with specific elements of law. This advice will fall between private practitioners and law centre advice. A better demarcation of the work which law centres will and will not undertake, should enable the advisory worker to direct the citizen between the two options. The possibility of access to legal aid may influence the citizen's decision. With the introduction of small claims and fast-track procedures, together with the withdrawal of civil legal aid in favour of conditional fee arrangements, it will become ever more critical for citizens to be able to receive free advice in situations where they are required to represent themselves or use an advice worker or trade union representative.

The third category mirrors most closely the work currently undertaken by the Citizens' Advice Bureau network and consumer advice services, which do not offer specifically legal advice but rather advise the citizen on dispute resolution or complaints mechanisms outside the sphere of legal advice.

The possibility for overlap clearly exists between these three functions. Each agency will be able to undertake the work of the other in part, if not in whole. Therefore, what is needed is better co-ordination to bring those advice workers together and to enable them to share best practice and development areas of expertise. The limited reservoir of lawyers available in the public sector in this type of work ought to be shared more evenly in training advice workers and in helping them to categorize particular casework files as raising, or not raising, legal issues. This would be apart from conducting legal advisory work in the usual way. Similarly, the advisory workers with experience of local government and central government procedures which are informal, characterized by their own dispute resolution culture, and non-legal, can help advise other workers with their expertise of best practice, the best means of approaching the procedure and reasonable prognoses for success or failure.

The only means by which this goal can be achieved is by the creation of a national advisory service. This structure would enable information technology to be put in place between the different agencies to develop software and websites that enable citizens to access information independently. It will also enable the sharing of best practice in areas of law and advisory work which receive little concerted intellectual concentration and development beyond the work of highly-motivated individuals concerned to enlarge the potential for such services. Significantly, public money and charitable funding which at present is supplied to various agencies performing similar functions in relation (often) to the same communities, can be brought together. Premises and facilities could be shared to enable the small amount of money that is currently available to be disseminated to the more crucial aspects of the work, for example, investing in information technology and in the training of more advice workers. A national advisory service on this model would be able to compete for legal aid franchises and other government money available to advice agencies at the present time. Within that national structure would be sufficient reservoirs of shared experience in particular fields, thus making it possible to support specialist initiatives like the National Homelessness Advice Service set up by NACAB and funded in part by the Department of the Environment at a mere cost of £300,000.[12]

How a national advisory service would fit into an integrated justice system is explored in Part V. Put simply, the NAS should be brought under the control of the Ministry of Justice and its expenses met out of that budget, after collecting from the Departments for Trade and Industry and for the Environment the money which is currently expended on such facilities. Co-ordinating this reform, with a reform of legal aid and the introduction of a form of national legal service, will facilitate a greatly expanded availability of access to information about rights than is currently possible. This proposal is similar in thrust to that considered by the Legal Action Group in their policy document, *A Strategy for Justice*.[13]

NOTES AND REFERENCES

1 As defined by the Bar Council and identified in returns to Bar Council surveys.
2 See M. Foucault, *The Archaeology of Knowledge* (London, Routledge, 1989).
3 The *Observer*, 21 June 1998.
4 The *Guardian*, 19 June 1998.
5 The *Observer*, 21 June 1998.
6 Griffith, *Politics of the Judiciary* (5th edn., London, Fontana Press, 1997).
7 For example, in December 1995, Lord Chief Justice Taylor complained that government policies to introduce minimum sentences for many crimes would hamper the independence of the judiciary in sentencing.
8 See, the *Observer*, October 1997.
9 On the decisions of Hobhouse J. in the local authority swaps cases, see, Hudson, *Swaps, Restitution and Trusts* (Sweet & Maxwell, 1999), generally.
10 Considered in Part V, *Models for Reform*.
11 www.courtservice.gov.uk.
12 NACAB, *Delivering Human Rights*, Annual Report 1995/96, p. 24.
13 Smith *et al.*, *A Strategy for Justice* (London, Legal Action Group, 1992).

Part V

Models for Reform

7

Structural Change in the Public Sector

Thus far we have considered the case for reform and the different factional approaches to change in the justice system. The hard policy-making comes, however, in relation to the specific models for reform. The following chapter forms something of a mix-and-match discussion of the available structures. The trick is to analyse those options in the context of the preceding discussion of the best approach to the reform of the justice system. The models set out here are a collection of disparate proposals made since the 1970s concerning the administration of justice. A number of alternative proposals for reform have been made by politicians or have been considered, often informally, by the policy-making bodies. The common objection is a lack of focus on *producing* social justice. Hence each of the models is adapted to correlate with the underlying thrust of this book that the business of the justice system is to provide a service to society at large.

PUBLIC SERVICE ETHOS

The central tenet of this book has been the need for the development of a public service ethos within the legal system and related services, concomitant with the development of other services provided under the welfare state. The models for reform must be required to live up to that principle. Rather than seeing justice as a principle that exists entirely independently of other political arenas, within the sole competence of the lawyers and the judiciary, it must be seen as a social good which is accountable to the public, responsive to the public, and accessible by the public without discrimination.

The development of the New Labour approach to welfare state benefits and to healthcare is predicated on the rights of citizens and the responsibilities of those same citizens one to another. Policy in relation to justice must be similarly organized around the rights–responsibilities divide – that is, after all, the essence of the language of the common law in deciding who has a right and who bears an obligation. The judiciary and the courts structure must be reorganized away from notions of rank and privilege in favour of the needs of the public seeking redress. It is considerably more simple to conceive of law centres and Citizens' Advice Bureaux along the lines of public service, allied as they are to local authorities and community-based advice work. Yet the court system remains at one removed from that level of genuine democratic accountability.[1] In this sense there is a ground to be identified between the closeted, autopoietic English legal system, and the democratically elected judicial structures funded in many states of the USA.

The focus of the New Labour programme is predicated on the relationship between the individual and the state, between the private and the public spheres. In ideological terms, it accepts that times have moved beyond the convictions of left and right, requiring some new epithet to indicate that, rather than simply establishing a new point on the left/right spectrum, the new politics occupies an entirely different dimension.

This new politics has proved difficult to discuss and to conceive of, either because it requires an entirely new language to be discussed properly or because it is simply a vacuous exercise. Understood from the point of view of a Labour Party emerging from received notions of its socialism, however, it is rather easier to make concrete. The received notion is that the Labour Party has always been a socialist party. Its brand of socialism is, however, properly described as social democracy on the European model. The New Labour project has grown out of a Party wedded to its welfare state institutions and its trade union heritage into successive attempts to embrace the electoral affections of the British people increasingly desirous of liberty and suspicious of inefficient state industries and institutions. The response has been to develop a language of interdependent rights and responsibilities in which the desires for a rhetoric of freedom can be tempered with an understanding of social and communal obligation. This model of a radical centrism, which talks of self-help for citizens, matches very closely a vision of a justice system in which those same citizens are able to define the extent of their rights and the responsibilities of other actors in their community.

In contradistinction to centralized power held at a distance from 'the people', the talk of the third way is for the individual to connect with the community.[2] Interestingly, government's role is seen to be setting standards and regulating overall performance against centrally-set objectives. The context of 'community' is therefore more critical. It might involve greater self-help, greater power for local government, or new regional assemblies involved in setting local priorities. The leading ideal of the community agenda (as opposed to the communitarian agenda considered below) is for decisions having a local impact to be decided locally, or at least as closely as possible to the place of impact.

By reducing the role of the state in the provision of public services, it is hoped that reinvigorated local communities will evolve to provide local solutions. In this way devolved budgets follow the granting of responsibility to local communities. The role of public services is redefined by some commentators[3] to be to enhance the opportunities of individuals and communities rather than to respond specifically to alleviate need. Existing public services are seen as having been designed at a time when needs were more uniform and were made by a less demanding public. The command economy controlled from the centre is not considered to be sufficiently responsive to local needs to provide the particular form of service which particular communities or regions may require. Therefore, devolution of responsibility is preferred together with an increase in accountability for those local providers. The systems creating public service providers are consequently required to incorporate a new set of functions to enhance the efficiency and accountability of the services they offer: performance management, benchmarking, local scrutiny, incentives for good performers, and sanctions from the state in the case of under-performance. The redrawn public service structure aims to provide more than simply rights of access, but also rights to information and rights to shape the services available. This thinking must be adapted to the legal system.

A COMMUNITY LEGAL SERVICE

The creation of a 'Community Legal Service' is Lord Irvine's grand design. However, beyond a catchy title for a system of block contracts, it is not clear precisely how it is expected to operate. At one level it seems designed to work little differently from a renamed version of Conservative proposals for block contracting and NHS-style trust reforms.

The community legal service is a devolved bureaucratic structure. Rather than fix legal aid priorities from the centre, it is proposed that such decisions be made at a more local level. Central government will set budget limits for each region. It is then for the regions to allocate parts of their budget to different aspects of legal practice. This raises issues of the manner in which such local decision-making is to be carried out, and the agencies which ought to be entitled to contribute to those decisions. The allocation of budgets will run in parallel with the allocation of franchises to private practitioners and other advisory agencies, entitling them to call on the devolved legal aid budget. The community legal service will decide how much of its budget is to be used to defray legal fees for which type of work in each financial year. The money allocated will then be divided between the franchise-holders in each area. Those firms who have a contract entitling them to perform matrimonial work in, say, Greater Manchester will be entitled to a portion of that budget in that financial year for services in that region. The operation of franchises in this sense is more closely akin to block contracts than franchising, and the legal aid system is closer to the reformed system of NHS trusts than to a welfare state benefits system.

A community legal service will only work where there is flexibility in funding and a freedom to be bloody-minded in the choice of priorities for which money will be applied. The most important point is that the creation of a community legal service will create differences between the nature and composition of legal services delivery in different areas. The notion of equal rights for all citizens will therefore be made impossible, although that is not necessarily to say that the situation would be made worse, depending on how that it done.

What is new about the community legal service is its intention to devolve power for spending legal aid budgets to local control. The level of local control, the 'community' inherent in the name, is to be based on the regional legal aid boards. As considered below, there is some difficulty in defining how that regional level operates as a viable community and how it would be possible to measure needs and allocate resources at such a level. The issue of the democratic content of the community legal services is something which has yet to be considered. The central political notion behind the idea of local control is that the legal aid budget needs to be stretched into areas which currently receive no, or only a little, legal aid support. For example, in the traditional Labour heartlands[4] there is no access to legal aid funding for industrial tribunal representation, something which the TUC has sought to make a part of Labour Party policy. Under John Smith, Labour was prepared to give such an undertaking that it would be possible for individuals seeking redress for unfair dismissal and other matters before an industrial tribunal to call on the legal aid fund to provide them with appropriate representation. The community legal service idea enables responsibility for making a decision as to the extension of entitlement to be made by the regional authority where it decides that there is local need for industrial tribunal representation rather than other forms of service. Meanwhile, the bureaucratic attraction of local control is that it enables budgets to be set and priorities allocated.

This aspect of the community legal service deserves closer attention. For the welfare state socialist, the loss of control over the allocation of eligibility is problematic. Aside from the important question of removing the universality principle (a concept which never applied neatly to legal aid in any event[5]), there is the problem of the provision of welfare benefits by a body other than the state. The clue is in the name: the welfare state is predicated on exactly that principle, that it is for the state to provide welfare benefits. There has been, as yet, no suggestion that budgets ought to be allocated to local authorities for them to distribute, at a locally decided level, unemployment and incapacity benefits. The welfare state maintains benefit levels at a centrally determined level. The introduction of a minimum wage will ensure that centrally determined wage policy is introduced. The social fund is an exceptional discretionary budget allocated to local areas to distribute to those who apply for it. However, the social fund is properly considered as a means for local authorities to meet cases of exceptional hardship outwith the strictures of central control. It is not a general, parallel means of benefit provision. Therefore, the community legal service continues the conception of legal aid as something other than a welfare state benefit because it is something which can be controlled locally from a centrally-allocated budget. Again, it has more in common with the NHS system than with social security payments.

For the radical centre, devolution of control to a regional level matches the central policy objective of having decisions made as close to the impact of that decision as possible. There are two virtues in this scheme. The first is that it recognizes diversity: diversity both in terms of regional variations and in terms of individual differences. The community legal service focuses provision on the 'sharp end' where need is considered most acute. Rather than rely on the blunt instrument of central planning, it is more efficient for local officers to assess local needs and allocate money to meet them.

The second point is that it offers a possibility of satisfying two seemingly irreconcilable problems at once: reducing the cost of legal aid and at the same time widening access to it. By empowering the community legal service to distribute money, it is possible to target those sections of society which government wishes to bless with legal aid funding, if they are identified as a target for eligibility. Thus access can be widened. At the same time it is possible to force other sections to be removed from eligibility by setting a low local budget which requires the regional board to exclude some areas of practice from access to legal aid altogether. In reality what happens is that some people are brought into the eligibility net who were not previously included, while others are excluded who had been previously included. To some this looks like allowing politics to interfere again in the provision of justice. To a socialist it looks suspiciously like redistribution and is therefore a good thing, provided the Robin Hood principle of transferring from the rich to the poor is observed.

Beneath New Labour's 'newspeak' lies a straightforward commitment to making a palpable difference rather than satisfying political-ideological standards, such as the principle of universality, if those standards are not providing effective solutions to local problems. This can be described as New Labour's 'virtuous face'. The benefits of the community legal service are therefore to be emphasized, in terms of focusing limited resources on particular problems. Unfortunately, nothing is quite as simple as the view of a fairer distribution system as set out above in the context of legal aid. Aside from the problem of legal aid being provided for the apparently wealthy as considered in Chapter 5, it is not a case of taking legal aid from the rich recipients and passing it on to the poor, who were previously deprived simply because recipients of legal aid are disadvantaged. Therefore, redistribution of eligibility will always cause as many political problems as it solves. From a machiavellian viewpoint, the establishment of a community legal service to carry the blame for those decisions is attractive to central government. This could be dubbed New Labour's 'spin face'. The trade-off is between the virtuous face, which genuinely seeks solutions to problems of social exclusion, and the spin face, which seeks to make hard choices while staying away from their ramifications.

There is a further problem with the virtuous face of these proposals. The community legal service is a mechanism for addressing resources to the areas of greatest need. In that sense it is demand-led public expenditure, where that demand is backed up by genuine need, rather than supply-led expenditure which makes money available and asks people to come and collect it. The existing legal aid system makes money available and asks lawyers to claim that money from the Legal Aid Board. The problem is reconciling the policy of central government with the actions of the local community legal service board. While the Labour administration will perceive the community legal service as either a means of enfranchising a particular social community, or of achieving broader access to justice, local priorities will not correspond to those central desires unless there is specific legislation to ensure that local spending plans are targeted at centrally conceived priorities.

The Community Legal Service in the 1999 Bill

The remit set out for the CLS in the legislation (at cl. 5) is:

> ... for the purpose of promoting the availability to
> individuals of services [to do with general information,
> advice, dispute resolution, enforcing decisions and other
> forms of legal dispute] and, in particular, for securing (within
> the resources made available, and priorities set ...) that
> individuals have access to services of a type and quality
> appropriate to meet their needs.

Clearly, there is still great scope for the Commission and the Lord Chancellor to make regulations as to the nature of 'priorities' which the CLS is expected to address. The issues surrounding the setting of priorities are considered in greater detail below in *Models for Reform – Community Legal Service*. There remains also the vexed issues of the resources which are to be made available by the Lord Chancellor's Department through the old legal aid fund. Lord Irvine has announced that that budget will remain at the level last set by the Major administration. As set out in *Models for Reform*, the issue for the Blair administration is to make better use of those resources in a more integrated approach to the justice system as a whole.

The underlying quest is then for the CLS to deliver in relation to 'services of a type and a quality appropriate to meet their needs'. What is not clear is how the level of appropriateness necessary to meet needs is to be isolated. Within a welfare state structure of need identification and a structure for seeking to meet that need, it would be easier to predict how that would operate in practice. In line with the Woolf Report, this may mean that the CLS is entitled to refuse to fund litigation if it is not 'appropriate' for the citizen, even though that citizen might otherwise fall within the category of 'need'.

What is somewhat out of place within this context is the rider (in cl. 6(6)) that '[i]n funding services as part of the Community Legal Service the Commission shall aim to obtain the best possible value for money.' This is a straightforward nod back to the Economic System Management Approach identified in Part I. While the rhetoric may be focused on increasing access for the citizen through a web of new structures that are (at the time of writing) unpiloted and mapped only in outline, the practice is focused on keeping a tight rein on public finances. It is suggested in *Models for Reform* that the only means by which it will be possible to maintain control on the budget and also achieve a better service for the end-user is by the adoption of a more integrated approach to advice, assistance and representation across the entire justice system. Economies of scale on the welfare state model are the only means by which access to justice can be increased at a measured cost.

As part of its broader remit, the CLS is empowered to enter into co-operation with other agencies (cl. 5(5)) but there is no formal structure to link the Community Legal Service to any of the agencies of local government. It is argued in *Models for Reform* that there is a need for a national advisory service which will pull together local government advisory frameworks with CABx and law centres, as well as the existing framework of legal aid advice through private practice. The failure to provide for express links between the CLS and any of the organs of local government is a weakness of this programme. It is necessarily the case that links will tend to be stronger in some parts of the country than in others, that synergies will therefore lead to savings in some areas more effectively than in others, and that there will be a greater unevenness across the justice system as a whole rather than a greater holism in approach.

One of the strengths of the CLS structure also ought to be a facility for monitoring the standard of service provided to the citizen by those empowered to give advice through the franchising structure. Indeed, it ought to be a natural extension of franchising that decisions as to those service providers who are entitled to draw on the legal aid fund have their competence and standard of service monitored by the body which provides those funds.

The Criminal Defence Service in the 1999 Bill

To deal with the criminal legal aid system, a Criminal Defence Service is created. There is a subtle distinction between the CDS remit and the CLS remit. The CDS is created to secure 'that individuals involved in criminal investigations or criminal proceedings have access to such advice, assistance and representation as the interests of justice require'. Therefore, the focus is not on the needs of the applicant but rather on the interests of justice. A benign interpretation of that provision would be that justice would always require the provision of publicly funded assistance. There is no mention of the 'means' of the applicant either. A benign interpretation of that omission would suggest that (as with the system of legal aid at present) publicly funded assistance is more likely to be granted in the majority of cases with reduced focus on the defendant's means. However, a less benign interpretation would suggest that justice may also involve facilitating the prosecution's desire for an efficient trial process which may not account for the needs or means of the defendant.

In line with the CLS structure outlined above, through the CDS structure the Commission is empowered to delegate its functions to other persons by means of an authorisation 'to accredit, or authorise others to accredit, persons or bodies providing services which may be funded by the Commission as part of the Criminal Defence Service' (in cl.13(5)). Again, it is for the Commission to fund advice and assistance as '*it* considers appropriate' (cl.14(1)). The responsibility for this policy is therefore removed from Parliamentary control and placed in the person of the Commission, under the approval of the Lord Chancellor (who is similarly beyond Parliamentary control). The result is a worrying delegation of responsibility to bureaucracy away from effective political scrutiny. Similarly concerning is the possibility of delegation of some of these functions in practice to other persons.

In relation to the funding of the CDS, the Lord Chancellor undertakes to provide such sums as are 'required to meet the costs of any advice, assistance or representation' (cl. 18) rather than requiring the Commission to work to a fixed budget. However, this may be tempered by the Commission's ability to decide which forms of criminal defence it will and will not fund. What would be more difficult to work through would be a situation in which the Lord Chancellor wished to cap criminal legal aid spending but in which the Commission refused to restrict those situations in which public moneys would be made available for criminal defence. What is clear, however, is that the Lord Chancellor is not capable of giving directions to the Commission as to decisions in individual cases (cl. 25(5)). However, that does not appear to prevent the Lord Chancellor from interfering on matters of policy which may have necessarily direct effects in relation to particular cases.

These issues are pursued below in relation to the democratic aspects of the community legal service. First, it is important to consider precisely the structure of the community legal service as disclosed by the published policy documents.

The detail of the community legal service

The community legal service is the Labour administration's proposal for the reform of legal aid provision.[6] It is not a new system in itself; instead it is part of a restructuring of the legal aid system. Rather than set nationally applicable levels of income below which a person is entitled to receive legal aid, the aim is to give greater local control over the manner in which legal aid money is used. By creating distinct community legal service boards, based on the model of existing Legal Aid Boards, local budgets can be set to achieve locally prioritized objectives for legal services. For example, some areas have more of a need for representation in employment disputes, whereas others see housing and social welfare as their priority. The community legal service, in conjunction with the Legal Aid Board and the Lord Chancellor's Department, would set priorities for the expenditure of legal aid in those areas within budget constraints. While the detail of the Labour Party's policy is not clear, it might be that the community legal service would come to replace the Legal Aid Board, retaining a central core to administer the budgets and policy directions of the regional community legal service boards.

The central policy statement is contained in the appendix to *Access to Justice*:

> In place of the waste and inefficiency of the current system, we propose to create a Community Legal Service, co-ordinated by existing regional legal aid board offices. This will assume responsibility for disbursing the entire national legal aid budget on a regional basis. In addition to providing basic legal services, each local board will be able to bid for earmarked funds from within the existing legal aid budget to establish innovative schemes to meet particular local needs.[7]

The political slant on the community legal service is clear. It is aimed at the free market's favourite demons of inefficiency and ever-increasing public expenditure, while reflecting the lawyers' concerns of excessive cost and delay. While one of the perennial criticisms of the Blair administration is a reluctance to increase taxation to pay for public services, there remains the need to examine what is being paid for with public money. Legal aid expenditure in its present form is a particularly bad thing on which to spend public money. Expenditure on legal aid does not correlate to greater access to justice, rather it correlates to more money for lawyers.

Therefore, the efficient use of public money is a contentious issue. Also an issue is the local requirement for legal aid money for services other than straightforward advisory work by lawyers. As considered below in relation to a Law Foundation (see p. 229), there has been little work done on the alternative uses of legal aid funding. However, this could stretch from legal advice provided outside the usual eligibility criteria to advisory services provided by non-lawyers or charitable organizations. The example considered below is that of the Law for All charity which combines charitable advisory work with legal expertise to provide a legal advice and representation service which is free at the point of use for local residents. The Labour Party's policy expressly embraces such progressive initiatives provided that they acquire suitable local accreditation. As considered in Chapter 5 in relation to advice agencies, the forward movement of service provision for local communities is an important part of the development of legal services in the UK.

Within that general schema are a list of more specific priorities:[8]

Within the budget allocated for their area, each regional office of the Community Legal Service will carry out a number of core functions:

- Assessing the legal needs of its area. This will include assessing the demand for alternative forms of dispute resolution such as mediation and arbitration as well as for legal advice and representation.
- Drawing up a detailed strategy to meet those needs in consultation with local authorities and new advisory regional legal services committees.
- Agreeing priorities for legal services with the help of legal services committees chosen to be representative of the local communities they serve.
- Ensuring access to high quality legal representation through local lawyers in private practice and through making much more use of Citizens' Advice Bureaux, law centres and other independent advice units. The aim will be to build on existing provision and good practice initiatives wherever established in order to create a comprehensive, nationwide network of outlets for legal advice, assistance and, where appropriate, representation. The Community Legal Service will be expected to work closely with local authorities with whom there will be significant overlap of interest (for example in relation to local advice centre provision).
- Using the existing legal aid budget to expand access to alternative forms of dispute resolution such as mediation, arbitration and tribunals.
- Promoting public legal education, preventative work and liaison with other local and regional agencies. Law centres and advice agencies also have an important role to play in the vocational training of the legal profession and this should be expanded.
- Monitoring the quality of local legal provision.

To take each of these statements in turn. The community legal service will be required to perform specific functions and thus take both direction from central government and take responsibility for specific decisions off local government. The core responsibility is the assessment of local needs. At one level this requires an audit of the manner in which money is being spent locally and a decision as to whether or not that direction is deemed acceptable. It is likely in most areas that matrimonial legal aid will be identified as a particularly prevalent burden on local budgets, tempting provision away from non-domestic violence cases into increased use of mediation.

Since the 1997 election, Lord Irvine has set out some skeletal tasks which the community legal service would undertake:

> The Service could provide telephone helplines, education in rights and obligations; legal advice on the Internet; referrals to alternative dispute resolution; legal representation in tribunals; even interactive kiosks in every high street or supermarket dispensing information about the law and the legal system.[9]

There are two disappointing words in this thumb-nail glimpse of the community legal service. The first is the use of the word 'could' which indicates that, despite the example of successful services in Ontario and New South Wales (see Part III) there has been no blueprint set out for the British model. The second disappointment is the word 'referrals' indicating that there is no plan to integrate these services within the community legal service structure or under another umbrella to share cost and expertise.

Unless local community legal service boards are given the authority to make choices as to the precise allocation of resources in this way, they will have little effective power to shape the manner in which justice is administered in their region. To empower them to examine the way in which alternative services could be used is futile unless they are then enabled to put those powers into effect.

There are a number of problems with this level of regional control. First, to enable local community legal service boards to be truly flexible, it would be necessary to give them quasi-legislative powers to increase the obligation to use mediation rather than receive legal aid for all stages of matrimonial disputes. Second, this will lead to a different treatment of the family, in the case of matrimonial law, in different regions: some favouring legal, mechanistic divorce proceedings without any obligation to save the familial relationship through counselling, while others would make mediation obligatory by withholding eligibility for legal aid in practice until after alternative means of dispute resolution had been tried.

Third, the community legal service would require a means of measuring, researching and evaluating those local requirements. In effect, something akin to the disbanded policy unit of the Legal Aid Board, which would be able to run pilot schemes, perform statistical analysis and develop new ideas. Replicating that level of intensive work across the country in different regions would be inefficient and a strain on regional budgets otherwise used for legal aid spending. If there were no local policy unit, then the regional board would be required to make its decisions based on approximations derived from national statistics and from representations made to it by pressure groups.

The risk of using pressure group politics in relation to the community legal service is that the people who need the favours of the community legal service to enfranchise them are typically those who are not able to represent themselves and are not represented by pressure groups. If they were represented by effective political lobbying or political pressure, it is less likely that they would require access to the justice system on an individual basis in the first place. Therefore, the pressure group model of access to local government and regional boards seems likely to ignore the needs of those very people who require the help of a revamped justice system. It is not obvious how the community legal service boards are to be able to translate political objectives from central government into local, directed action.

At the time of writing, it is not clear what form the consultation process with local government will take. As considered below, it might be seen as a sop to concerns about the democratic account-ability of the community legal service. It is unlikely that the intention is for local authorities to be empowered to administer legal aid expenditure in a similar form to housing policy or the interaction with police committees. Similarly, the composition and role of 'new advisory regional legal services committees' is unclear. The possible models are considered below in relation to the democratic issues of community legal services.

The networked use of advice agencies and local practitioners is an important element of the strategy: in particular the creation of 'a comprehensive, nationwide network of outlets for legal advice, assistance and where appropriate representation'. As highlighted in Chapter 5, there are problems of integrating advice functions into a coherent strategy. At one level, advice agencies and private practice can duplicate efforts, at another they are straightforwardly in com-petition to provide services to the public. Sharing best practice is one criticism of the current composition of the justice system. In terms of private practice, it is difficult to bring together a disparate commu-nity of mainly high street practitioners to analyse best practice, rather than simply to gather Law Society obligatory continuing education accreditation points. The possibilities offered by technol-ogy (as considered below) and a Law Foundation (also considered below) present more possibilities for integration than a bureaucratically-focused community legal service. In the same way, loading the education function on to the community legal service appears to be placing too much responsibility in one place. The community legal service will have sufficient calls on its time with the creation and monitoring of local requirements, without the added duty of educating the public and running pilot projects.

The monitoring of legal provision is an important role for the body making decisions as to the use of public money in justice provision. The publication of the results of that monitoring is an important part of retaining the accountability of the community legal service. Given the role of the community legal service in block contracting or franchising (depending on the system) it is also important that that institution has responsibility for monitoring the performance of those practitioners and other agencies which are entitled to draw on public funds by way of legal aid. However, the full monitoring function requires a national agency to co-ordinate the provision of legal/justice services and to co-ordinate pilot projects to develop new means of delivering services and the sharing of best practice. As developed below these two functions are possibly best divided between two bodies. The existing Legal Aid Board is best placed to co-ordinate national monitoring of the legal aid system. A Law Foundation, mimicking perhaps the functions of the Legal Aid Board's policy unit, would administer pilot projects and best practice.

Tied in with the debate about the restructuring of the legal aid system, is the broader context of a system which is focused primarily on traditional, expensive court-based legal action rather than on alternative, more appropriate means of dispute resolution. As the Labour Party policy document *Access to Justice* identified the problem, 'This concentration of resources on the courts has acted as a brake on long overdue consumer orientated reform of both the legal profession and dispute resolution'.[10] The contentious issue of using the language of consumer rights is raised here, rather than talking straightforwardly of democratic rights. A more intricate problem is the notion that the use of legal aid as the primary means of providing access to rights for citizens. This focus by policy-makers has long meant that the political debate about democratic empowerment has ignored the question whether lawyers and the legal system are the most appropriate forums in which to play out these issues. The possibility opened up by the community legal service is the ability of each region to examine its needs and available expenditure to allocate money not only to defray legal fees in advice and litigation, but also to use the services of non-legal professionals or to pay legal aid to advice agencies which are not made up exclusively of lawyers or which are not organized as conventional legal practices.

Within this maelstrom of questions raised by the implementation of a community legal service, the ultimate policy statement sets out the polemical basis for the service:

> The development of the Community Legal Service will be achieved within the legal aid budget through reducing the exorbitant cost and waste inherent in the current system. Spending will be strictly monitored and controlled by the use of block franchises.[11]

In short, it is hoped that the community legal service will both cut costs and raise access. This is the philosopher's stone of legal affairs policy. The theme running through this book is that there is no simple 'quick fix' for legal affairs spending. The effective solutions will only come about through integrated reform. The community legal service will only offer a lifeline for those reforms if it deals with problems of democratic accountability and a re-emphasis on non-legal solutions to disputes.

Structure of the community legal service – issues of democracy

The precise structure of the mooted community legal service is, at the time of writing, uncertain. What is clear is that the core idea of a community legal service will only work where there is flexibility in funding and a freedom to be bloody-minded in the choice of priorities for which money will be applied. The community legal service complies with the policy of devolution of responsibility for services to a local level. It permits spending priorities to be fixed by regional boards. Consequently, it becomes impossible to administer a single policy on a national basis. It moves from the basic premise of the welfare state: that there are sufficient resources to fund universal benefits, which are designed from a central point.

The democratic aspect of this policy is the most intriguing issue. It is possible to justify differential spending only if a means of democratic approval can be achieved. That democratic approval would need to be more than voting for a local councillor, it would probably require specific approval for a package of measures by local consensus. The introduction of 'virtual town halls' would enable local people to vote for a specific package of local community legal service spending plans. However, the further problem arises of defining the constituency appropriate to fit with each community legal service region. One of the factors which is not clear is the regions which would be covered by each community legal service board and the possibility of defining those constituents. Given the apathy with which local government elections are met, it is unlikely that popular mandate will be the most effective means of ratifying complex spending plans.

If there is no electoral approval for these spending plans, a difficulty arises in the context of the body that makes the choices and frames the spending choices. Where bureaucrats make the choices bureaucratically, there will be talk of hidden agendas. It is only if the selection is seen to be the result of choice made by some body representative of local people that this problem can be circumvented. Responsibility could be devolved to local councillors. However, local government might resist this. Local magistrates' committees and local legal aid boards carry the problem of being apolitical appointees who could not command any seeming of representation. Perhaps local committees made up of people selected on a focus group basis would be a closer approximation – however, educating them as to the complexities of legal aid budgeting would not be an easy task.

The argument for a community-level selection of requisite spending priorities is that there can be a political discussion as to the needs and priorities that affect the community. The presumption that this is a matter for expert decision-making masks the fact that it is a discussion about the entitlement to public resources. In any other context, this is a straightforwardly political matter. Therefore, the solution to the operation of a community legal service must be a political matter too.

The alternative is, therefore, to have centrally-controlled delivery of legal services. All that the community legal service will do at that stage is to channel funds. The community legal service will not be responsive to local needs for justice provision.

Altering the eligibility criteria

The extreme cultural shift this represents is the movement towards a system of *vertical* eligibility for legal aid, rather than *horizontal* eligibility on the basis of income.[12] The community legal service requires that there be choices as to the availability of legal aid for categories of case, rather than by reference to particular individuals satisfying a means test. That eligibility is decided by reference to categories of case is not unusual given that defamation and industrial tribunal cases do not currently receive legal aid. Therefore, refusal of eligibility is already governed by category of case. However, it is a change to require that it be categories which are the primary determining factor in the eligibility for legal aid. This vertical eligibility means that an individual is entitled to legal aid simply because (s)he is within a certain category – that is, there is universal access to legal aid where one's circumstances satisfy with the requirements, in the same way that there is entitlement to benefit where the applicant is unemployed.[13] This is distinct from means-testing before permitting entitlement to legal aid, regardless of the purpose for which that legal aid is to be used.[14] This would make it possible for Lord Woolf's prognosis that particular types of case be subject to different forms of litigation procedure to be adapted to the availability of legal aid. There would be a coherent logic to the application of those principles which is currently not expressed in the two halves of Lord Irvine's plans to reform civil justice and legal aid.

Costs provision

There are many features of the current system of awarding costs which deter litigants, mainly to do with the risk that they will be made responsible for the costs of the other side. In the case of medical negligence cases or cases against employers, this usually means paying for the fees of the other side's lawyers. Often legal aid will not be available in these amounts and therefore the litigant decides not to run the risk of suing for what he or she is rightfully owed. By requiring costs to be borne by the defendant in some cases where litigation can be shown to be well-founded, the plaintiff who has suffered injury might be able to embark upon litigation. The points made earlier with reference to insurance might also provide a means of enabling defendants and plaintiffs to participate in necessary litigation without having to bear undue costs.

By removing the fear of paying the plaintiff's legal costs, the defendant is less likely to settle as a result of duress. The risk of having to meet the whole of one's legal bill does provide an incentive for settlement, however. Further, the rich client or the legally-aided client is likely to be less pressured than the private-paying client in considering litigation tactics. On balance, it does not appear that in all cases there is any one remedy offered by alteration of costs award rules.

Costs rules could be altered similarly in cases that are brought in the public interest. One example of this would be the recent proposals for the creation of an environmental court. Another example would be the possibility of litigation being brought on behalf of the estimated 4 million people addicted to Benzodiazepene prescription tranquillizers in the UK. By expanding alternative dispute resolution into areas such as employer/employee disputes, the cost of litigation is reduced while making it possible in many circumstances to provide a more appropriate method of justice.

Building the best community legal service

While much of the preceding discussion appears critical of the community legal service, there is much to be said for the development of the public service ethos through local control of legal aid spending, in tandem with greater accountability of the judicial role in court services.[15] What is important is to ensure that the best principles are preserved in any community legal service structure.

The community legal service must operate as part of an integrated strategy for local justice. Using the term 'community' in its broadest sense, or simply as a catchy slogan, will not ensure the generation of successful communities. An integrated strategy requires that advice agencies, private legal practitioners, and the courts and tribunal system in each area operate to share best practice. The community legal service is the umbrella under which these different actors gather together. Legal aid must be made available according to local priorities, within the confines of a nationally-determined strategy. That means that the community legal service is required to police private practitioners and contract-holders closely.

Where there are gaps in the provision of access by means of legally-aided advice and representation, advice agencies and courts must be prepared to give advice and administer (respectively) claims and disputes raised by individual citizens. Therefore, for example, where mediation is provided in place of legal aid in a region, it is necessary for advice agencies to replace the advisory role otherwise performed by lawyers in providing that mediation service. If the community legal service is prepared to fund divorce proceedings, there is a reduced need for local government or other agencies to be funded to replicate that legal advice. Rather, it is better for local government, the Department of the Environment and the Ministry of Justice (see p. 225) to co-ordinate the means by which such services are funded such that citizens are able to access all of the services which they need from whatever source.

In another example of this movement towards co-ordinated advice and representation, small claims courts should adapt their procedures to meet the requirements of the unaided litigant, while advice agencies must make their service available in an accessible form for such a person, for instance, by relocating the agency to premises adjoining the court. Standard form pleadings and claim forms, in which each party sets out their case and evidence, should be developed by the courts together with advice agencies to facilitate claims. The use of networked information technology in each region is therefore important to enable best practice to be shared and centres of excellence to be developed.

The suggestions outlined here would mean local initiatives could create integrated community legal services on a micro level. To function on a macro level, it is important to integrate these initiatives into a national strategy by correlating local developments into work carried out by the Law Foundation to develop technology, to carry out pilot projects and to share best practice between advisory agencies and the courts service. As mentioned above, the Ministry of Justice would play a supervisory role to ensure the effective progression of justice policy.

As a further point, it is essential that the franchising system be refocused away from compulsory competitive tendering and used to provide contracts to solicitors' firms and advice agencies who can demonstrate an ability to give advice and representation of a suitable quality. This would represent a move away from the requirement that solicitors' firms show they can manage the paperwork involved in litigation. Clearly, there is also a role for cost control in the setting of legal aid fees in this area.[16]

What is most contentious about the community legal service proposal is the very idea that such decisions should be made at the local level, rather than merely administered at that level in response to standard, national policy initiatives. This issue will be pursued in the following chapters. The term community legal service conjures up notions of advisory services made available to the public. The term 'community legal aid board' fits the picture more exactly, even though it is a little less catchy. To allow the service to expand its competence more broadly than the administration of public funds and their use to provide advice and representation, would be to confuse the cost control function with the policy development and democratic function.

The final dilemma, and the core problem in practical terms, is the democratic context considered above. If the community legal service is designed to serve a particular community then there is a problem of the manner in which it is to be made accountable to that community. The creation of legal services committees is expected to enable local people to participate in these decisions. However, the selection of such committees is likely to mimic the problems of the selection of magistrates and the appointment to police committees of citizens who are perceived as merely reinforcing particular political viewpoints or perpetuating social hierarchies. Simply linking the community legal service to local government is unlikely to increase the democratic content of legal aid funding beyond reflecting the success of pressure groups to ensure their concerns are reflected in spending priorities.

The answer appears to be to approach the issue from the

perspective of the activities undertaken by the community legal service. The priority of the service is to measure and administer the public funds available for these services. By integrating the services into a national strategy, it should be possible to measure the use of legal aid in each region so that typical budgets can be predicted for future years. The Law Foundation, considered below (p. 229), is the body, together with the Legal Aid Board centrally, which will pilot approaches to funding and the award of franchise contracts within each region. The service should set its budgets in conjunction with the central authority and after consultation with local government as to local priorities and existing advisory services on offer.

At this stage it is important to ask to what extent the civil service model of a community legal service is important, perhaps in parallel to the national legal service outlined in Chapter 8.

NOTES AND REFERENCES

1 Despite the ethos of magistrates' courts and county courts being responsive to the requirements of local justice.
2 T. Blair, *The Third Way*, Fabian Pamphlet 588 (London, Fabian Society, 1998).
3 See, Alan Milburn MP, 'Mapping the Third Way', Nexus Conference, 3 July 1998.
4 Although New Labour would be quick to dispel the idea that there are any heartlands after their 1997 landslide victory.
5 As considered in Chapter 5.
6 The term 'community' is clearly a fashionable one. The Commission for Social Justice, set up by the late Labour leader John Smith, indicated the need for an 'investor's Britain' in which institutions and citizens work together to enhance the growth of communities: see *Strategies for National Renewal* (London, Vintage, 1994). The term community has been used more broadly under the influence of Etzioni by the New Labour administration.
7 Labour Party, *Access to Justice* (London, Labour Party, 1995).
8 See the Appendix to this book.
9 Lord Irvine, speech to the House of Lords, 9 December 1997; www.open.gov/lcd/speeches/1997/adjn-deb.htm.
10 Labour Party, *Access to Justice* (London, Labour Party, 1995).
11 See the Appendix to this book.
12 The vertical/horizontal distinction has been considered on p. 155.
13 Albeit there is a level of means-testing currently before some benefits are payable.

14 Within the exceptions for cases such as defamation and industrial tribunal proceedings.

15 As considered in Part IV, *Components of Delivery, The judiciary*.

16 For an amplified discussion of this point, see the detailed proposals concerning legal aid on pp. 70, 145.

8

New Structures

A NATIONAL LEGAL SERVICE

The national legal service is suggested as a replacement for legal aid in many circumstances.[1] Rather than use public money to pay lawyers in private practice, it is argued that it would be more efficient and more socially useful to provide free legal advice to all who need it from lawyers employed by the state. A national legal service is therefore a civil service department made up of lawyers who will provide legal advice in the same manner as NHS doctors provide healthcare services. It is proposed in the first place to pursue the comparison between the NHS and the national legal service so as to examine the strengths and weaknesses of the proposal.

At one level the national legal service proposal is little more than a Citizens' Advice Bureau system where the advice workers are legally qualified and able to appear in all courts on behalf of their clients. This model is extended in some cases to include a Public Defender function. The Labour Party document, *Access to Justice*, makes it plain that there is no intention to create a national legal service within the remit of the community legal service:

> We are not intending to establish a salaried public legal
> service, but one in which a range of services is offered by
> independent providers. The franchising system will be
> improved and used to monitor and maintain high standards
> of service delivery and value for money. We do however
> envisage that over time the Community Legal Service will
> expand its employment of salaried lawyers with rights of
> audience in the courts so as to provide high quality,

affordable representation at lower cost to the taxpayer than the existing system.[2]

The national legal service could not simply adopt the Citizens' Advice Bureau model because a national legal service would be required to provide representation, as well as simply advice. Otherwise, it would be simply a Citizens' Advice Bureau or a law centre. At this level it is difficult to see what would be achieved by a national legal service beyond the mass employment of lawyers by the state. What is essential is that any form of national legal service satisfy the core policy goal of providing near total equality of access for citizens to legal remedies and assistance.

As to the criticism that the national legal service would merely operate as a means of employing thousands of lawyers, it could be said that the NHS does nothing more than provide doctors and nurses with guaranteed employment. However, healthcare is generally considered to be of greater significance than legal advice. That said, legal advice may, in some cases, relate to critical aspects of the individual's well-being such as, for example, cases as to housing or rights to particular forms of healthcare. What is more straightforward in relation to healthcare is the measurement of success or failure in most circumstances: in a medical scenario, the patient either becomes more or less healthy. In a legal case the litigant may become housed or divorced, and therefore the situation is capable of observation and measurement in terms of success or failure too. In many cases, the success or failure of the advice will be more difficult to measure in absolute terms. Depending on cases, the qualitative differences between the two systems are not always immediately obvious.

The huge attraction of the national legal service to a socialist is its rough approximation to the NHS. Alongside hospitals full of professionals retained by the state to help citizens without prejudice or favour, would be lawyers' offices and courts teeming with professionals retained by the state ardently ensuring that the liberties and responsibilities of its citizens were activated without prejudice or favour. The difference between the two is the nature of medicine as a science where needs and responses can be identified with much greater certainty, compared to the comparatively nebulous content of law. Typically legal argument requiring trial necessarily involves the interrogation of matters of fact and matters of the nature and content of the law. The diagnosis of illness, while requiring analysis and professional discretion, operates by reference to Cartesian, scientific principle.[3]

Structural problems with the national legal service

A number of questions arise. What happens in situations in which two citizens approach different officers within the national legal service in respect of the same case? The suspicion would be that bureaucratic inertia would operate in favour of early settlement of the dispute by means of negotiation between the officers concerned. Under the current system, the lawyer in private practice is more likely to take up the cudgels on behalf of the client and see the matter through to the bitter end. In many circumstances that lawyer will benefit personally from extended litigation. It is arguable that this vested interest causes extra cost and delay to the system of legal aid because lawyers will not see speed of completion as being the most important aspect of a case.

Alternatively, the consensual attitude of civil servants to allowing only triable issues to proceed to court has two potential problems. First, the civil servant comes to occupy a quasi-judicial role. If the civil servant lawyer strongly advises settlement or that the litigant refrain from action, that person is effectively denying a remedy to the claimant. It is true to say that lawyers in private practice occupy the same position but they are motivated by a desire to keep litigation alive if possible, rather than to dismiss it. From the point of view of the citizen, the private practitioner is more likely to work harder to protect her interests. Second, following from the first, the nature of the private practitioner as a 'hired gun' presents the citizen with a greater likelihood that she will be represented with as much gusto as is possible. To the extent that some private practitioners do not live up to these expectations, the combined effect of awards of franchises on grounds of competence and the operation of complaints proce-dures should weed out the ineffective lawyers. In terms of claiming against a civil servant, it is less likely that the citizen will be able to ensure the quality of service by direct contact than with a private practitioner. The example of the Crown Prosecution Service does not offer much hope for the operation of a dynamic cadre of lawyers in the public sector.

In terms of the generation of a market in legal services, the availability of legal services which are free at the point of use (or subject to minimal cost) would provide the 'budget' end of the market which is currently missing. Lawyers in private practice would be required to offer their services at reduced rates to encourage clients away from the free service offered by the state. Alternatively, lawyers in private practice would be required to offer specialist services not available from the state lawyers. If a national legal service were restricted to criminal defence work only, along the lines of a public defender system, this would leave private practice free to concentrate on civil work. If the national legal service expanded to offer housing law advice, or advice on access to state benefits, it would be left to private practice to provide the service for private clients in other areas of law.

On a practical note, the creation of a national legal service on any of these models would require the employment of many thousands of lawyers to meet the volume of service currently made available by lawyers in private practice claiming from the legal aid fund. It is difficult to see how standards would be maintained in this context in ways that are materially different from the current system of awarding contracts and ensuring the quality of advice given by supervizing the use of those franchises. In effect, the only difference would be that many of the lawyers currently in private practice, regulated by the body operating the legal aid system, would be employed directly by the state and provided with civil service pensions.

A summary of the objections

The objections to a national legal service are primarily twofold. First, there would a great increase in cost to the state of handling the extra claims and paying salaries to all the lawyers involved and managing the system. Given the current strictures on legal aid spending, this would appear to dismiss this proposal in practical terms. Second, there is no guarantee of the quality of advice. The experience of some national legal service-style programmes in the USA, for example, has been a haphazard ability to advise citizens effectively as to their rights because of a lack of time and expertise, and because of bureaucratic inertia to bring the sort of seemingly speculative arguments which a privately-paid lawyer would advance to protect a client. The 'dead hand' of the bureaucrats has been a great obstacle to such schemes in practice.

Viable uses of the national legal service

The national legal service proposal suffers from the breadth of its vision. The costs of introducing such an initiative are potentially prohibitive and there is no guarantee that the reform would automatically lead to tangible improvement in the lot of ordinary litigants. However, there is much in the strategy that is worthy of being pursued. The most attractive aspect of the proposal is the scope it offers on a national basis to provide advice and assistance to citizens, aside from the bureaucratic questions of controlling budgets and allocating public funds. The main drawback with the legal aid scheme is that it is restricted to cost control and public spending, there is little role for the public bodies to seek to direct the manner in which services are provided. Public bodies like the Legal Aid Board respond to demands made on it by the professions. There is no similar public body with particular responsibility for examining the manner in which specific services are delivered and best practice shared. The only public body in anything like this role is the Lord Chancellor's Department, considered below. Rather, legal aid is a state subsidy of private legal practice. The use of a national legal service enables a strategy to be created in which goals orientated around the strategic provision of advice services to the citizen can be generated.

Once the national legal service is expanded to such an extent that trained and qualified advocates are made available on demand to any citizen for any type of case, then different arguments obtain. That all citizens are able to defend litigation without fear of cost would enfranchise many more citizens. For those currently unable to gain access to justice through legal aid, it would remove many of the pressures on them to settle litigation. At that level the civil liberties aspects for reform are compelling. However, where the national legal service is extended to provide advice for anyone wanting to bring a claim (i.e., to act as plaintiff) without any concern as to the cost, the context changes slightly. Clearly, there is a public service available to all citizens which has great impact for the quality of citizenship.

As considered below, there are a number of other functions which the justice system must provide. Many of those tasks – public education as to legal rights and litigious procedures, the development of information technology as part of the advisory process, and the opening up of court buildings – are important tasks related to the management of public funds which fall outwith the role of the Legal Aid Board or possibly of the Community Legal Service. A national legal service strategy would enable the development of this type of idea, in tandem with the Law Foundation considered below, outside the limits of the cost management function.

The form of national legal service proposed would be closer to a national *advisory* service that co-ordinated more closely the work of Citizens' Advice Bureaux, law centres and local government advisory services. With the ever-growing scope of national and local government, bringing with it new forms of advice workers, counsellors, telephone help-lines and appeals procedures, there is a need to guide citizens through the maze of legal, quasi-legal and administrative methods of complaint, dispute and redress. A national advisory service co-ordinating these services seems the most effective mechanism for sharing resources in areas where Citizens' Advice Bureaux, local authority employees and law centre personnel are offering the same service.

The primary drawback with the national legal service proposal is that it focuses too much on lawyers and not enough on helping citizens. By looking at the needs of citizens, and accepting that that will include legal advice in some circumstances, it should be possible to bring together law centres, Citizens' Advice Bureaux and other advisers to share their own best practice, to develop their own national and regional centres of expertise and excellence. Just as some lawyers develop expertise in particular areas of private practice, so advice workers and lawyers in the public sector similarly develop expertise which should be shared on a national level between agencies. By building in incentives to national advisory service budgets to develop and promulgate efficient means of working (perhaps in tandem with the Law Foundation, below) the quality of the service as a whole is developed together with mechanisms for better serving the public.

The use of information technology and the generation of pilot projects are essential in this area. These ideas are developed below. However, before moving to those specifics, the issue of national co-ordination of legal affairs policy is one which still requires some consideration. In particular, the need for reform at the level of governmental accountability for the justice system.

A MINISTRY OF JUSTICE

The principal benefit of the national legal service strategy, as considered in the previous section, was identified as being the opportunity to co-ordinate policy in the justice system on a national level while developing better means of serving the public. The community legal service proposal focuses on local needs, within the context of a national strategy. The issue not yet considered in this discussion is the manner in which that national strategy is to be isolated. At present this is the task of the Lord Chancellor's Department. The patronage of the Lord Chancellor is something which has been considered in an earlier chapter. In relation to the conferment of awards and badges of achievement, both to the legal profession and the judiciary, the Lord Chancellor has complete competence. In the particular example of the Blair administration, the Lord Chancellor appears to be omnipresent. It is not a novel point to make to suggest that the office of Lord Chancellor creates the only ministry headed by an unelected politician. Aside from a junior minister[4] to carry the Lord Chancellor's bags in the House of Commons, there is little direct accountability within the Parliamentary system. It is ironic that the government department which is most closely connected to the operation of citizens' liberties seems to be the least accountable.

What is immediately apparent about the government of the justice system is that it is not the responsibility of one single department. The Courts Service and legal aid fall within the remit of the Lord Chancellor's Department. Within the purview of the Lord Chancellor personally are issues relating to judicial appointments (including the magistracy) and promotions within the legal profession. The Lord Chancellor retains an advisory body in relation to legal education and training. Of the advice agencies, the law centres are administered from the Lord Chancellor's Department too. Peculiarly, the budget for the Citizens' Advice Bureau system is administered by the Department of Trade and Industry. Issues to do with criminal justice, sentencing and prisons are administered by the Home Office – outwith the responsibilities of the Courts Services Agency. At present, there is a turf war between the Lord Chancellor's Department and the Home Office as to responsibility for juvenile justice, which is an even more important political issue given the rise in media interest in juvenile crime and in the family. It is then the Department of the Environment which has responsibility for local authority advice agencies and appeal procedures by means of guidance notes in support of subordinate and primary legislation, as well as direct bureaucratic control of certain aspects of local authority funding.

In short, there is a confusion of departments overseeing the access of citizens to their rights. The lack of a clear strategy in providing advisory, educational and representation services is bound up in the administrative duplication of tasks. This issue was considered in relation to advice agencies in Chapter 5. What is required for a progressive and effective means of giving advice to citizens, whether legal or otherwise, is the co-ordination of these services under a single, uniform structure. While there is a need for local government to retain responsibility for its advice and appeal procedures, there needs to be closer contact with other agencies. However, there is no justifiable reason for continuing the schism between the Citizens' Advice Bureau, law centre and private legal aid schemes. Indeed, given the political priority of cutting the cost of legal aid, it is likely that the only means of reducing the cost to central taxation is the integration of services and the sharing of costs. This integration issue, in relation to legal aid spending, is considered below.

There are therefore two problems arising from the current administration of the various justice responsibilities. First, the Lord Chancellor's Department is not fully democratically accountable.

Second, supervision is splintered between a number of departments. The immediate answer to both of these problems is the creation of a Ministry of Justice.

The creation of a Ministry of Justice

The Ministry of Justice was a long-standing commitment in Labour policy that was dropped in 1995 by the Labour Party and absent from its 1997 manifesto. As discussed in Part I, in respect of the Blair administration, there was discussion as to whether, in dropping this long-term pledge, much of the responsibility of the Lord Chancellor's Department for criminal justice should move to the Home Office. However, given the need for proper development of citizens' rights administration and dissemination, further breaking down the responsibilities of that department would militate against the efficient management of Labour's goal of greater democratic empowerment. The Ministry of Justice proposed here is therefore slightly different from the Labour Party's original proposal.

A Ministry of Justice as proposed under the leadership of John Smith, would have relocated the existing Lord Chancellor's Department into the control of a full Cabinet minister drawn from the House of Commons (and therefore elected), rather than from the House of Lords (and therefore unelected). In effect this would have constituted a retitling of the department. Significantly, though, the department would then have been subject to a ministerial question time, as with all other government departments, in which the Cabinet minister (rather than a junior minister) would be required to answer questions in the House. Furthermore, the new Ministry of Justice would have been shadowed by its own select committee, as is currently the case with all Cabinet departments. The intention was therefore to solve the problem of a democratic deficit in the administration of justice, and to use that department as a platform for progressive reform of the legal system, as outlined in Chapter 1.

A number of savings to central spending budgets could be made by integrating many of the duplication of functions. The second advantage would be in the quality of representation and advice that could be provided to the citizen by having the expertise that is currently dispersed made available through an integrated advice mechanism. While the process of making legal affairs and citizens' rights reviewable in the Commons is important, policy concerning Industrial, Social Security and other tribunals must be centred in one place so that efficient working practices, costs savings and better administration can be concentrated together. The binding together of these various bodies under one department should enable their independence to be enhanced in terms of industrial and social policy while their administration and support functions are improved.

The scope of the Ministry of Justice would be to look broadly at the following issues concerning access to justice from the point of view of cost, standard of service and the organization of the justice system.

Building an effective Ministry of Justice

The form of the Ministry of Justice as advanced here, builds on the John Smith proposal to address the second shortcoming identified above: the lack of a single administrative organ. The Ministry of Justice should take on a role that reflects the broadest sense of the term 'justice'. While there are historical complications with amalgamating law centres and Citizens' Advice Bureaux, there is no reason for duplication of effort, separation in their governmental administration, or a failure to share know-how. The activities of these agencies should be separate, in that the Citizens' Advice Bureau system provides general advice, which will often be specifically legal, whereas law centres provide specifically legal advice in particular subject areas, which may occasionally stray outside the legal area. Two similar structures would benefit from co-ordinated information technology systems, library resources and training. Given the complementary nature of the tasks which they carry out, there are obvious synergies for their activities.

This is one practical dimension to the Ministry of Justice, beyond the constitutional accountability issue considered above. Another dimension builds on the co-ordination of advice and is pursued in subsequent sections. In short, having introduced some local control over legal aid allocation, central control of franchise standards and co-ordination in advice work, the Ministry will need to develop ways in which these parallel agencies can best provide services to the public. Rather than keep advice agencies as a passive, responsive service, it is important to be pro-active in explaining rights and governmental policies to local communities. Much of this work is done by local government at the moment in terms of housing services, environmental health, individual healthcare initiatives and benefit entitlements. It is not enough to develop reservoirs of expertise in legal aid franchised private practitioners and public sector advice workers, simply to leave that knowledge passively in those bodies. The local community can best assess its requirements for community legal service budgets and local authority services if that information is disseminated among the population. The Ministry of Justice will therefore need to become involved in developing the best means of delivering those services through centrally controlled pilot schemes, including the collection of information from other jurisdictions or sharing information about initiatives within the UK, and enabling the transmission of that information to the public more generally.

The Ministry of Justice will therefore be an important department in support of the public initiatives of departments relating to health, social security, education, environment and trade and industry, without needing to become a major department of state in itself.

A LAW FOUNDATION

The innovative, developmental role of the Ministry of Justice would rely on combining governmental priorities with private and public sector know-how. The legal system, as the hub of the justice system, languishes under labyrinthine procedures and archaic ceremonies. The task of generating a legal system capable of delivering an effective code of human rights law and able to respond to citizens' increasing need for advice and dispute resolution, requires a body capable of looking broadly at the issues and developing new working practices. The suggestion is the development of a law foundation.

The law foundation is a model for a policy development unit which would exist independently of the Ministry of Justice. However, the work of the law foundation would be on subjects given to it by the Ministry or developed by it to satisfy requests made of it by the Ministry. Therefore, priorities such as the development of means of establishing local need for community legal service boards could be developed by the law foundation in chosen areas. It would be for the Ministry either to direct the models which the foundation were required to test or to permit it to formulate its own models (after consultation with appropriate bodies) to be researched and developed. The strength of the law foundation would be that it would draw existing agencies, private practice, and citizens' groups under its umbrella to carry out particular projects – thus ensuring policy-making through a public–private partnership. Funding the organization would be possible through professional sponsorship of its independent research and reallocation of some existing LCD research funding money, as considered below.[5] This body would also be able to draw on the expertise of the Judicial Studies Board in considering new developments. In effect, the foundation would become a legal services comparator of the work done by the Law Commission on substantive law reform.

A law foundation is a form of organization that has been used to great effect in other jurisdictions as a non-governmental means of examining the way in which the justice system operates and of creating pilot projects for new techniques in dealing with disputes. The British justice system is currently riddled with examples of inefficiency and waste. Little work has been done to quantify the extent of this problem, but on a purely anecdotal level there is a large amount of time wasted during litigation in preparing documents and waiting for a case to be listed. Court buildings are also under-used in many circumstances. Much of the ADR work could be conducted in court buildings when the courts are not sitting or in areas where there is capacity which is surplus to court requirements. There are clearly efficiency savings to be made in this area. Similarly, new information technology will require testing in an advice centre environment and integration into the court building infrastructure in many places so that the court buildings and the advice agencies continue to be brought closer together.

In such a structure, the co-ordination of the research work in this area and the pilot schemes that will be necessary for the above proposals to cope with the implementation of the Middleton and the Woolf Reports, would be the responsibility of the law foundation. By having the law foundation exist separately from the Ministry of Justice, it is possible for the profession, the advice agencies and consumer organizations to feed into the innovation process their individual concerns, and thus ensure that the justice system does not evolve in a way that is determined solely by civil servants or a central political agenda.

The cost of organizing pilot schemes would be relatively inexpensive, as has been shown in other Commonwealth jurisdictions. The law foundation does have the advantage of being an easily accessible source of publicity for innovative ideas and Labour government developments in justice policy. In practice, clearly, the law foundation would work closely with the Legal Aid Board, the ADR administrative function and the advice agencies, responsibility for which remain with the Ministry of Justice. The result is a strengthening of the partnership between the private and public sectors in advancing the work of the justice system at a low cost with the production of efficient and effective working practices.

The justice system must be reactive to the needs of the society that it serves. For too long the British legal system has been rigid and has set itself up against the needs of the citizen. This rigidity is epitomized by the cost and the length of time involved in any litigation. The legal system is not responsive to the needs of the citizen because it cannot change its own nature as circumstances require. The way in which the system can be made more responsive is to provide alternatives to the legal system in which people can receive the remedies they require at low cost. To develop appropriate alternative methods and to ensure that any forms of ADR are properly serviced, there must be a body that is independent of government control and which can oversee the justice system and monitor its progress and the quality of the service provided.

The New South Wales model

The idea of a law foundation is most clearly visible in New South Wales, where the model has been used to generate a large number of projects. It should be noted that the law foundation suggested in this discussion is more closely linked to the Ministry of Justice and that Australia has a better history of progressive initiatives than England and Wales.

The American, Canadian and Australian jurisdictions are more advanced in their use of a multitude of legal and quasi-legal agencies to develop access to justice programmes. The marketplace for information and computer-based technology in the USA is ahead of the UK generally.[6] In New South Wales, a network of Community Justice Centres provide advice for citizens in a number of specific contexts.[7]

The Law Commission

The Law Commission was created originally by the Labour Party and is seen by some as remaining an essential part of the process of educating people as to their rights. In fact its current role is that of a technical law reform commission, producing reports which are comprehensible only to the practitioner, not to the general public. The specific role of the Law Commission is to consider substantive areas of law and the way in which these should be reformed. The process of simplifying the law is essential in encouraging people to believe that they own their rights because those rights are clearly expressed and comprehensible to them. It has been suggested in Labour Party policy documents that the work of the Law Commission should be directed towards the means of achieving this project rather than simply the reform of technical rules.

One of the difficulties faced by the Law Commission has been making its voice heard. Its work has long been overlooked, with its proposals taking many years to be adopted into legislation. The adoption of the Jellicoe procedure in the House of Commons, to speech legislation through committee, together with the increased use of the House of Lords as a chamber in which purportedly non-controversial legislation can be commenced, has made it possible for more Law Commission draft bills to be considered by Parliament than was possible hitherto. The Law Foundation will enable the co-ordination of the results of its monitoring of the legal system with the tasks that the Law Commission is set. One body to produce the technical reform proposal, and the other to ensure the possibility of its smooth implementation in systemic terms. By networking these resources, the talent that is latent or active but disparately located, can be galvanized and used to work for the improvement of the rights of citizens.

CONTINGENCY AND CONDITIONAL FEES

The proposals made by Lord Irvine in relation to contingency fees have been considered in detail in Part III. The matter of contingency fees is often discussed in this area as a means of cutting the costs of legal aid. Contingency fees enable the litigant to meet the cost of legal fees entirely (in most cases) by paying a percentage of a damages award to the lawyers if successful, and nothing if unsuccessful. In personal injury cases, this enables many litigants to bring actions without worries as to meeting the legal bill. Alternatively, the 'conditional fee arrangement' has been proposed by the Middleton Review under which parties would obtain insurance to cover the cost of fees if litigation is unsuccessful.

There are a number of objections, however. First, a court awards damages to a plaintiff on the basis of her loss. Therefore, if the damages are to compensate the wrong suffered by measuring the size of the loss, there is no calculation to take into account legal expenses – that is the purpose of the costs award. To give away a part of the damages is to rob the plaintiff of a necessary part of the compensation for her loss. The result would be the alteration of the tone or manner in which litigation is conducted with out a corresponding increase in the quality of justice received by the citizen, with the danger of it worsening.

Second, contingency fees open the client to bartering with lawyers from a position of weakness. Third, contingency fees do not guarantee the increased representation of those whom the Labour Party would wish to see represented more. Indeed it is likely that only the high-profile defamation cases would attract the interest of the lawyers, rather than the benefits of representing those who have suffered small industrial injuries which may yet affect their ability to work.

Fourth, contingency fees only work in the case of claims for amounts of money. A claim to be housed on grounds of homelessness does not carry with it any award of money ordinarily. Therefore, there would be no possibility of contingency fees. Similarly, injunctive relief carries little likelihood of damages. Defending actions rarely carries any likelihood of damages awards, other than costs orders.

Contingency fees, therefore, cannot offer an entire answer. In many commercial cases, however, it is only the lawyers and the commercial litigants who stand to lose by the arrangement. In that context they should be permitted to enter into whatever arrangements they can negotiate between themselves.

Lord Irvine has accepted the case for conditional fee arrangements to cut the legal aid budget. It remains to see how he intends, in the detail of his proposals, to replace the welfare state benefit, legal aid, with a partial system based on insurance-based conditional fees for money damages claims. It would appear that the upfront cost required from the litigant to enter into conditional fee arrangements will exclude those who are unable to afford it. The solution would appear to be a concessionary, means-tested system as suggested by his lordship before the Home Affairs Select Committee.[8] It is difficult to see how this proposal differs from the provision of legal aid.

Legal insurance

Rather than rely on central legal aid funds, there may be circumstances in which it would be reasonable for some parties to take out insurance against successful litigation. Two contexts should be considered here: first, legal insurance as a complete replacement for legal aid and, second, as a support for a contingency fee system. The result would be that successful litigants would recover their costs from the insurance companies of those whom they have sued. One example of this would be potential polluters of water systems and air, as required in some jurisdictions in the USA. This alternative would be of limited impact on the legal aid budget because it cannot be guaranteed that the bulk of litigants would fall within legal aid eligibility guidelines, but it would have the effect of increasing the ability of citizens to seek equal access to remedies against corporations.

Lord Irvine has supported the availability of insurance for use by practitioners entering into conditional fee arrangements in claims for money damages. The proposals suggest that litigants should pay the cost of the premium to acquire insurance to cover the legal adviser for the risk of losing the litigation. However, no pilot schemes have been set up as yet, and insurers have shown reluctance to support the scheme in public. Aside from this practical problem is the further issue of litigants finding the lump sum to pay for the premium when they are already too straitened to afford legal fees.

One alternative is that the insurance-based system would be similar to the Japanese one of compulsory insurance for healthcare, or the German system of legal insurance. Common to all such systems is the notion that the citizen pays for private insurance through taxation. That insurance then pays for the whole of, or most of, the cost of any litigation. The state is required to provide the funds for those citizens who are unable to afford the increased tax burden, or do not pay tax at all. Issues then arise as to whether the insurance should entitle the citizen to choose a lawyer themselves, or whether they are required to use a lawyer appointed for them by the state. This brings in some of the arguments raised by a national legal service, considered above.

It is submitted that this proposal would constitute a reversal of the core policy of the 1949 Legal Aid Act and the welfare state motivation that lay behind it which is 'to make legal aid and advice more readily available for persons of small or moderate means, to enable the cost of legal aid or advice for such persons to be defrayed wholly or partly out of moneys provided by Parliament'.

Obtaining suitable insurance in the market would not necessarily guarantee that suitable advice could be obtained or paid for. It would rob the state of the ability to select priorities for state funding through the current legal aid system. The final objection is that legal aid is already paid for through central taxation, and therefore there is no need to increase the tax burden to pay for a new system. It would be better to make the current welfare state model (albeit a means-tested one) operate more effectively for the achievement of greater social justice.

There is an argument for investigating methods of legal insurance which would require certain types of litigant (such as companies dealing with environmentally harmful chemicals) to insure themselves against litigation as well as the risks of losing law suits. In the cases of drugs companies or large employers this would mean that the insured party would have the resources to pay for the costs and the damages of the other side. The next section explains how the procedural rules could be altered to enable citizens to sue those who have caused them damage without having to enter into a pessimistic cost-benefit analysis of their chances of success.

ACCESS TO LEGAL INFORMATION THROUGH NEW TECHNOLOGY

The introduction of groundbreaking new technology is one way in which the Labour government can achieve the twin objectives of empowering the citizen and cutting the cost incurred in consulting with lawyers. Systems pioneered in New South Wales and in Arizona, USA, enable courts systems and library facilities to educate the citizen as to her rights and the means of activating them, without the need for paying for a lawyer. This information technology resembles the system used by tourist authorities to enable visitors to locate points of interest and hotels. The citizen can follow a series of questions which locate the individual's complaint. Once the individual has decided which claim is involved, videos of proceedings can be screened which demonstrate the procedure before the requisite tribunal. The technology can also produce *pro forma* legal documents to cover the claim that the individual wishes to bring.

The extension of the availability of para-legals, supported by libraries of relevant materials in the current law centre setting, could assist the citizen in locating the type of claim that is to be brought and the way in which it can be conducted. This would enable citizens to access justice without the need for undue legalism. The operation of these systems would be overseen by the law foundation (discussed above), as part of its watching brief. Money raised from charitable donations could be used to fund the comparatively inexpensive pilot projects in the UK, which would mimic the work being done in other jurisdictions already. This will undoubtedly revolutionize the conduct of litigation by using technology that already exists.

The reorganization of law centres, Citizens' Advice Bureaux and the other private charitable organizations which offer similar services, is necessary to co-ordinate the scarce resources which exist in terms of equipment, reference materials and human expertise. The use of this technology would enable the advice agencies to offer a unique new service. It would also confirm the need for the training of para-legal personnel to ensure that they are able to meet the public demand.

The result of introducing new technology as a legal tool is that it would produce a net saving in legal aid by enabling litigation and legal redress to be conducted with a reduced legal representation that would normally require a high level of cost.

The use of technology in other jurisdictions

In Australia, information technology is available on a far more accessible basis than at present in England and Wales. Legal information in the UK remains restricted by the control of legal publishers in terms of texts and by Crown copyright over HMSO publication of legislation. Australia has a network of on-line advice, one such being Lawlink[9] which provides text on legal rules in relation to a list of common claims, such as divorce, noisy neighbours and contract claims. In the USA there is even more of this type of material available on websites, such as 'Free Advice'[10] and 'Law Guru'.[11] These American sites operate as a text base, giving information to anyone accessing the material, and also providing access to legal advice from specific law firms, and therefore acting as a means of gaining business from Internet users.

IT and the future of law

There has been some debate about IT as the future for large commercial firms; some consider it the tool of the millennium for the City solicitor practices. However, it does not provide much help for smaller firms who are unable to afford large amounts of information technology not tailored to their specific needs, nor does it help the individual litigant learn more about his/her rights. The thrall of the future, the first whiff of the white heat of technology, provokes a kind of literature that is excitable and drunk with possibility. Its premise is simple: information technology will revolutionize the way that *law can be done*. I accept that is an inelegant phrasing of anyone's core thesis but I think it is accurate. The 'way law can be done' is a subject that occupies Susskind.[12] As he says: 'it is argued that information technology will eventually help to engineer the entire legal process and result in a major change in the predominate ways that legal services are delivered and justice is administered'.[13] Perhaps that is even worse.

What lies beyond his analysis is the real nature of the English legal system. Eighty-five per cent of solicitors' firms in the UK have four partners or less.[14] The vast bulk of the English legal establishment is made up of small firms of solicitors dealing with problems brought to them by individuals coming in off the street. The majority of the legal system is concerned with the availability of legal aid. The central crisis facing the legal system is the lack of any feasible access to justice for the majority of the population. The core problem is not the use of IT in the system, but rather the question of access to the system at all.

To give Susskind the benefit of the doubt, his book is couched primarily in terms of 'what might become', rather than what is. Further, he has worked in a City legal practice for fifteen years and therefore his perspective is slewed in favour of commercial practice. What Susskind is not clear about it seems, is precisely *how* the extension of information technology will revolutionize law. Clearly, there are computers rather than electric typewriters in most legal offices now. The advantages of storage on disk are easy to see. What is not obvious is why using raw data from electronic rather than written sources *necessarily* makes lawyers more efficient. Output might be more efficient but input need not be.

The second opportunity seen by Susskind is that citizens will be able to be educated about the laws and their rights. He sees the end for the advisory role of the lawyer – changing the role instead into 'a form of information service'.[15] This presumes that information technology will have the effect not only of making law accessible but also of making the law simpler. This misses the obvious truth that making something available does not make it easier to understand.

Putting access to laws on the information superhighway will not solve an insatiable thirst for knowledge that people are presumed to have. All of this material is currently available in public libraries but there are not huge queues waiting for a particular volume of the *Weekly Law Reports*. This is the chimera that we are offered: putting something on a web page does not equate to educating the entire population. The lawyer will never simply operate as an information feed. The solicitor will not be replaced by the modem. Contrary to Susskind's utopian world view, lawyers will still need to explain citizens' rights to them. Citizens will still enter a lawyer's office with little idea that their *real world* problem is also a *legal problem* with a specific legal source of redress.

In this new world, there will be a reliance on law firms who can prepare legal materials on a variety of computer applications which are then made available to clients. This will only be possible for firms which are large enough to cope with this up-front expenditure (i.e., some of the 5 per cent of solicitors in the English legal system with more than ten partners). Similarly, they will need clients who will come into the building to seek out general legal information. Most citizens will not use this resource unless they have a legal problem. At that stage they will want *advice* from a lawyer and not a computer system proposing a menu of possible approaches.

Providing a law-based information superhighway on the level suggested by Susskind would require an enormous injection of funds that do not exist. No political party is prepared to increase the Lord Chancellor's Department budget by the volume needed to sustain such proposals. Putting all of the available statutory material on the Internet currently carries enormous copyright problems. Simply making that material available will not help decipher it. Lord Irvine's long-standing proposal that legislation itself needs to be made simpler is a necessary first step.

The other problem is that the legal profession itself will be required to make an enormous investment in information technology. For the big City firms this is a necessary part of economic survival in a market where everyone is wired up to e-mail. The opportunities offered by e-mailing across time zones such that documentation can be considered, redrafted and altered without needing to spend a day 'in typing' is a huge efficiency gain. However, it cannot be expected that there will be such dramatic changes in two partner firms of solicitors in, say, small towns. Those small firms are the majority of service providers in our legal system. The threats to their marketplace are not lack of information technology, as Susskind thinks, but the more recent threat of the introduction of compulsory competitive tendering or the challenges posed by the introduction of community legal service boards. The central issue facing publicly funded legal services in Britain today is the greater demand by citizens for access to new and broader social, economic and political rights. It is the legal system which has to bear the brunt of this in resources terms.

The only two sectors of society that are able to access our justice system at present are the very wealthy, or those who are entitled to legal aid. The majority of British citizens, typically those who are in work or who have only modest savings, are unable to access legal advice. The huge capital expenditure necessary to introduce information technology at the level proposed by Susskind will not address these core problems in the system. Therefore, we have to be concerned with the ability of citizens in their day-to-day lives to receive high quality advice and assistance. This stretches from the offices of barristers and solicitors to the incredibly valuable work that is done by Citizens' Advice Bureaux, law centres and voluntary agencies.

Undoubtedly, information technology has a part to play in this process. Susskind spends too little time considering the application of this technology outside a 'business' context.[16] What is important is to understand that information technology is a tool and not a saviour. The opportunity that is offered by the use of new technology is one of providing advice in a way that is comprehensible *to* the citizen and accessible *for* the citizen.

Too much of our law, and too much of the operation of the legal system in practice, is shrouded in mystery. Video technology used by advice agencies, offers us the opportunity to make that process more comprehensible and offers advice agencies the opportunity to share information and have greater access to it. The systems pioneered in New South Wales and in Arizona, USA, have enabled courts systems and library facilities to educate citizens as to their rights and the means of activating them, without the need for paying for a lawyer. These technologies are discussed only briefly by Susskind, and with a surprising hesitancy given their potentially huge application and very encouraging results in the USA.[17] Instead, he prefers taking accessible, tactile machines out of the advice agency front rooms and using computer-based systems. This defeats Susskind's own core aim: making all the systems a slave to computers requires a computer technician to operate them. The citizen is simply unable to use the very systems that are designed to improve citizen access to legal services.

Susskind's weakness in his argument is that he is concerned with a particular vision of the legal system that does not require explaining rights to citizens, nor does it see the need to educate rather than simply inform. The business of reforming the legal system does include provision of information – but it requires more fundamental work than that.

Integration with other agencies

The significance of new information technology is its role as a tool that can mean the sharing of data between the community legal service, the national advisory service and the law foundation. However, the development of information technology is frequently seen as an end in itself; all that it really offers is a new means of accessing information. The task which has yet to be performed is the creation of that information, in many circumstances. It is the content of the information which will be the success or failure of the project. Aside from the copyright issue, legislation can be transferred to a database without too much trouble. The value-added material would be the text that explains to citizens logging on to the database the content and nature of the available legal forms of redress. This combined with video examples of the tribunals in action means that the technology does offer the possibility of para-legals employed by advice agencies providing the initial advice to citizens as to the possibility of bringing a claim and the mechanism by which it is to be brought.

The development of information technology by the law foundation, in parallel to its increasing use by private practice, is an essential element of the educational function and also of the drive to provide a national advisory service capable of imparting information to citizens.

CODIFICATION AND SIMPLIFICATION

Examining the substantive law is a major part of the overall strategy. The simplification of litigation will reduce costs in itself. One example is that suggested by the Law Commission's finding, that in matrimonial cases there are many unnecessary allegations of adultery and unreasonable behaviour. If divorce were to be granted on consensual grounds, much of this unpleasantness and unnecessary cost could be removed. The money saved could be transferred to mediation projects which would help to remove matrimonial cases from the courts structure altogether.

Above and beyond the costs implications of simplification, there are the democratic advantages of making law easier to understand and access. The humane use of civil codes published at affordable prices and readily available in bookshops, enables citizens to know the core content of their rights and obligations. In the same way that many domestic bookshelves will have a dictionary, there is much to be said for the availability of a single volume containing the core rules of the English legal system. Mystification and systemic closure is the enemy of the democratic utility of law.

The Lord Chancellor's Advisory Committee on Education and Training should be co-opted into the Ministry of Justice framework to work on the quality of legal training and the ensuing quality of representation of the public. The work involved in this area would also involve a remit to examine the work of bodies like the Citizenship Foundation and to consider the means of introducing legal education into schools as part of education into citizens' rights.

EDUCATION

Together with a programme of greater simplification of the law is the need to educate the public as to their legal rights and, more practically, the means by which they can be advised about those rights. The very volume of law generated by central government through primary and secondary legislation, makes it impossible for ordinary citizens to comprehend the nature of their rights. All that is before the proliferation of caselaw which is generally beyond access by citizens unless they embark on a large amount of research, coping with complex legal texts and terminology. Smith deals also with the need for citizens to be educated as to the means by which they access tribunals and courts, once they have been educated as to the content of their rights.[18] The discussion of new information technology and the creation of a national advisory service would seek to address this shortcoming in the democratic capabilities of citizens.

RETHINKING LEGAL AID

An integrated approach

An integrated approach will look at the justice system in the round. There is no single replacement for a legal aid system funded directly out of taxation, by contributions from clients and through costs awards. There is no single, comprehensive system of justice provision in this jurisdiction or in any other which could replace legal aid in its entirety. The possibility of access by citizens to the system of justice is an essential right in any democratic country which should be provided as a priority, among other political priorities such as education and healthcare, out of central treasury funds. The question is: how can legal aid be provided differently in particular types of case so that the citizen receives an equivalent or improved form of representation and justice, in line with the basic principles outlined above? There are partial alternatives to the present legal aid system which, in particular instances, would offer suitable alternatives and generate costs savings over the life of a Parliament.

Labour is committed to the retention of the legal aid system. It is also committed to undoing the harm inflicted by the removal of civil legal aid entitlement for 14 million people in 1993, as part of a fifteen-year programme of reduction. The difficulties are twofold: the cost of simple legal aid provision, and the inappropriateness of many legal remedies. By seeking alternatives to legal aid provision out of central funds in the way that it is currently administered and by better budgeting it is possible to reduce the amount of the Lord Chancellor's departmental budget. By developing alternative remedies and continuing the programme of funding resources provided by non-lawyers, cheaper, quicker and often better quality justice can be provided to the citizen. The remainder of this section outlines some of the possibilities which Labour has developed together with members of the profession and consumer groups.

Will these alternatives produce a reduction in the LCD budget?

The answer is a qualified 'Yes'. The cost of legal aid will be reduced by increased use of ADR at the cost of producing more litigation, at least initially, which will require some investment in tribunal infrastructure. This financial cost is not expected to increase the present legal aid budget. It will have the palpable benefit of convincing many more people that they are empowered under a Labour government. The end result is expected to be that these reforms would be politically difficult to reverse. Franchising will enable the provision of central funds to legal aid work to be controlled by managing the levels of fees charged by law practices.

Inflows of money from the legal profession to a law foundation, whether mandatory or voluntary, will enable research and monitoring work that will produce medium-term cost benefits over the life of a Parliament. The examination of waste and unnecessary procedural rules will achieve reductions in the Lord Chancellor's Department budget. The centralization of tribunal functions in a Ministry of Justice will introduce new central funding resources which can be managed more efficiently.

There are aspects of the Lord Chancellor's Department budget which could produce costs savings in themselves. There was a shortfall in the take-up of criminal legal aid which was not reapportioned to the civil legal aid budget. There are costs savings to be made in the area of judicial services, which were identified during the passage of the Judicial Pensions Act in 1992, in the manner in which the costs of judicial services are controlled.

There are other cost savings which can be made by reference to the following principled alterations to the way in which justice is administered in the UK. By investing in the creation of a new type of justice system, more citizens can have access to it at lower incremental cost to central budgeting: producing a net reduction in the cost of providing justice for the individual citizen.

Answer: A Ministry of Justice

As considered in Part IV, it is vital that there is co-ordination between the legal profession, the judiciary and the broad range of advisory agencies so as to provide a unified means for citizens to gain access to information about their rights. The suggestion has been made that a National Advisory Service should be established to bring together the Citizens' Advice Bureau network, law centres and local authority agencies to provide services where private practitioners (through the legal aid scheme or otherwise) are unable to supply the public's needs.

Information technology matched with suitable training for advice workers will enable many more citizens to learn about their rights and to understand better the agencies from which they can receive practical advice about their protection.

The reform of legal aid must be seen in the context of these other developments. Through a Ministry of Justice it is possible to integrate legal aid advice by rationing the use of legal aid money to pay for legal fees associated with restricted forms of work. The decision as to which forms of work are to be covered by legal aid should be a political one given that it relates to the manner in which public money is spent. Similarly, political criteria to do with the accountability of the judiciary and the courts system ought to be introduced to ensure that litigants receive a service, rather than the current, arrogant subjugation of the citizen to the whim and ceremony of the wig and the bench.

To bring all of this together requires reallocating responsibility from departments of government to a Ministry of Justice that is democratically accountable through a select committee and a minister required to attend in the House of Commons to answer questions like other ministers. The developing politicization of the management of the justice system is to be encouraged because it enables a public debate about the manner in which the system operates, rather than the *laissez-faire* approach which leaves it to the lawyers and the judiciary to look after their own interests. Public scrutiny is a necessary step along the road to reshaping the justice system as a public service like the National Health Service.

NOTES AND REFERENCES

1 See, generally, the campaign of Austin Mitchell MP, and Cranston, 'Delivering Civil Justice: alternatives to Legal Aid', in *Law Reform for All*, Bean (ed.) (Blackstone Press, 1996), p. 59, *et seq.*
2 Labour Party, *Access to Justice* (London, Labour Party, 1995).
3 I am conscious that this distinction is a little rough and ready, but the point is made.
4 Promoted in July 1998 to Minister of State – although it is not clear whether this is a promotion for Geoff Hoon personally or an elevation in the office.
5 Some initial, unpublished research of these funding possibilities in 1995 indicated the probability of great enthusiasm for sponsorship without the need for firms to acquire influence or proprietary rights in any research, if the funding structure were allied to a *pro bono* professional qualification requirement.
6 See such websites as Legal Tech (www.legaltechshow.com) and the digital lawyer products (www.digital-lawyer.com), for the range of computer-based applications aimed specifically at lawyers in those jurisdictions.
7 For details see the Community Justice Centres website at www.nsw.gov.au.
8 October 1997.
9 On the New South Wales government website, www.lawlink.nsw.gov.au.
10 www.freeadvice.com.
11 www.lawguru.com.
12 Richard Susskind, *The Future of Law* (Oxford, Clarendon Press, 1996).
13 *Ibid.*, p. 3.
14 Law Society statistics, 1995.
15 Susskind, *op. cit.*, p. 3.
16 *Ibid.*, Part IV, pp. 105–49.
17 *Ibid.*, pp. 212–15.
18 Smith, *op cit.*

Part VI

In Place of Injustice

9

Citizen, Judge and the Public Sphere

This chapter's aim is to consider the role of the justice system in relation to the vast array of legislation which is dispensed through local government. A number of complex or expensive procedures have grown up around the access to rights which are the prerogative of local authorities. The complex procedures include the appeal procedures, required by statute in most instances, which local authorities create to hear appeals from those denied services or treated in unacceptable ways. Acquiring information about these procedures and proceeding through judicial review is an expensive and complex process. The prophylactic initial procedure to gain leave for judicial review, followed by the judicial review hearing itself, is an elongated procedure for those claiming benefits or services, when receipt of those benefits or services is critical on a day-to-day basis, let alone the month-to-month pace of the legal system.

This chapter will therefore isolate some specific instances in which the law muddies what appears otherwise to be straightforward legislation. More significantly, perhaps, it also explores a judicial reluctance to hold local authorities to account for the services which they are statutorily bound to provide, on the basis of *ad hoc* judicial policy to do with pressure on local government financing. The particular instances chosen relate to the much-litigated law on homelessness, an aspect of child law and the law on social security. These issues are central to the rights of many millions of people and yet they are only lightly analysed compared to the weight of words poured over developments in commercial and tax law. The justice system, while needing to address many of the issues to do with access, personnel and procedure discussed in earlier chapters, also needs to recognize the political content of the common law development of principles to do with local government law.

Homelessness

In Francis Fukyama's *The End of History and the Last Man*, we are encouraged to believe that our world will cease to have anything deserving of the name 'history' as a result of the victory of capitalism over state socialism. One of the great objections to this notion of a happy social equilibrium is the worsening of poverty across the world – and its alarming resurgence in the purportedly prosperous capitalist countries. That homelessness does not feature in many university law programmes, despite being the most litigated area of housing law in England and Wales, is perhaps symbolic of our consideration of it as something hidden. As Robert Wilson puts it in *The Dispossessed*:

> the true poverty opera takes place in the tiny rooms of
> council flats and houses. You have to get inside to see how
> bad it is. It is conducted in privacy.[1]

It is a fact of our society's approach to the homeless that they are a phenomenon removed from 'real life' as lived by most of our society. That attitude is identifiable in much of the case law in this area and in the Parliamentary debates about the housing legislation. There is a general consensus which runs from the Poor Law of 1530 through to the decisions of the House of Lords in 1997:[2] that is, that the poor do not have a stake in our society and are not deserving of any special favours from it. The poor have always suffered before the English courts. At one level they suffer because there is only a scrappy availability of access to courts via the legal aid system and a hotchpotch of tribunals which, typically, deal with the legal problems of this constituency of the rejected.[3]

Lord Brightman's speech in *Pulhofer v. Hillingdon BC*[4] was central to the development of the law relating to homeless people. His lordship took the view that, while local authorities had to find 'accommodation' for homeless people (in some circumstances, under the 1977 Housing (Homeless Persons) Act), that accommodation did not have to be 'reasonable accommodation'. The statute was deliberately altered in the wake of this decision to include a standard of suitability of the accommodation in the legislation. However, *Pulhofer* remains a seminal decision affecting the subsequent case law. It is seminal not because it represents current law but because the policy pronouncements which it makes still represent the underlying attitude of much of the current case law concerning the homelessness legislation.

The issue of the suitability of accommodation became the battleground between the warring permissive and restrictive interpreters of the homelessness legislation. The permissive school sought to encourage local authorities to live up to the letter of the law. The restrictive school sought to limit the scope of the authorities' obligations under the statute. Some of the early decisions, principally those of Lord Denning, sought to read in standards of appropriateness of accommodation. As a result of these decisions, local authorities would be required to live up to a spirit, identified by these permissive judges in the legislation, that homeless people are to be housed *suitably* wherever circumstances require it.

It is worth noting the accommodation that was being considered in *Pulhofer*. The applicants were a married couple with two young children who were provided with accommodation in a bed and breakfast guest house by the respondent local authority. The authority had provided them with 'occupation of one room at the guest house containing a double and a single bed, a baby's cradle, dressing table, pram and steriliser unit. There were three bathrooms in the guest house, the total capacity of the guest house being thirty-six people, or thereabouts. The applicants were in consequence compelled to eat out and to use a launderette ... This expense absorbed most of their state benefit of £78 a week'.

Lord Brightman found, with the unanimous support of the House of Lords, that the accommodation described was satisfactory 'accommodation' for the Pulhofer family. In Lord Brightman's view, the 1977 Act is an Act which saves the homeless from a lack of any help rather than imposing an obligation on local authorities to house them. In his words, while the Act had the word 'housing' in its short title, 'it [was] not an act which impose[d] any duty on a local authority to house the homeless'. Rather the Act was intended 'to assist persons who are homeless, not an Act to provide them with homes'. Lord Brightman was concerned, *inter alia*, that in the immediate wake of the introduction of the new legislation, the local authorities would not have had the time to increase the size of their housing stock to meet demand.

Significantly the purpose of the legislation, in Lord Brightman's opinion, is that it 'is intended to provide for the homeless a lifeline of last resort; not to enable them to make inroads into the local authority's waiting lists for applicants'. The local authority are required to 'balance the priority needs of the homeless on the one hand, and the *legitimate aspirations* of those of their housing waiting list on the other hand'. The homeless are therefore categorized by Lord Brightman as the undeserving poor. They are not identified as having 'legitimate aspirations' of their own to be housed. The homeless do not have equal rights to other citizens for consideration in housing terms. On the one hand, there are those with legitimate aspirations, and on the other hand there are the homeless who impliedly lack such legitimacy.

The recent House of Lords decision in *Awua v. Brent LBC*,[5] in the leading speech of Lord Hoffmann, explicitly approves much of what is said in *Pulhofer*. Lord Hoffmann distinguished between the time for which accommodation was offered and the quality of that accommodation. With reference to the time for which accommodation was offered, he held that it need be neither permanent nor settled, provided that it was 'accommodation'. Further, he conceded that the legislation introduced after *Pulhofer* had reversed the precise ratio decidendi of that judgment but that the underlying approach of *Pulhofer* was nevertheless correct.

It would, of course, have been possible for Lord Hoffmann to hold to the contrary: that accommodation could not be suitable where it was only offered for a short period of time. Lord Hoffmann's decision means that accommodation which is made available for only a short time will be more likely to be considered suitable because the applicant need only occupy it for a short while. The opposite view is that the homeless applicant needs some secure accommodation and therefore the authority should not be allowed to avoid its obligations by offering only short-term accommodation. In this writer's opinion, *Awua* continues a judicial tradition in the higher courts of seeking to limit the utility of the accommodation which must be provided to the applicant.

This test mirrors the approach taken in *Pulhofer* that the court may be concerned about the impact on local authority housing stocks of any decision that is made. A claim as to whether or not the authority has been rational in its decision-making in this context is therefore necessarily delimited by the broader exigencies of the housing management function. This is a movement away from the use of objective standards of what does and does not constitute compliance by local authorities with their statutory obligations. Consequently, the ability of the applicant to assert that accommodation is unsuitable will be reduced in an area where there is great pressure for public sector housing. Lord Hoffmann identified as merely 'inconvenient'[6] the result that *Pulhofer* required applicants to put themselves on to the street before they would be homeless because unsuitability of accommodation was not ground enough to make them homeless.

Further, Lord Brightman in *Pulhofer* considered that those people who were contending that they were homeless should only be allowed to commence judicial proceedings in 'exceptional cases'. (This was at a time when judicial review was the only remedy available to applicants.) This statement constituted the effective withdrawal of the ability of many people to access their rights under the homelessness legislation. It is hoped that the new appeals procedure introduced in the 1996 Act will enable applicants to question decisions without the complication of judicial review proceedings and without needing to cross the barrier erected in the way of access to those court remedies.

This attitude has been promulgated by a similarly constituted House of Lords in *O'Rourke v. Camden London Borough Council*[7] where the plaintiff had applied to the defendant local authority to be housed on leaving prison, under the terms of the homelessness provisions of the Housing Act 1985. The plaintiff sought to be housed, *inter alia*, on the basis that he was in priority need. The local authority provided him with temporary accommodation and then evicted him on the basis that he was not, in their opinion, in priority need.

The plaintiff brought an action for damages for unlawful eviction without provision of alternative accommodation, as required by Section 63 of the 1985 Act. The county court judge struck out the plaintiff's claim on the basis that it disclosed no cause of action – the only course, in his opinion, being to bring proceedings for judicial review of the defendant local authority's decision. The House of Lords followed *Cooks v. Thanet D.C.*[8] and took the view that it was unlikely that Parliament had intended the legislation to create private law rights of action in favour of the plaintiffs. Therefore, he was not entitled to damages for wrongful eviction.

The plaintiff argued that the legislation sought to provide protection for a limited class of person and therefore ought to be construed as creating a private right of action. The defendant contended, successfully, that the legislation ought to be construed as being enforceable in public law by individual homeless people who then have *locus standi* to bring judicial review proceedings. In the words of Lord Hoffmann, delivering the leading judgment: 'the Act is a scheme of social welfare, intended to confer benefits at the public expense on grounds of public policy'.[9] The view is that it is public money which is being spent to house homeless people on the grounds of 'general public interest'. The judiciary is abstracting to itself, again, the power to identify that public policy.

While it is true to say that local authorities are acting in their public function when they exercise their powers under the housing legislation, it is difficult to see why this should excuse them from private law claims which would obtain against a private landlord simply because the wrong was committed while performing its statutory function. It is submitted that there is no external factor, in the context of housing the homeless, which ought to excuse the local authority from this liability. Unlike cases of *force majeure* where governmental powers are exercised *in extremis* (as under war condi-tions), the local authorities should be required to refrain from committing civil wrongs, such as wrongful eviction, or face the usual civil penalties in damages when they do.

The second reason for Lord Hoffmann's excuse of the local author-ity in *O'Rourke* was that the authority was required to exercise a large degree of judgement by the legislation, in a way that made his lordship reluctant to impose the usual civil penalties on the public body in the ordinary course of their activities.[10] Again, local author-ities are excused strict liability on the grounds of the perceived scope of their responsibility. Failure to impose a scheme of stricter liability in the courts simply enables local authorities carrying out their duties in a less rigorous fashion.

The ancient legislation, and even that of the nineteenth century, referred to the homeless as 'rogues and vagabonds'. The Poor Law passed in 1530 aimed to licence begging and to 'outlaw vagabondage by the imposition of severe punishments'. The Vagrancy Act of 1824 was enacted 'For the punishment of idle and disorderly Persons, and rogues and vagabonds, in that part of Great Britain called England'. A disorderly person was defined in Section 3 as including 'every person ... placing himself in any public place ... to beg or gather alms'. Section 4 empowered to the courts to sentence 'incorrigible rogues' in this context to imprisonment or hard labour. Thus, the poorer you were, the greater the punishment you faced.

It is important to note that the 1824 Act had been introduced at the time of enormous social unrest with the reformist agitation of groups like the Chartists and the utilitarian zeal of the Benthamites. Street-level agitation caused by the new poor in the new industrial towns was the heart of the problem. Incarcerating people begging on the street fitted into a pattern of combating street-level activity with physical force. Similarly, the 1935 Vagrancy Act was enacted during the Great Depression at a time of agitation and profound economic hardship. Criminalizing and marginalizing those who are most poor has established itself as a feature of British history at times of social upheaval and economic difficulty.

Therefore, it is ironic that, just as Fukyama is reading the runes for the 'End of History' and victory of capitalism, our courts are working overtime once again to deny the indigent poor access to social resources, as economic insecurity begins to rise in the wake of the global recession of the early 1990s. The English courts have fallen back on to notions of the 'undeserving poor'. The disturbing fact of the law on homelessness is that such attitudes are not confined to blather of the Elizabethan Privy Council that introduced the Poor Law but also underpin judicial decisions in the 1990s.

Children in care

The judiciary's permissive approach to the elasticity of local government obligations can also be seen in the context of their responsibilities to children in their care. In *Barrett v. Enfield London Borough Council*[11] the plaintiff had been in the care of the local authority from the age of ten months. In the following seventeen years, the plaintiff was moved to nine different homes and sought to bring an action against the local authority claiming damages in respect of the development of psychiatric illness caused by the frequent re-locations. The plaintiff claimed that the local authority had failed to show the standard care that would be expected of a responsible parent. This standard of care was said to include an obligation to plan for the child's future as well as an obligation to ensure the plaintiff's security and to provide suitable social workers.

The Court of Appeal held that it would be contrary to public policy to impose a duty of care on a local authority in this situation. The reasoning was that the obligation would have had to be fixed in relation to decisions which ordinary parents are required to make on a daily basis. The Court of Appeal held that, on the basis that it would be unreasonable to impose the obligation on ordinary parents, such an obligation could not be imposed on local authorities standing *in loco parentis*. The Court of Appeal accepted that liability could attach vicariously to the authority in respect of social workers' negligence in implementing local authority decisions. Oddly, the Court of Appeal also accepted that this would create a liability for the local authority where its officers negligently implemented a policy but, seemingly, it would not create a private civil liability for the local authority for failing to have a policy or for having a negligent policy. In the latter case, the only redress would be by judicial review.

A social security example

Circumstances where individuals are reliant on state benefits do not offer any buffer against legalistic, overly-subtle distinctions between those who are, and those who are not, entitled to receipt of benefits. In joined appeals before the House of Lords,[12] the applicants sought attendance allowances in respect of 'frequent attention throughout the day in connection with bodily functions', further to the Social Security Contributions and Benefits Act 1992.[13] F was deaf and required an interpreter to use sign language to communicate with others. It was held that the inability to hear and the requirement for an interpreter arose in connection with a 'bodily function'. In the court's view, the frequency with which the attention was required depended on the need to enable the applicant to live a 'normal life'.

C was incontinent and sought the benefit in connection with the cost of her daughter cleaning her laundry. C's daughter collected the laundry, took it away, washed it, and then returned it to C. The majority opinion of the House of Lords was that there was no 'attention' within the statute because the laundry was *taken away* to be washed. The practice of taking the washing away could not be 'frequent attention' designed to assist the claimant with her bodily functions. Therefore, C's claim was dismissed, while F's claim was upheld.

The distinction between these cases is extremely narrow. C's requirement for attention was equally directly as a result of a mis-performing 'bodily function'. However, benefit was denied where the aid is provided by alternative means. The court did not consider the need which had to be met by the benefit, but rather the means by which the benefit was being met. 'How' was elided with 'why'.

Conclusion

The conclusion drawn from this necessarily brief survey is that local authorities' statutory obligations are not being enforced by the higher courts in a way that imposes strict interpretations of those duties on them. The reason for this drift in judicial largess is an informal development of policy based on an assumed scarcity of local authority resources and a concomitant reluctance to overstretch social welfare budgets.

This policy is ill-informed and, worse, it is straightforwardly unconstitutional. There can be no doubt that judicial policy-making in the area of local government obligations amounts to legislation by the back door. Policy pronouncements in Supreme Court decisions are made without any expert knowledge of local government financing. Moreover, deliberate curtailing of statutory obligations constitutes an infringement on the intention of Parliament with reference to the provision of social welfare services. Judicial attitudes to local authority obligations under statute therefore impact directly on individual citizens' access to social welfare benefits.

NOTES AND REFERENCES

1 R. Wilson, *The Dispossessed* (Picador, 1992), p. 52.
2 See *O'Rourke v. Camden London Borough Council* [1997] 3 All ER 23.
3 For a detailed analysis of the law relating to the homeless, see Hudson, *The Law on Homelessness* (London, Sweet & Maxwell, 1997), generally.
4 *Pulhofer v. Hillingdon BC* [1986] AC 484.
5 *Awua v. Brent LBC* [1995] 3 All ER 493.
6 *Ibid.*, p. 497.
7 *O'Rourke v. Camden LBC* [1997] 3 All ER 23.
8 *Cooks v. Thanet D.C.* [1982] 3 All ER 1135.
9 *Ibid.*, p. 26.
10 *Ibid.*, p. 26.
11 *Barrett v. Enfield LBC* [1997] 3 All ER 171.
12 *Cockburn v. Chief Adjudication Officer; Secretary of State for Social Security v. Fairey* [1997] 3 All ER 844.
13 Specifically ss. 72(1)(b) and 64(2)(a).

10

Conclusions: In Place of Injustice

Not even the apparently enlightened principle of the 'greatest good for the greatest number' can excuse indifference to individual suffering. There is no test for progress other than its impact on the individual. If the policies of statesmen, the enactments of legislatures, the impulses of group activity, do not have for their object the enlargement and cultivation of the individual life, they do not deserve to be called civilized.   *Aneurin Bevan,* In Place of Fear[1]

The constitutional settlement

The English legal system is proof that there is no truly democratic settlement in the UK. At the root of the British constitution is an understanding in the 'rule of law'. An assertion, in Dicey's terms, that no-one is above the law, that the law should apply equally to everyone, and that the role of law is to regulate the relationship between the individual and the state. I say it is 'an assertion' because, in truth, it can be nothing more than that. For the majority of citizens in the UK it is impossible to gain access to justice through law or quasi-legal forums. To maintain that there is a theoretical entitlement to equal treatment before the law is nothing more than a chimera which serves to shore up the legitimacy of an undemocratic system.

These are unpalatable truths for a nation that prides itself on a Parliamentary democracy which it brandishes as a model for the rest of the world. This is despite the decrepit working practices of the House of Commons, inherited from a time before the right to vote was extended to women, and the House of Lords' embodiment of the legacy of inherited wealth and status through the hereditary voting privilege. These are not the democratic structures of a democracy about to enter the twenty-first century. They are the relics of British history and, in tune with the climatic of marketing and service industries, a model of heritage theme-park politics.

The reality of the situation is that legal advice is available only to those with the wherewithal to pay for it. Legal aid for civil claims is available to those on income support levels of income only. It is proposed that that scheme will be removed and replaced with

256

conditional fee arrangements, requiring the citizen to negotiate a fee with the lawyer to be deducted from his/her winnings, if any. Therefore, only those with large enough claims will be able to acquire such agreements. Legal aid for criminal claims is still broadly available.

In Hutton's analysis of the British social class system, society can be divided into those who are financially insulated and comfortable, those who are in work but not comfortable, and those who are reliant in some part on benefits and not at all comfortable. In terms of access to democratic, rather than economic, freedoms, there are those who are able to access legal advice (corporations and affluent individuals), those who are eligible to receive legal aid (the socially disadvantaged on benefit levels of income), and the remainder who are working families not eligible for legal aid but unable to afford lawyers' fees for litigation.

It is worth considering in more detail the last category from Hutton's 40:30:30 society as applied to law. There is a shortcoming in a society in which the majority of its people are unable to gain access to the justice system so that their democratic rights can be put to work. The citizen who suffers in this situation is typically a person in work who has a dispute. That dispute might be a conflict with a neighbour or a complaint against treatment by an employer, it might be contested access to a governmental service or issues arising from family breakdown. Out of necessity, the person with a dispute will seek assistance from an outside agency. That is the first step in democratic empowerment, before having the ability to act is the need for knowledge in what action is possible. The citizen requires information: what action can be taken? Who can advise me on that action? How do I act? What are the implications?

For most citizens, problems of this sort will present, first of all, a powerlessness such that legal action is not possible. Unless the citizen is able to access advice or legal representation, no action will be possible. This book has considered the broad range of legal and non-legal advice mechanisms which are open to the citizen. The theme that has run through the discussion in this book, has been that these issues are fundamentally political. It is a political question whether or not citizens are empowered by making access to justice possible. It is a political question deciding what public resources are to made available. Citizens require this access to rise from being 'subjects' in a monarchical system of political power, to being 'citizens' of a mature democracy. For most citizens access to legal advice is an impossibility as a result of cost, delay and complexity.

The result is that those people who deserve to feel a part of society through their employment or familial status, are in fact disenfranchised from the logic of our putative democracy: that all are equal under the rule of law. This farcical social arrangement requires a strategy for its implementation through universal access to justice. Without the possibility of universality of *access*, let alone uniformity of outcome, the British constitution cannot be said to be the foundation of a functioning democracy. As British politics wakes up to the democratic deficit in our society, made flesh in terms of increasing social exclusion, our citizens are alive to the shortcomings in their liberty and the absence of a vibrant communal spirit which will support our individual, familial and societal aspirations. What is needed is a different understanding of the term 'democracy'. Democratic rights must be seen as extending beyond the ballot paper to an ongoing right to challenge and to shape the legal context in which the British polity sets out rights and responsibilities. Such a form for democratic rights can only be said to exist in circumstances where citizens can put those rights to work. To do that they need education, advice, and frequently representation.

The individual in relation to the social

At the heart of the debate about access to social justice is the relationship between the individual and the social. The debate about a 'third way', which currently occupies the collegiate mind of the centre-left in Western politics, is based on the nature of the relationship between the individual and the state. This debate has crystallized in a new understanding of the way in which public services and the state must be responsive to citizens. What has yet to be embraced wholeheartedly is the need for an honest discussion of the political dimension to setting priorities. Simply to talk of an active citizenry 'making it plain what their requirements are' will not help governments choose between the various courses of action on offer. Rather, it is important that *politics* is the arena in which social priorities are debated and public resources allocated. Access to effective justice offers citizens one important means of challenging iniquities in the administration of those priorities or in resolving disputes with other people as to those or other social goods. However, that right to challenge is only useful as a means of contesting and debating with an executive decision. In deciding how to allocate the legal aid budget, there ought to be a clear decision about the cases which are to be supported by the state. Allied with that is the need for a discussion about how much the state is prepared to subsidize lawyers' fees to conduct particular kinds of work.

In the passage from Bevan quoted at the beginning of this chapter, an important facet of his vision of democratic socialism is developed.

This book's discussion of equality in Part II, uncovered the acceptance by bodies like the Commission for Social Justice that it is possible to have justifiable inequality in society. This stands in opposition to the welfare state commitment to universal benefits. Bevan focused on the relationship between the individual and the state, and the need for socialist institutions to ensure that the position of the individual is not sacrificed in the cause of creating structures which have utilitarian appeal. Within welfare state socialism it is important to hit a middle line between the individual's potential for self-improvement and the broader context of providing for social need.

Law – incorruptible or incorrigible?

> Here one comes upon an all-important English trait: the respect for constitutionalism and legality, the belief in 'the law' as something above the State and above the individual, something which is cruel and stupid of course, but at any rate *incorruptible*.
>
> George Orwell, *The Lion and the Unicorn – Socialism and the English Genius*[2]

Orwell outlined the instinctive affection of the British citizen for 'the law', typically rendered in inverted commas. Like the constitution, 'the law' is understood to be a good and necessary thing, but it remains beyond precise definition. It exists in symbolic presentations of its power – in today's world this means photographs of elderly men in wigs or newspaper reports of judicial sentences. It occupies an ideological place which is bound up with a veneration for law as something necessarily correct because it has the legitimacy to speak. This is despite the effort which is expended in satirising it. Stories of judges who do not know the household names of pop stars and footballers are a staple of tabloid newspapers. There was the classic *Not the Nine O'Clock News* sketch which played up the supposed hidden life of public school educated judges, in the portrayal of a Crown Court judge who had never heard of video recorders or personal stereos but who could identify with great precision a particular brand of sex toy. The law is also represented in a plethora of TV series about criminal barristers or police officers – sometimes presented as staid and traditional (*Rumpole of the Bailey, Kavanagh QC*) at other times as young and sexy (*This Life, Blues and Twos*).

However, the power of the law is far more pervasive and deep-rooted than that. Law is the logic which underpins every action. Hardly a human interaction passes without being capable of some legal analysis of the rights and obligations created or abrogated. The result is that each right or obligation is capable of enforcement by lawyers and judges. In Foucauldian terms, this is truly power because it is exercised in the detail of our lives, frequently without our knowing it, and has claims to its own self-generating legitimacy. It is in the language of law, as Foucault says, that power is exercised and discussed. The language of law is important because it is the law which tells us that certain things are so. Property rights are only organized in the way that they are because our discourse about property rights, and in particular the law of property, says so.

The same point can be made about the lawyers who people 'the law'. Their words and opinions become powerful texts in the allocation of power. Orwell's sentiments rest on the acceptance of the incorruptibility of law. It is no accident that one talks of legal 'rights', a word which operates both in the sense of 'entitlements' and in the sense of 'assertions of truth'. The power of the lawyers remains in their own restrictive practices. The allocation of work between the solicitors' branch of the profession and the barristers' branch was the result of historical accident as other forms of legal professional (such as the serjeants, attorneys and scriveners) disappeared from the Dickensian England of *Bleak House*. The ceremonial forms of dress and address in which the Bar and the judiciary perform their roles continue to dominate not only court proceedings, but also the way in which all lawyers are required to talk about law. The common law system means that 'the law' can create its own language within its own closed system and thus manage its dissemination into society more broadly.

The control of the legal aid fund by the Law Society, and the professions' constant reaction against proposals for change, have kept the citizens at a distance from access to conversation about their rights. A closed professional system has managed to keep prices high. The allocation of tasks between lawyers and non-legal professionals has resulted in a situation in which all the public money available for use in the justice system is applied to paying private lawyers' fees from taxpayers' funds via the legal aid scheme.

The most welcome trend in recent years has therefore been the developing politicization of the way in which the use of public money is to be organized. The growing power of the Lord Chancellor's Department, bringing control of more and more of this debate under its own provenance, is to be celebrated to the extent that it results in a department of government treating the use of public money as a political issue about citizens' rights. However, the ultimate political responsibility for this system must be placed in an elected Cabinet minister and organized under a Ministry of Justice.

Adoption of concepts into legal language brings them to life. This is why the access to the language and to the discourse of the content of legal rights and responsibilities is so important for citizens. Unless we can speak of our rights and challenge the law's conceptions of them, we are unable to shape them. At the heart of the third way for an empowered citizenry operating within permissive social structures, it is essential that the promulgation of this discourse through law is permitted. Ensuring that the needs of the individual are not lost within an ideological drive towards the greater economic good, as was the case in the Thatcher years, that individual must be empowered. The issue is then creating the necessary structures to ensure that access to discourse.

Modelling the future

The development of a Ministry of Justice is, then, the next step in bringing together all of the agencies and resources (human as well as financial) to advance the democratization of society through a responsive and accessible system of justice provision. In Part II, a survey of the fundamental principles of the new programme was attempted. The resultant core values revolve around several key principles. Equality is the main objective of any left of centre political project. In the rhetoric of New Labour it is a goal which has lost it primary status although it retains a place. Tony Blair talks of individuals having 'equal worth'[3] whereas Giddens seeks a more prominent position for notions of equality. In coming to the notion of equality in relation to law, it is comparatively easy to decide that all citizens ought to be equal in terms of their access to the legal system, to legal advice and to tribunals. It is a fundamental aspect of social justice that there be equality of access to the legal system and it satellites.

At present, there is not equality of access, nor is there a reasonable distribution of forums in which law is discussed and through which it is disseminated. The issue of legal aid being available on unequal terms to only the very rich or the very poor means that the current system is failing the populace. The courts themselves are structured with the interests of the lawyers and judges in mind. Archaic ceremonies surrounding dress, forms of address and the procedures for conducting litigation perpetuate this inequality of access. The remedy is in the establishment of a national advisory service, creating access to advice and assistance on everything from local authority services to technical legal problems. This twinned with the development of a national legal service to support the work of advice agencies would mean that best practice and expertise could be shared around the system. The result would be greater equality in the ability of citizens to know about their rights and the means for redress.

Bound up with this allocation of ability to access advice, assistance and representation is the allocation of power. The present legal system claims the right to speak authoritatively about moral, political and other issues in society. Thus to be outwith that system is to be without power. Citizens who cannot access the legal system are effectively disenfranchised. There is then a hegemony in favour of those who speak through the legal system. Moral questions are resolved into a language of lawfulness and unlawfulness in which a prevailing ideology of what is acceptable and not acceptable is promulgated. The question of access cuts to the very heart of what it is to be a democratic society. The exclusion of some ensures they have no stake in the New Britain which the third way would otherwise seek to forge.

Where there is a hegemonic distribution of power through the legal system in favour of the lawyers and those who can bring their claims to law, the only possibility of change is to overthrow that system or to develop a new means of allocating those rights through discourse. Law becomes a means of communicating about the content of rights and responsibilities. The justice system is the place that makes this form of communication possible. An inability to communicate, or an obstacle to communication, constitutes a hazing of that discourse. In a world where communication is ever more important as economies expand, as communities are formed on a broader basis, drawing together the means of promoting connexity becomes a task for the justice system. Among the many effects of globalization are the commonality of goals, of attitudes and of needs.

There is a new form of politics required to reflect and to shape this massive movement of ideas and actions. A responsive justice system is one of the most important, flexible ways of permitting individuals and groups to communicate about their mutual rights and responsibilities in a legitimate forum. Such a system makes that communication possible. It is this writer's view that closed social systems would tend to disturb the free flow of such ideas and activities, requiring them to be channelled through a predetermined, narrow form of discourse. Thus a legal system hidebound by tradition and inflexible ways of thinking seals itself off from other social systems, promoting systemic irritation. More significantly, however, it allows individuals to be relegated in a game of social systems working out their respective modes of communication. Ours is a society of increasing chaos and complexity in which the justice system must respond equally to all, accepting all into its portals to hammer out their respective interests, obsessions and needs. Social justice can only be promoted through this humane activation of discourse where one is truly equal with another in bringing concerns to law.

Towards a just society – a map

The proposal for the remit of a Ministry of Justice is the culmination of a much more fundamental conversation about the nature of British democracy. At the outset of this book, the approach was taken that British society remains in a pre-modern state with regard to its justice system. Contrary to the modernist line, it is not possible at this stage to create a just society. First, the means by which social communication and democratic enfranchisement are to be facilitated need to be put in place. This requires a justice system that works more effectively than the present antiquated system, and a cluster of satellite advice agencies and tribunals. Through these new structures it is possible to give citizens, whether individually or acting collectively, the ability to move towards a just society.

The Ministry of Justice would enable the legal system to be scrutinized as a political entity as in the case of healthcare and education. To tie the citizen into this process it is vital that the means of providing advice and assistance are made accessible to the many and not simply the few. Legal aid must not disappear down the route of contingency fees as this would result in a reduction of the service. Individuals would as a consequence be forced to become speculators on their own success, with the insurance premium as the stake. For many, this would act as a straightforward deterrent from litigating in the first place. In any event, it would not pay for initial consultations with lawyers. Contingency fees are a retrograde proposal which should be avoided, except in the case of those who are financially secure enough to decide it is a viable option.

Block contracted legal aid runs the risk of becoming merely another form of withered public service which is extended as a form of welfare benefit, as is increasingly true of healthcare, to those who cannot afford to litigate privately. The introduction of block contracting requires a laudable political element in deciding the forms of litigation which public money ought to help. Its downside is that it breaks completely from legal aid as a universal welfare state benefit. The democratic cost is the restriction on citizens who are therefore able to come to law. The financial cost will be a legal aid bill at the same level at present but providing help for fewer citizens.

The way of breaking out of this vicious circle is to look at the problem of legal aid from the angle of the citizen. The primary goal of legal aid is to serve the citizen. The difficulty with legal aid funding is that lawyers' fees are, in many cases too high. While caps are being placed on criminal practitioners through standard legal aid fees, matrimonial law practitioners are charging much higher fees and absorbing one third of the total legal aid budget. The logic of deciding on the types of case for which legal aid ought to be available and the level of fee which should be paid for certain types of legal work, would enable the justice system to require that some issues are reserved exclusively for mediators and that the money saved in lawyers' fees is reapplied to enable more people to come to justice.

It is the lawyers who are stripping this money from the legal aid budget and therefore it is the legal professions who should be the focus of the cost-cutting bravado which infects legal affairs policy-makers. For too long, the three lawyers' trades unions (the Bar Council, the Law Society and the judiciary) have clubbed together to demand that the status quo be defended to ensure their own profita-bility and to protect civil liberties. The problem lies with the level of their fees and their insistence on exclusive competence in so many areas of work, which results in the absorbing of resources that would otherwise be used to extend access to those same civil liberties.

In part, the debate about lawyers' exclusive competence is tied into the role for advice agencies. There is significant expertise in many parts of the advisory sector which should be networked through better use of information technology as well as through consistent funding on a unified basis, rather than the present system of scattered funding between numerous agencies from public and private sources. A law foundation is the type of body necessary to stand between public and private sectors to administer the money raised through public funding, charitable donations and a tax on lawyers who do not undertake sufficient legal aid work. Such a co-ordinating structure could pilot the schemes which would change the legal system and could disseminate best practice between lawyers and non-lawyers alike. The increasing use of arbitration and media-tion services could be finessed through increased availability of information for citizens and their advisors.

Above all, what is required, is a willingness to create a justice system which is concerned with the democratic rights and responsi-bilities of its citizens, and not to perpetuate one which serves the vested interests of those already initiated into it. Law is the product of politics, in the democratic sense through the legislature, and in a practical sense of power as an effect wrought on one person by another person in the body of judicial application of the common law. The law and the justice system must therefore become the place in which citizens and public bodies can communicate and act on the issues which face our nation.

CONCLUSION

What is key is that, in developing the policies of the democratic socialist New Labour government, Bevan's imprecation is borne in mind. In the search for cost-cutting and models which provide more efficient government, we must not overlook the democratic deficit which already exists in our nation as a result of a legal system that underpins our constitution but which is out of the reach of most people. For many millions of people, this means an abrogation of their rights as citizens. Those individuals are prevented from claiming their stake in our society through lack of education about law, lack of information about the means of protecting their rights, and a lack of access to justice. Our apparently enlightened principles about responsive and efficient government are allowing us to remain indifferent to the individual suffering of many.

NOTES AND REFERENCES

1 A. Bevan, *In Place of Fear* (first published 1952; Quartet Books, 1990).
2 G. Orwell, *The Lion and the Unicorn – Socialism and the English Genius.*
3 T. Blair, *The Third Way*, Fabian Pamphlet 588 (London, The Fabian Society, 1998).

Appendix

The following is a reproduction of the bulk of the text from the Labour Party's policy document *Access to Justice* (1995) prepared before the 1997 General Election, as discussed in Part I of this book.

Access to justice: Labour's proposals for reforming the civil justice system

INTRODUCTION

As our new statement of aims and values makes clear, Labour is committed to working for a 'just society, which judges its strength by the condition of the weak as much as the strong, provides security against fear, and justice at work ... and delivers people from the tyranny of poverty, prejudice and the abuse of power.'

Under the Conservatives our society has become more unequal, more fearful, more divided. In short, more unjust. Nowhere is this clearer than in relation to our civil justice system. Most people now feel that the legal system does not work for them. The vast majority of people on middle and low incomes are effectively denied access to justice. The courts are seen as slow, inaccessible and increasingly expensive to use. The law and access to justice are available now only to the rich and, as the number of people eligible to receive civil legal aid has been reduced, the very poor.

Ever since Magna Carta we have rightly given the principle of equality before the law a place of paramount importance in our nation's affairs. This principle is now under threat because, in practice, it is meaningless and worthless to the millions of people who can no longer get proper access to legal advice, assistance and representation.

Yet our justice system could and should be a vital public amenity for individuals and their families, empowering people to defend their interests, to assert their rights, to enforce the responsibilities of others to them and to challenge abuses of power and authority.

Labour is determined to shape the justice system so that it is on the side of the ordinary citizen rather than on the side of the lawyers.

The combination of an undue emphasis on traditional, expensive court based procedures and our antiquated and unsustainable legal aid system has resulted in a majority of the population being unable to assert their rights or enforce the responsibilities of others to them. Justice is one of the foundations on which the next Labour Government will build, and, as Tony Blair said in Sedgefield on January 28th this year 'it is social justice which requires that there must be access to the law for all'.

This document sets out Labour's plans for fundamental reform of the civil justice system of England and Wales. The systems operating in Scotland and Northern Ireland are rather different and are not specifically addressed in this paper although many of the general principles will apply.

PART ONE: THE SCALE OF THE PROBLEM

Record waits in the civil courts

Users of the civil justice system are suffering record delays in getting their cases dealt with. The availability of alternative dispute resolution remains extremely limited and the Government's over-hyped Courts Charter has failed to improve either the speed or the quality of service provided to litigants. Since it came into force in January 1993 there have been nearly 10,000 complaints about delays and errors. Consequently the Court Service has been forced to pay out over £600,000 in compensation for breaches of the Courts Charter's own standards and targets. Yet at the same time we are failing to make efficient use of our existing facilities and many courts are only in use part-time.

Soaring Costs and the Court Service Agency

Court fees have rocketed by up to 400% in the last three years alone and six new ones have been introduced. The Lord Chancellor has announced his intention to introduce daily hearing fees, too – up to £200 for the county court and £500 for the High Court. Consumer groups and lawyers have condemned this further restriction on access to justice. The Court Service Agency reduces the political account-ability of the court service and cost over £900,000 in consultancy fees to set up, including £32,000 for designing the logo and stationary. Labour has made clear its opposition to the creeping commercialisation of the courts system and the waste and deterioration in service quality that this has caused as well as the damaging effects this has had on staff working conditions and morale.

267

The Legal Aid Crisis

It was Labour that established the legal aid scheme. The Legal Aid and Advice Act 1949, with its principal aim of providing legal help to those of 'small or modest means', was a giant step towards access to justice for all. We remain committed to that aim.

Since 1979, however, the cost of the legal aid budget for civil and criminal cases has risen 600% to over £1.4 billion per annum. By 1994–95 total expenditure on civil legal aid exceeded £600 million, whilst the costs of criminal legal aid approached £470 million. The costs of advice and assistance were in the region of £235 million. This is an increase fuelled by outdated, complex court procedures, rising crime, rising unemployment and increased debt, family breakdown and homelessness as more and more of the very poorest in our society come before our courts. Abuses of the system have also played a part. So, instead of this massive increase in public expenditure preserving access to justice for the majority of society, it has actually been accompanied by savage cut-backs in legal aid eligibility, as the costs imposed on the legal aid fund by social breakdown have escalated. In 1979 79% of the population was eligible for civil legal aid. That figure is now down to 48%. In April 1993 alone, an estimated 12 million middle and low income people lost their eligibility for legal aid. Nobody whose pay packet exceeds the Income Support threshold or who has modest savings is now eligible for civil legal aid.

The recent history of legal aid exposes the incompetence and lack of compassion of a Government that has failed to monitor or control its cost and highlights fundamental flaws in the existing scheme. The scheme is ripe for reform that will both widen and improve access to justice and give greater value to money to the taxpayer.

PART 2: PROMOTING ACCESS TO JUSTICE

Access to Justice for All

Labour is committed to putting the needs of the consumer of legal services at the centre of our justice system. Access to justice for all and the creation of a consumer orientated legal system are the fundamental aims of our policy. Achieving these goals requires action in four key areas.

First, our aim must be to maximise access to justice, by ensuring that proper legal advice and assistance is available to all citizens. We must also promote a range of appropriate forums for dispute resolution, in whose competence and impartiality both parties have confidence. Labour will enhance consumer choice by encouraging the development of alternative, less expensive and more flexible means of resolving disputes than the court system. We propose to create a Community Legal Service, through radically reforming the legal aid scheme to reduce reliance on expensive lawyers operating through the court system and incorporating and improving provision for alternative dispute resolution.

Second, we need to empower our citizens by ensuring that people know what their legal rights and responsibilities are and are clear about how to assert those rights and enforce the responsibilities of others to them. Schools, advice centres, libraries and court buildings all have a role to play in providing information and promoting public legal education. And legislators and other officials have a responsibility to ensure that our laws are as concise and easy to understand as possible. Empowerment also depends crucially on ensuring that people's rights are adequately protected in legislation. Labour is committed to incorporating the European Convention on Human Rights into UK law and to enhancing anti-discrimination legislation, for example by strengthening the rights of people with disabilities.

Third, we must make the best possible use of the public and private resources available for legal services. The Government has failed to monitor or control the rising costs of legal aid and the courts system over the last 16 years. Labour wants a justice system that is speedy, cost effective and accessible to all. The current publicly funded system and, in particular, its almost exclusive reliance on lawyers in private practice to undertake legal aid work is expensive and inefficient. We also propose a range of measures to make access to justice cheaper and easier for those paying their own legal bills. Resources will continue to be wasted unless the way in which the legal profession operates is made to serve the interests of consumers.

Fourth, the justice system must be seen to work for all citizens, not just a privileged few, and must command public confidence. As far as possible the judiciary and the legal professions should become representative of the society they serve. The selection of judges is too important to be conducted in secret and legal and judicial training needs to be overhauled.

1   EXTENDING ACCESS TO JUSTICE

A Community Legal Service

The present system of publicly funded legal services is costly, inefficient and available to only a small section of society. The system is biased towards traditional, expensive court based legal action rather than other ways of resolving disputes. This concentration of resources on the courts has acted as a brake on long overdue consumer orientated reform of both the legal profession and dispute resolution. A radical new approach to publicly funded legal services is required if we are to get better value for money and broader access to justice.

In place of the waste and inefficiency of the current system, we propose to create a Community Legal Service, co-ordinated by existing regional legal aid board offices. This will assume responsibility for disbursing the entire national legal aid budget on a regional basis. In addition to providing basic legal services, each local board will be able to bid for earmarked funds from within the existing legal aid budget to establish innovative schemes to meet particular local needs.

Within the budget allocated for their area, each regional office of the Community Legal Service will carry out a number of core functions:

• Assessing the legal needs of its area. This will include assessing the demand for alternative forms of dispute resolution such as mediation and arbitration as well as for legal advice and representation.
• Drawing up a detailed strategy to meet those needs in consultation with local authorities and new advisory regional legal services committees.
• Agreeing priorities for legal services with the help of legal services committees chosen to be representative of the local communities they serve.
• Ensuring access to high quality legal representation through local lawyers in private practice and through making much more use of Citizens' Advice Bureaux, law centres and other independent advice units. The aim will be to build on existing provision and good practice initiatives wherever established in order to create a comprehensive, nationwide network of outlets for legal advice, assistance and, where appropriate, representation. The Community Legal Service will be expected to work closely with local authorities with whom there will be significant overlap of interest (for example in relation to local advice centre provision).
• Using the existing legal aid budget to expand access to alternative forms of dispute resolution such as mediation, arbitration and tribunals.
• Promoting public legal education, preventative work and liaison with other local and regional agencies. Law centres and advice

agencies also have an important role to play in the vocational training of the legal profession and this should be expanded.
• Monitoring the quality of local legal provision.

The development of the Community Legal Service will be achieved within the legal aid budget through reducing the exorbitant cost and waste inherent in the current system. Spending will be strictly monitored and controlled by the use of block franchises.

The Service will have as part of its remit the delivery of high-quality legal services to private clients at an appropriate charge, as well as publicly-funded clients.

We are not intending to establish a salaried public legal service, but one in which a range of services is offered by independent providers. The franchising system will be improved and used to monitor and maintain high standards of service delivery and value for money. We do however envisage that over time the Community Legal Service will expand its employment of salaried lawyers with rights of audience in the courts so as to provide high quality, affordable representation at lower cost to the taxpayer than the existing system.

Non-court Dispute Resolution

It is widely acknowledged that many disputes that are currently resolved through the courts could and should be resolved more satisfactorily, appropriately and cheaply through some means of alternative dispute resolution (ADR). Though some cases will inevitably require a court hearing to ensure that justice is done, the courts are not the only place where disputes can be settled. Conflicts at a relatively personal level in particular often benefit from a procedure that is less formal and adversarial, and for plaintiffs with small claims a process such as mediation is a far less hazardous option than litigation.

There are many different alternatives to traditional court-based litigation. These include tribunals, arbitration and ombudsmen as well as mediation. Current ADR provision is very inadequate and will need to be developed to ensure that individuals can choose from a wide range of such alternatives so that each dispute is dealt with in the most appropriate way. Existing means of alternative dispute resolution (ADR) must be made more effective and more widely available to the public.

The Industrial Tribunal system is failing to provide an effective, non-legalistic forum for the resolution of employment-related disputes. We remain committed to the tribunal system but believe that a fundamental overhaul is required to ensure that the system returns to the original principles laid down by the Donovan Commission in 1968, that tribunals should be 'easily accessible, informal, speedy and inexpensive'. A number of proposals in the Government's recent green paper, 'Resolving Employment Rights Disputes: Options for Reform', for example reducing the role of lay members by increasing the number of cases in which the Chair sits alone, will make the system more, not less, legalistic. We will enhance not reduce the lay element of tribunals and will work to ensure appropriate training for tribunal staff and fair treatment of women and minorities. We will continue to consult with the Trade Union Congress and the Confederation of British Industry in this regard, with a view to early reform.

Wherever possible our aim is to reduce the need for legal representation within the tribunal system. We shall aim to encourage the use of preliminary assessment hearings to provide incentives for earlier settlement of disputes and will promote the use of mediation and arbitration. Where appropriate arbitration should be available on a voluntary basis as an alternative to the tribunal itself. Improved industrial relations procedures should stop cases coming before tribunals in the first place and we have suggested a range of measures to strengthen the rights of those in work.

For cases where complexity necessitates the presence of a lawyer to represent those coming before the tribunal, we shall examine how legal aid might be made available without increasing overall legal aid costs, for example by encouraging the new Community Legal Service to target its resources accordingly.

We propose that the jurisdiction of the Council on Tribunals, which will continue to be directly responsible to the Lord Chancellor's Department and to Parliament, be extended so as to give it a supervisory role in the development of all mediation, conciliation and arbitration services, including the training and accreditation of such practitioners.

Mediation

We believe that the wider use of mediation, in particular, has enormous potential for both using more effectively existing resources for publicly funded legal services and for resolving everyday disputes quickly and satisfactorily.

The Lord Chancellor's proposals for divorce law reform, which we welcome in principle and which envisage a far greater role for mediation, make it all the more necessary to encourage the growth of non-court dispute resolution. We recognize that mediation may not always be appropriate (for example where one partner has suffered violence or intimidation) and in these circumstances we will continue to ensure access to legal representation in publicly funded cases.

There is currently an imbalance between public provision for traditional litigation on the one hand and mediation services on the other. We propose to transfer resources from the former to the latter through dealing with less by litigation and more through mediation. Comprehensive delivery of such mediation services must be built up through a nationally accredited structure.

The benefits of mediation can be harnessed not only to allow more people to resolve their disputes more appropriately, but also to help change for the better the current culture of conflict resolution. Lawyers will have a part to play in mediation, but a part that will require a considerably altered attitude. As former Chief Justice of the United States, Warren Burger observed, in the twenty first century most people will expect lawyers to be 'reconcilers, not warriors: healers not hired guns'. Development of mediation in matrimonial cases and landlord and tenant disputes will be a priority.

Personal injury claims

The current no-costs regime in the small claims court works well for most litigants, but precludes those with minor personal injuries from hiring the expert legal and medical back-up that they need, thereby discouraging defendants, usually large insurance companies, from settling at an early stage if at all.

The system by which compensation awards are clawed back from those on social security benefits can leave some litigants worse off than if they had not pursued their claim, a situation the Social Services Select Committee recently called 'revolting to the ordinary man's sense of justice'. As the Committee points out this appears to be deterring some people from making claims for damages for personal injury at all. The present system is manifestly wrong and should be changed. Labour has called for an urgent review of the compensation recovery scheme.

Any increase in the small claims limit would bring an even greater number of personal injury claims into the no-cost regime. We therefore remain opposed to increases in the small claims limit in the county courts without considerable allowances being made for the special nature of personal injury cases with respect to costs. We must ensure that changes in civil procedure do not disadvantage claimants.

A New Focus for the Lord Chancellor's Department

The Lord Chancellor's Department has traditionally had as its focus the judiciary and the legal professions. This must change. The first priority of the Lord Chancellor's Department under Labour will be the individual citizen and consumer of legal services, and the Department will be re-structured in such a way as to ensure that a dynamic, coherent approach to the delivery of legal services is pursued.

The first stage of this process must be to assess the changing legal needs of the British people and then to develop, with the Legal Aid Board and the regional legal services committees, a strategy to meet those needs.

The role, status and executive responsibilities of the Lord Chancellor's Department's Minister in the House of Commons will be enhanced, and the Department as a whole will be made more accountable to the Commons by the creation of a Select Committee on Justice and Legal Services.

2   EMPOWERING THE CONSUMER

Giving Consumers a Voice

The civil justice system is antiquated, fragmented and incomprehensible to most of the people it is meant to serve. Court users and the consumers of legal services have no say in how it is run. We intend to give the consumers of legal services a new voice in the reform, operation and co-ordination of the administration of justice.

We intend to build on the success already being demonstrated by the North-West Legal Services Committee. Each region will have a similar body consisting of court service officials, lawyers, local authority and consumer representatives, all serving on a voluntary basis. We will ensure that legal services committees draw their members from a wide cross-section of relevant consumer and community groups so that they are truly representative of the local communities that they serve.

These advisory committees will help to put an end to the current, crisis-driven approach to civil justice reform and to provide in its place a genuinely coherent, consumer-orientated policy on access to justice nationwide.

The committees will be able to recommend to the Lord Chancellor's Department particular types of research and reform that they believe should be undertaken.

Public Legal Education

A just society depends on people knowing their legal rights and responsibilities. We intend to encourage the promotion of public legal education and awareness of the rights and responsibilities of citizenship through all schools, advice centres, libraries and court-rooms.

We will work in partnership with the Law Commission and other organisations to ensure that statutes and other legal instruments are as concise and comprehensible as possible. All new Bills should include a clear statement of their policy objectives, in order to assist citizens with understanding them.

The Role of the Law Commission

The Law Commission, established by the 1964–70 Labour Government, has a vital role to play in promoting access to justice by ensuring that the law is as clear, comprehensible and up-to-date as possible. At present its ability to achieve this aim is hampered by the difficulties in getting Law Commission reports on particular areas of the law enacted by Parliament. At present 36 such reports remain unimplemented.

We intend to reform Parliamentary procedure to ensure that important, non-controversial law reform measures, both civil and criminal, are swiftly enacted so that the law does not become antiquated, confusing and unnecessarily expensive to use.

We also intend to make it the responsibility of the Law Commission to keep under review the effectiveness and fairness of the adversarial system in both the civil and criminal courts and to recommend to the Lord Chancellor measures in the public interest that would allow a more inquisitorial approach, as well as to recommend to the Lord Chancellor and to the Judicial Appointments and Training Commission the necessary changes to legal and judicial training these measures would require.

The Role of the Courts

Justice demands that some cases are dealt with in court, but the courts should be more than just places where judges hear cases. A lot of space in court buildings is at present under-used. Labour intends to utilise the existing network of court buildings more effectively, and to use the courts and other public buildings to make legal information and advice readily available to all citizens. There are already good examples from around the country of court buildings acting as information centres (for example through the provision of a CAB office, as happens in Stoke on Trent and at the Royal Courts of Justice in London) and we should build on this experience.

The design and operation of court buildings and facilities must serve the needs of victims and witnesses, not just those of judges and lawyers. We are committed to improving access at courts and other centres of dispute resolution for people with a disability.

As is made clear in *Safer Communities, Safer Britain*, Labour's policy statement on crime reduction, our whole justice system must become more victim focused. A key part of this is ensuring that courts are made more victim friendly, for example through the provision of separate waiting facilities for witnesses and victims. Courts must also reflect the particular needs of children.

In order to improve access to justice we will re-allocate resources within the Court Service for the benefit of court-users. We will make full and cost-effective use of the latest information technology, so as to empower individuals to undertake the initial stages of their cases themselves. We will ensure that there is effective training for court staff.

Courtrooms are under-used and we are committed to exploring ways in which they could be used outside the usual sitting hours, on a self-financing basis, for the benefit of those in full-time work.

A review and overhaul of the current court listing system is urgently required.

Empowering the consumer – bringing justice closer

We are committed to incorporating the European Convention on Human Rights and Fundamental Freedoms into British law. This will make the remedies afforded by the Convention available in our own courts, thus saving litigants the expense and delay of taking their cases to the European Court of Justice.

We intend to allow High Court centres other than the Royal Courts of Justice on the Strand to hear actions for judicial review and applications for leave to apply for judicial review. This reform will increase the availability and the affordability to litigants of this important and growing area of jurisprudence.

We will amend the rules of procedure in the civil courts to allow multi-party actions as an effective means of enforcing group rights in product liability, environmental damage and landlord and tenant cases in particular.

3 MAKING THE BEST USE OF RESOURCES

Reducing the Cost of Access to Justice

Britain has some of the highest legal costs in the world. We believe that there is great potential in the court service, the legal aid scheme and the legal professions for efficiency savings and for providing greater value for money for private and publicly-funded clients alike.

Court procedures

We recognise that reforming the rules of court and improving case management is the key to making significant and permanent reductions in the delays and costs of litigation and we await with interest the publication of the final report of Lord Woolf's Civil Justice Review.

We intend to amend the rules on procedure and costs so as to introduce incentives for the early resolution or settlement of disputes as well as strong disincentives for the delay or protraction of litigation by lawyers.

We remain opposed to the introduction of exorbitant, catch-all daily hearing fees for all litigants. This Government has introduced massive increases in court fees as well as new court charges whilst failing to safeguard the interests of the ordinary individual litigant in this respect. Large commercial bulk users of the courts can and should be expected to make a proportionately larger contribution to the cost of running the court system. The individual litigant and small- and medium-sized businesses must not be penalised in seeking access to justice by having to bear a disproportionate share of these costs.

Reforming Legal Aid

Legal aid now accounts for more than half of the Lord Chancellor's Department's total budget. The Government has allowed the cost of legal aid to soar by 600% since 1979 without tackling the fundamental flaws in the scheme. At the same time they have slashed eligibility so that less than one half of the population now qualifies for assistance, compared to almost four fifths in 1979. The current legal aid system is far too concerned with lawyers and the courts. Our plans for a Community Legal Service provide the far reaching reform required to put a proper emphasis on meeting the needs of individual citizens, and will allow us to use resources more strategically to improve and extend publicly-funded legal services. At present a massive 97.7% of the £1.4 billion annual legal aid budget is paid directly to lawyers in private practice on a case by case basis. This leaves only 0.3% for deployment through advice agencies. This system is an extremely expensive and inefficient way of providing publicly-funded legal services in all cases and its deficiencies are, in part, responsible for the recent cut-backs in legal aid eligibility.

We accept that the franchising scheme will be clearly established by the time of the next Labour Government. Franchising will play a key role in the development of a Community Legal Service. However, we remain unconvinced about the merits of compulsory competitive tendering for franchising contracts. We believe that this could undermine the whole franchising project, driving some firms away from the scheme and encouraging others to emphasise cost control at the expense of quality assurance for the client.

We favour the introduction of more stringent and sophisticated quality control standards for franchised firms, together with improved assessment and compliance mechanisms, to ensure that the quality of the advice and of the service provided to clients, as well as the level of administrative competence, is enhanced.

Labour's proposed reform of the legal aid system will control costs more effectively and fairly than the proposals outlined in the Lord Chancellor's Green Paper on legal aid for regionally cash-limited budgets for criminal, family and civil non-family legal aid. These reforms fail to address the deep structural problems that underlie the crisis in our legal system. They will deny access to justice to people eligible for legal aid, and who have a reasonable case, simply because of where they live or what time of the financial year they apply for help. The problems which have resulted from the introduction of the Social Fund clearly demonstrate the injustices that can be caused when this type of regional cash limit is imposed.

The proposal to cap the criminal legal aid budget has serious implications for the liberty of individuals and the quality of representation in court.

We firmly oppose the introduction of an application fee for legal aid. We believe that a catch-all application fee would deny access to justice to the poorest and most vulnerable in society and that a means-tested application fee would cost far more to administer than it might save.

We advocate the introduction of more stringent measures to detect and eliminate abuses of the legal aid scheme. The rules for court approval of costs, should reflect the difficulty and complexity of the case and the value of the work done rather than the seniority of the lawyer delivering the service.

Alternative ways of funding legal action

i *Legal expenses insurance*

Some have suggested that legal expenses insurance has a significant role to play in extending access to justice. We are not convinced that there is a case to be made for the introduction of compulsory personal legal expenses insurance as a means of reducing the costs of legal aid.

We shall consult further with the insurance industry on whether, both in terms of desirability and feasibility, there is a case for introducing compulsory legal expenses insurance for companies with respect to environmental damages claims.

ii *'No Win, No Fee'*

We do not oppose in principle the introduction of conditional fees, which allow a client to obtain the services of a lawyer without paying fees unless and until he or she receives an award of damages. A certain amount of money will then be paid to the lawyer out of the damages. We remain adamant, however, that any 'no win, no fee' regime must safeguard the interests of consumers against those of lawyers, who are usually in a superior bargaining position.

In addition to a reasonable statutory maximum uplift on lawyers' fees when a plaintiff wins, which should be very much lower than 100%, we favour the introduction of a statutory cap on the percentage of a successful plaintiff's damages that can be paid to his or her lawyers. Such a cap should not just be a matter for negotiation between lawyer and client. If the total amount payable under a fee uplift agreement exceeded the sum representing the maximum percentage of the damages payable to the lawyer, the statutory cap would take precedence over the uplift contracted for between lawyer and client, and the client would only be liable for the maximum percentage of the damages payable.

We regard conditional fees as an experiment to be monitored closely and, in the light of the Scottish experience, do not expect their introduction to make a significant improvement to access to justice. They are, at present, little more than a gimmick designed to mask the chaotic state of the legal aid scheme and the court service.

Tackling restrictive practices – reforming the Legal Profession

A reformed legal profession has a vital contribution to make to the provision of accessible and affordable legal services. This requires both the profession and Government, in partnership, to address the need to remove practices that currently operate to reduce access and inflate cost.

We will ensure that the structure and practices of the legal profession are made subject to the strictest public interest criteria. An incoming Labour Government will formally refer the legal profession to the Monopolies and Mergers Commission (which is to combine forces with the Office of Fair Trading to become the Competition and Consumer Standards Office) so that existing structure and practices can be tested by reference to their ability to meet consumer needs.

This rigorous, independent examination of the operations of the legal professions will help to ensure that the interests of the consumers of legal services, together with the wider public interest in the efficient administration of justice, are properly protected and enhanced, and no longer subordinated to any vested professional interests. Detailed information about the fees charged by lawyers must be made more readily available to the public.

We are also anxious to work with the profession to ensure that its rules and practices do not operate to restrict the development of legal services. At present it is not possible for lawyers to join together with other professionals to provide a range of services under one roof. We believe that there is nothing inherently objectionable to multi-disciplinary practices involving lawyers (either solicitors, barristers or both), accountants, surveyors and other professionals.

We believe that the rule prohibiting direct access to barristers by lay people can no longer be justified. Barristers should be free, subject to appropriate standards of service and safeguards for the consumer, to enter into such arrangements as are necessary, either amongst themselves or with solicitors, to facilitate one-stop legal service shops.

We believe that solicitor advocates should be treated in exactly the same way as barristers in matters of court dress, the use of court facilities and applications to become Queen's Counsel.

The Lord Chancellor's Advisory Committee on Legal Education and Conduct (ACLEC), which includes lawyers and consumer representatives, will be retained and directed to advise on the changes to the profession's rule books necessary to bring these reforms about.

We believe that this package of reforms will set in train a process that will better equip the legal profession to deliver accessible and affordable services to the consumer as we approach the 21st century.

Queen's Counsel

There are a number of aspects of the current arrangements for the appointment of Queen's Counsel that require reform. The mechanisms by which this rank is conferred are unnecessarily secretive, providing neither reasons nor redress for unsuccessful applicants.

Consistent with the protection of confidentiality it should be the rule that anyone who may be turned down for silk because of an allegation to their discredit should be given full particulars of that allegation and the opportunity to refute it.

The responsibilities of the legal profession

There can be no substitute for a properly reformed and broadened publicly-funded legal service. Whilst we recognise the value of the work done by many lawyers on a low-paid or voluntary basis, we intend to ensure that the legal profession as a whole, and particularly those lawyers who do little or no legally-aided or *pro bono* work, makes a greater contribution to access to justice for all.

We want to see the Law Society and the Bar Council make greater efforts to co-ordinate and to develop their *pro bono* activities. We would like to see, in particular, a system designed to initiate and to foster long-term relationships between particular firms and chambers and particular community legal services, and an appropriate flow of both financial and human resources from one to the other.

4 STRENGTHENING CONFIDENCE IN THE LEGAL PROFESSIONS

A Judicial Appointments and Training Commission

The system for selecting and training those who preside as judges in civil and criminal cases must command public confidence. Winning this confidence is crucial to giving the public a real sense that justice is accessible through the courts. We are committed to the development of a more rational training and career structure for the judiciary together with a more open and objective selection process that can better identify and harnesses judicial talent from sources other than the bar, to include solicitors and academics.

The current system is widely perceived as being defective in several respects. We seek to remedy this by the creation of a Judicial Appointments and Training Commission, which will take over work currently carried out by the Lord Chancellor's Department and the Judicial Studies Board.

This body will be independent of the Lord Chancellor's Department and answerable solely to the Lord Chancellor, whom it will advise on all aspects of judicial appointments and training. Commission Members will be appointed from amongst suitably qualified lawyers, academics and lay people with relevant experience.

The Commission will have oversight of the advertisement of all judicial posts and of selection procedures and responsibility for the training functions currently performed by the Judicial Studies Board.

We are committed to maintaining the highest judicial standards and to ensuring that judges are appointed purely on merit. We are anxious to ensure that the judicial selection process is open, fair and accessible to all. Special efforts should be made by the Commission to develop a strong equal opportunities policy and to encourage members of all those groups currently under-represented in the ranks of the judiciary to apply for appointment.

The widest possible consultation on the suitability of candidates will continue, but the secretive aspects of judicial appointment will give way to a new principle of openness. In so far as confidentiality permits, candidates will have the opportunity to comment in detail on the substance of any objections made to their appointment.

We believe that this reformed system will ensure that the calibre of the judiciary is enhanced, because all the most able candidates will be encouraged to apply and fairly considered for appointment.

Judicial Training

The Judicial Appointments and Training Commission will conduct a review of judicial training which is the key to enhancing the accountability, the sensitivity and the effectiveness of the judiciary without jeopardising their independence.

A more coherent and systematic approach to judicial training is required, with closer links to academic research and teaching facilities.

Judicial Monitoring

The development of a more rational career pattern for judges, a greater emphasis on effective judicial training and a need to strengthen public confidence in the accountability of the judiciary make it all the more imperative that judicial performance appraisal, as recommended by the Royal Commission on Criminal Justice, be introduced without further delay. This appraisal will be carried out under the supervision of the Judicial Appointments and Training Commission and by senior members of the judiciary.

The Commission will also be responsible for producing a comprehensive code of practice for the judiciary and for monitoring judicial discipline, though judges of High Court level and above will still only be able to be removed from office by address to both Houses of Parliament.

Complaints about Judicial Conduct

Court users sometimes have cause to complain about the way a judge has behaved, notwithstanding the legal merits or demerits of their case. The current mechanisms within the Lord Chancellor's Department for investigating such complaints are woefully inadequate, and serve to undermine confidence in the judiciary.

The Commission will have an important role to play in ensuring that such complaints are taken seriously and properly investigated, and that appropriate action is taken.

Appointment of magistrates

The magistracy makes a vital contribution to the justice system. Magistrates hear 97% of all criminal cases in addition to many civil cases. The Judicial Appointments and Training Commission will advise on the appointment of both stipendiary and lay magistrates (JPs). Although steps have been taken to make the magistracy more representative of the population as a whole (for example by increasing the number of women appointed), in practice many people are still excluded from sitting as JPs. Employers are often reluctant to allow their employees time off and child care or other commitments can also interfere. Urgent action is needed to recruit JPs from a broader section of society and we will discuss with the Confederation of British Industry and local Chambers of Commerce, ways in which employers can be encouraged to release staff for civic duties of this type and can receive appropriate recognition for doing so.

The process by which magistrates are chosen needs to be made more transparent. Those who have their applications turned down should have the reasons explained. Vacancies should be advertised as widely as possible in order to maximise applications from those groups which are currently under-represented. Employers should be encouraged to release their employees for this type of civic duty. The law on paid time off for public duties should be reviewed in the light of changing work patterns and the increasing trend towards casualisation of employment. Adequate child care provision is also important in encouraging candidates to come forward and Labour is committed to extending the opportunities for high quality child care.

Legal Training

Legal training must constantly adapt to the changing nature of legal practice, including the wider use of alternative dispute resolution. It must also be of greater benefit to those not wanting to specialise in the commercial field.

Recent allegations of discrimination in the admissions policy for Bar School and the chronic shortage of course and training places for the two branches of the legal profession has brought both the Inns of Court School of Law (for barristers) and the College of Law (for solicitors) into disregard.

We welcome the proposal to validate institutions other than the Inns of Court School of Law to teach the Bar School course.

The crisis in the discretionary grants system means that the legal profession is increasingly becoming the preserve of the privileged. Urgent action is required. A Labour Government will carry out a review of the funding of legal vocational training, something that the Government has consistently refused to undertake, and explore the ways in which access to the legal profession can be broadened.

Greater steps must be made to allow para-legals and legal executives to up-grade their qualifications and hence increase their capacity to contribute to the provision of legal services.

Conclusion

Taken as a whole, new Labour's proposals represent the most far-reaching and comprehensive package of reforms since the 1945 Labour Government passed the Legal Aid and Advice Act 1949. We believe that they will assist in developing more accessible court and legal services, delivering higher quality and more affordable justice to all.

As a nation we urgently need, as the foundation of a radically reformed Parliamentary democracy, an independent, open and accessible justice system that is capable of underpinning a decent civic society. The rule of law and a properly reformed justice system have an invaluable role to play in empowering individuals and regenerating local communities.

We believe that the proposals contained in this policy statement have the potential to revitalise our legal system. We are committed to making the law a means of enhancing the life chances and realising the aspirations of the British people, and to transforming our antiquated legal system into a modern, efficient justice system that is worthy of the name and accessible to all who have need of it.

Index